AF483264

A PRIMER OF SPIRITUALITY

INDIC ACADEMY

Notion Press Media Pvt Ltd

No. 50, Chettiyar Agaram Main Road,
Vanagaram, Chennai, Tamil Nadu – 600 095

First Published by Notion Press 2021
Copyright © Prof. V. Krishnamurthy 2021
All Rights Reserved.

ISBN 978-1-68538-320-6

A PRIMER OF SPIRITUALITY

108 QUESTIONS & ANSWERS IN HINDUISM

PROF. V. KRISHNAMURTHY

Dedicated

To All My Friend-Seekers
Whose Incisive Questions
Constitute The Motivation For This Book

CONTENTS

PREFACE

This book arose from questions raised in various classroom lectures, face-to-face meetings and social media conversations by fellow travellers on the spiritual path. I have collated them over the duration of the pandemic and tried to answer them rather elaborately. I expect this compilation may clear the haze around the knowledge and understanding of Sanatana dharma, and clear the cobwebs around its vedantic aspects. Though it started as a self-education, I am glad it turned out to be an education on spiritual discipline for the community of seekers.

The subject matter has been broken into four parts. The first part (Part A) takes up general questions. Part B is confined to Hindu religion and its fundamental tenets, observances, practices, mantras, temples, gods and worship.. The third part, Part C, full of Vedanta, is what sets the style and title of this book, by taking up questions, mostly on spiritual sAdhanA, many of which tend to be almost a Purva-paksha argument (an opposing logic) type. Part D is a small synopsis of the Advaita of the Upanishads, as brought out by Acharya Shankara and is intended to give a background perspective to the rest of the book. One lesson imprinted in me by my father long ago, got thouroughly established in me now after the writing of the answers to the questions, namely, 'Nothing in Hinduism can be fully explained unless you take the help of the vedantic fundamentals'!

I should certainly record my indebtedness to various stalwarts, starting from my own father (Sri R. Visvanatha Sastrigal, 1882–1956) who planted the seeds of the philosophy in my mind even when I was a boy. And over the years it grew with my contacts with Swami Chin*mAyA*nanda, Swami Dayananda Saraswati of Arsha Vidya Gurukulam, Swami Paramarthananda, and other such masterly exponents, their expositions and their books and my own mild attempts to communicate.

I am happy to pay my reverential gratitude for the three inspirational forewords coupled with blessings for the book from Swamini Svatmavidyananda, Swami Shiva-rudra Bala Yogi and Shri C.L. Ramakrishnan.

I am extremely grateful to Shri Kiran Vadlamani, Founder of Indic Academy for sponsoring the publication of this work. I am indebted to the couple Usha Sekhar and K.C. Sekhar for an ever-present help on the style and presentation of the text. A special word of gratitude is due to my friend Sri R. Narayanan, for assistance in the formatting of the book. An appreciation is also due to the Publishing Team led by Hema Priyadharshni.

Finally I submit this book as a thankful offering of loka-sangraha at the lotus feet of the Guru ParamparA all the way down from Adi Shankaracharya.

Prof. V. Krishnamurthy

FOREWORD
BY SWAMINI SVATMAVIDYANANDA

I am very happy to write a foreword to this engaging and informative book on the Hindu tradition. The best of the teachings in the tradition—found in the Upanishads, the Bhagavad Gita, and the Puranas – are presented in the form of dialogues between preceptors and disciples, known as *saṃvāda*. This is because unlike many contemporary religions, Hinduism is not a belief-based tradition; rather it unfolds a vision of oneness and an ethical and prayerful way of life that is conducive to assimilating this vision. The truth of the self as whole and limitless can only be gained through self-enquiry, and by the systematic removal of doubts, errors and vagueness in one's understanding. Therefore, we have a rich hermeneutic tradition based on thousands of years of enquiry into its philosophy and practices.

True to this ancient precedent of the *sampradāya*, Professor Krishnamurthi's book is presented in the form of questions and answers. Neatly organized into helpful subheadings, the book is a handy and practical guide intended to clear common doubts and misperceptions about the Hindu dharma. Professor Krishnamurthi's erudition shines forth throughout the work without compromising its simplicity and elegance. The Pañcadasī, a highly regarded work on Vedanta says that the best way to assimilate self-knowledge is through the practice of deep contemplation, through talking about it and sharing it with others: *taccintanaṃ tatkathanaṃ anyonyaṃ tadprabodhanam*

(7.106). In this spirit, I commend Professor Krishnamurthi for his work, and wish him many years of *brahmābhyāsa*, contemplation upon *Brahman*.

Swamini Svatmavidyananda
Arsha Vijnana Gurukula.
1190, W 27ᵗʰ Ave., Eugene, OR97405
(541)684-0322 arshavm.org
8570, Village Place, Suwanee, GA 300024
(470)564-0644 arshavg.org

FOREWORD
BY SHRI SHIVA-RUDRA BALA YOGI

(Chairman of Shri Shivabalayogi Maharaj Trust, J.P. Nagar, Bengaluru, India – www.srby.org)

It gives me great pleasure to say a few words in appreciation of the book "A PRIMER OF SPIRITUALITY" via questions and answers on Hinduism. The author of the book, Prof. V. Krishnamurthy, is personally known to me. Besides a brilliant career as a professor of mathematics, he is also a great scholar on Hinduism and various Vedic scriptures. He has already written and published many books on Hinduism including his latest book *par excellence* on B.G. by the title "THUS SPAKE KRISHNA".

His latest book, "A PRIMER OF SPIRITUALITY" is a very novel propagation of knowledge, faiths and practices on Hinduism by sharing his life-long experience, knowledge, scholarship and wisdom in the form of questions and answers.

From his experience and knowledge, the author has selected and formed an excellent assortment of questions commonly asked by curious seekers of knowledge and truth about Hinduism. In all, the book covers the entire subject in about 108 questions and authentic answers grouped into four parts subject-wise.

As already explained by the author in his preface; the first part deals with general questions. The second part is confined to Hindu religion and its fundamental tenets. The third part is full of Vedanta that sets the trend of the contents of the book. Topped by a small synopsis as a "Basic Survey of the Message of Oneness" in part four.

As a yogi I have been answering similar questions on Hinduism and Spirituality over the past twenty years. Needless to say that this is an excellent selection of questions and nicely answered from his experience, knowledge and wisdom. Hence I do not wish to analyse and highlight them once again. I would make a special mention about the extensive and amazing cross-references to our scriptures which the author has provided for the benefit of the reader. This only shows the author's depth and thoroughness of knowledge of the subject to which he has dedicated his lifetime.

Another great aspect is that the author, a nonagenarian, at this ripe old age still has all the energy and enthusiasm to devote his time to the service of humanity in the propagation of this valuable knowledge. He is a true Jnana Yogi and Karma Yogi.

I would sincerely recommend this book as an excellent "PRIMER of SPIRITUALITY" to all inquisitive and enthusiastic readers. Over to the readers!

Blessings,

Shri Shiva Rudra Balayogi
26 August 2021 Bengaluru, India

FOREWORD BY SHRI C.L. RAMAKRISHNAN (IPS, RETIRED)

This thin volume is deceptively titled A Primer of Spirituality. It takes within its fold an extremely wide sweep of the entire philosophical concepts, heavily relying on advaitic tenets. The extensive knowledge of the author – a professor of Mathematics – is astounding. References and quotations abound – spread across the Vedas, the Upanishads, epics, purANAs, prakaraNa granthas, the B.G., Srimad Bhagavatham, the works of philosophers, the sayings of great seers like Adi Shankara, Sadashiva Brahmendra, Ramana Maharishi, Maha Periyava of Kanchi, Sri Ramakrishna Paramahamsa, Swami Vivekananda, Dr. S. Radhakrishnan and many other religious missionaries. Thus, it is a panorama encompassing the ancient to the present day, in spiritual quest.

The questions raised cover a wide canvas of spiritual thoughts, and which constitute the FAQs of the seekers of spiritual knowledge and serious students of philosophy. This publication needs to be read and re-read for assimilation and is not for casual reading.

It is difficult to list out the outstandingly illuminating answers given by the author to many of the questions. Applying the principle of *sthAli pulAka nyAya* – sample for bulk – the following will be enough to generate curiosity to study this book.

The apparent contradiction in the co-existence between science and religion has been raised in question two of Part A and the brilliant answer of reconciliation given thereto is memorable. Question six in this part refers to the mystical experience of the spiritual seekers – whether they appear logical or not – and has been clarified by the author through mathematical proof – his home ground. In the Sanatana dharma system, there is the concept of *svAnubhUti pramAna*. This is an individual experience of great souls, and is true for the dual reasons: They have no axe to grind to say so and more importantly, they will not force it on others. It is given for wholesome advancement of the seeker.

While dealing with Manu Smriti in B-11, the author has dispelled the misunderstanding in general regarding Manu's views on the status of women. This is a subtle point to be noted. Actually Manu gives a very high place for women. Under Question 13 in this part, regarding idol worship, the examples and the explanation are quite convincing. Perhaps it may be pointed out that Bhagavan Sathya Sai Baba answered this question in the following way: when a person pays respect to God, to the Acharya or his own elders, represented in a photograph, he is not respecting the photo as such, but what it represents. This is similar to idol worship. Again the venerable statesman Rajaji was once ridiculed by a person, who said: "worship of an idol is like respecting a stone (idol) standing on another stone (the floor)". Rajaji's repartee was that one's mother, wife, daughter, grandmother, granddaughter etc., are all females. But our behaviour and relationship with them will be different. There is need for *saguNa upAsana* – idol worship – to graduate to *nirguNa upAsana – Brahman*. This quotation is in Bhagavadpada's commentary on one of the Brahma Sutras where the acharya says that though *Brahman* is only one, these two approaches are for purpose of worship (*upAsana*) and for knowledge (*jnAna*) –

dvirUpaM hi brahma avagamyate/
nAma-rUpa-vikAra-bhedopAdhi-vishishhTaM tadviparItanca
sarvopAdhivarjitam/
evaM ekamapi brahma apekshhitopAdhi-sambandhaM
nirastopAdhisambandhaM ca upAsyatvena jneyatvena ca vedAnteshhu
upadishyate//

This can be seen in the references to *Brahman* in the Ch.U. (with *upAdhis)* and the Br.U. (without upAdhis). In the V.S. also, such apparent contradictions may be seen in *aNur-bRRihat-kRRisha-sthUlaH, guNabRRinnirguNo mahAn* etc.

Again, C-30 refers to the apparent conflict between bhakti (devotee and God) and advaita (non-difference between these two) and hence the argument that in advaita, there is no scope for bhakti. This conflict has been resolved by the author. Srimad Bhagavatam is a text predominantly on bhakti, as may be seen from the concluding verse:

nAma-sankIrtanaM yasya sarva-pApa-praNAshanam/
praNAmo duHkha-shamanaH taM namAmi hariM param//

This text speaks about bhakti in advaita

AtmArAmAshca munayaH nirgranthApi urukrame/
kurvanti ahaitukIM bhaktiM itthaMbhUta-guNo hariH//

C-3 raises the distinction among *Brahman*, Ishvara and the *JIva* has been convincingly explained by the author. The answer is: *Brahman* is uncontaminated by *MAyA*: Ishvara is with *MAyA* but the *MAyA* is under His control (Sv.U.)) and *JIva* is controlled by *MAyA*. Similarly, regarding question C-44, both the question and the answer are excellent.

Again, question 62 in this part, as to which of the three is superior, karma, bhakti and jnAna, has been clarified by the author succinctly. Perhaps, the order prescribed in the Vedas and also the B.G. (the essence of the Vedas), indicate that these three are said to be the stepping stones in the progress of a spiritual pilgrim. However, PUrva MImAmsa admits only karma, while the VishishhtAdvaita and Dvaita schools bank upon bhakti and the Advaita school declares that jnAna is the sole means of liberation. It is left to the belief and practice of those belonging to these schools.

yayA bhavetpumsAM vyutpattiH prayagAtmani./
sA saiva prakriyA jneyA sA sAdhvI cAnavasthitA//

For fear of the foreword becoming an addition to the text, as is the case in the plays of George Bernard Shaw, I stop here, though reluctantly, as the fare presented in this book is totally absorbing. The spiritual community stands indebted to the learned author for such a succinct and clear explanation of the nagging questions raised by seekers who have *jigjnAsA* and *shraddhA* as the twin requirements for spiritual elevation. It is my personal gain to have studied this compendium – which is short and sweet.

C.L. Ramakrishnan
Chennai
30-08-2021

HELP FOR TRANSLITERATION

**A possible help for transliteration of non-English words into English.
Kyoto-Harvard Convention (Modified)**

Vowels:		Consonants:					
a	as the 'u' in but	gutturals	*k*	*kh*	*g*	*gh*	*G*
A or Aa or aa	as the 'a' in father	palatals	*c*	*ch*	*j*	*jh*	*jna*
i	as the 'i' in mill	linguals	*T*	*Th*	*D*	*Dh*	*N*
I	as the 'ea' in meal	dentals	*t*	*th*	*d*	*dh*	*n*
u	as the 'u' in put	labials	*p*	*ph*	*b*	*bh*	*m*
U	as the 'u' in rule	semivowels	*y*	*r*	*l*	*v*	
e	as the 'ey' in they						
ai	as the 'ai' in aisle						
o	as the 'o' in go						
au	as the 'ou' in loud						
R or RRi	as the 'r' in Sanskrit*						

Note on*: For the English transliteration of Sanskrit *shlokas*, the Itranslator 2003 has been used. So words like Prakriti, nivRRitti, pravRRitti, AvRRitti, dhRRiti, require the 'RRi' for the input for the printing of the *shlokas* and transliteration process. But when we use such words in ordinary English sentences, we take the not-so-formidable spellings such as. 'prakriti', 'nivritti', 'pravritti', 'Avritti', 'dhriti'. Readers may kindly bear this incongruence in usage of Sanskrit words in English!

Sibilants

As in	Beginning of word	Middle of word	Sanskrit Examples
Palatal 's' as in the German word 'sprechen'	Sh	sh	*Ishvara*, darshana, pashyati, VishvaM Shankara, shAnti, Shiva
Shutter, shame	Shh or shh	shh	Vishhnu, Purushha, dveshha, eshhaH ShhaNmukha, mokshha
Sun, sand	S or s	s	samsAra, SamsAra, *Sattva*, VAsanA

In the pronunciation of the name 'shiva' of God the sh denotes the palatal 's' in the German word sprechen-, not 'siva' – where the 's' is as in 'sun' or the 'ss' in 'hiss' – nor as 'Shiva' – where the 'Sh' is as in the English word 'Show'-).

anusvAra   *M*   visarga   *H*   aspiration   *h*

Some contractions:

A.U. Aitareya Upanishad

B.G. Bhagavad Gita

Br.U. Brihadaranyaka Upanishad

Ch.U. Chandogya Upanishad

I.U. Ishopanishad

Katha U. Katha Upanishad

Kena U. Kenopanishad

K.Y.V. Krishna Yajur Veda

M.B. Mahabharata

M.N.U. Mahanarayanopaishad

S.L.: Shivananda Lahari

Sou.L.: Soundaryalahari

Sv.U.: Svetashvataropanishad

S.Y.V. Shukla Yajur Veda

T.U. Taittiriyopanishad.

V.R. Valmiki RAmAyaNa

V.S. Vishnu Sahasranama

PART A

QUESTIONS IN GENERAL

QUESTION A-1: What do you think is the right amount of time that one should devote for spiritual matters, as one progresses along his life in the midst of all his personal, domestic, professional and public responsibilities?

The answer is simple. In your nth decade of life if you can allot (n-1) per cent. of your time for spiritual learning and dharmic responsibilities, that should be good enough. For instance, when you have crossed twenty, 20% of your time and when you have crossed fifty, 50%. of your entire time should be for purposes beyond life! And so on. Once you are past ninety, you better devote 90% of your time for spirituality.

QUESTION A-2: Since Science and Religion are opposed to each other in their fundamentals, I think they cannot co-exist in the same personality. Do you agree?

It is totally wrong to think that Science and Religion are opposed to each other. It might have been true in the medieval world in reference to the religion of Christendom. The ancient Christian world was always afraid of the progress of Science because they scented through Science a danger to the opinions professed in the Bible. But this was never true of Hindu India with its roots going back to the Vedantic view of the Upanishads. Modern Science and Scientists all over the world have now started appreciating he Vedantic point of view trumpeted to the world by Swami Vivekananda himself at the end of the nineteenth century. Today Scientists are interested in recommending the Indian Vedanta for serious study by students of Science. This is so because, after the turbulence that the fundamentals of Physics underwent in the fourth and fifth decades of the last century Physics today is prepared to accept that the objective reality of the world is so much interlinked with the subject who observes it, that perhaps, as Vedanta would have it, it is only the Subject that is pervading the whole of the Object. This is actually the advaita point of view.

Indian Spirituality leans heavily on this viewpoint of the Upanishads. Indian History shows that this was the basis of the entire culture that runs as an undercurrent of everything in India – be it literature, music, painting and sculpture, the performing arts or religion. It is time that we switched back to this fountainhead of the culture. Once we do so the apparent contradiction between science and the so-called religion would all vanish. That religion is only a conglomeration of rituals and rites. But the essence of religion is the way of life which elevates one to an attitude of spirituality in every facet of one's life. Because of the advent of modern physics and the consequent philosophical implications, the West has now learnt to look at religion and spirituality more favourably. The West has now learnt to look at spiritual heritage of India with a spirit of learning. They seek India's Gurus, they read the Upanishads, they spend time in Indian spiritual centres and they struggle hard to assimilate he wisdom of the East. Centuries of misdirected western education have blunted our own tastes so far. It is now time for us to learn the futility of looking everywhere outside of Spirituality for the answers to the miseries of the human species.

QUESTION A-3: Is it true that even in the times of M.B. and before, fraudulent practices for acquisition of wealth were abundant? I thought Duryodhana's was a rare example!

For this question I take the help of Chaturvedi Badrinath's book: The Mahabharata – An enquiry into the human condition (2006). The teaching that one should not seek material prosperity at the expense of others was repeated in prudence literature for a long time. It was also recognised quite early in Indian thought that the teaching would be seldom remembered. The very long list of fines mentioned in Kautilya's Arthashastra (2nd cen. BCE) indicates the prevalence of deception and cheating in various ways: adulteration, false weights and measures; enhancing the values of articles and lowering their quality, deception in the manufacture of articles and in their sale, charging unauthorised rates of interest, claiming more than the amount loaned, manufacuring counterfeit notes, extortion and bribery etc. etc. Kautilya was evidently familiar with all the tricks of the trade. Cheating and fraudulent practices must have had a long history even before the writing of the Mahabharata. Hence the anguished and puzzled cry of Vyasa (almost at the end of the book: (*svargArohana parva*:5-62).

> *UrdhvabAhur-viraumyeshha na ca kashcit shRRiNoti me/*
> *dharmAd-arthashca kAmashca sa kimarthaM na sevate//*

With my arms raised, I am shouting; but nobody listens to me; when both wealth and pleasure can be had from dharma, why do people not follow it? Incidentally this shloka is called *MahAbhArata-SAvitrI*.

The Mahabharata leaves with us a last suggestion on material prosperity and wealth:

> *Dhanasya yasya rAjato bhayaM na cAsti corataH/*
> *mRRitaM ca yanna munchati samarjayasva taddhanaM//*

Earn that wealth which is free of the fear of the state, free of the fear of being stolen, and free of the fear that it will all end with one's death.

QUESTION A-4: Do you think religious education should be part of school curriculum? At what level?

1. From the age of 5, the practice of silent prayer should become a daily routine irrespective of the denomination or religion to which the child belongs or does not belong. The value of prayer can never

be overstated. No one can reveal God to another. But by revealing the value of prayer and inculcating the habit of prayer we place the child in a position to receive God-experience, in due time. Spiritual experience can come only through the correct understanding of prayer. Prayer is the point of contact with God. Silent prayer is the preparation of consciousness for the experience of Divinity within. The child should be tuned up from childhood well enough so that at adult age it is ready to receive the inevitable message that unhappiness and suffering are necessary for the unfolding of the soul within and to stand that unhappiness and suffering, prayer is the nutrition needed. So much does not have to be told to the child; but the habit of prayer must be made a second nature. This should not be left for the child to learn by itself after it reaches adult age – as is the experience of many a materialist adult who has learnt things the hard way and then, turned to the ways of the Orient in the past few decades. This is where it is not possible to accept the plea of the rationalist that, to pray or not to pray should be left to the individual for a decision on his own, when he becomes an adult. The plea assumes that each man, without standing on the shoulders of the men of earlier times, begins all over again to learn all that the earlier civilization has already discovered and recorded for us to take the torch from there. That is not the way Man has ascended to the present state of knowledge.

2. From the age of 7, children should know and learn the habit of sitting for an introspection and meditation. Any time the child errs in its social habits, obligations, table manners, discipline or routine, it should not receive corporal punishment but only an opportunity to introspect. The habit of introspection has all but disappeared in this modern age when everybody uses more than his leisure time to sit glued to the idiot box, without ever devoting any time to think about anything, not to speak of oneself – except of course, when they worry about something, which any way is not a productive activity.

3. From the age of 11 onwards, regular lessons on meditation should form part of the curriculum. Meditation need not be sectarian. But meditation is an effort to be done at the individual level and since Indian culture has an under-current of unity in spite of its plurality of traditions, it should be possible certainly in India which has the advantage (see No.8 further on) of several religions coexisting over the centuries, to integrate sectarian meditation into a classroom activity.

4. From the age of 15, the child should be educated on the positive aspects – not the bizarre, not the fantastic, not the strange, habits and customs – of all world religions by competent teachers, who, while they themselves would be students of comparative religion, would keep their own bias, if any, towards a particular faith or opinion, in abeyance as best as possible in order to present objectively the commonness of spirituality in all religions. Comparative religion is not competitive religion. Every religion is a blend of macro principles and micro setting. The latter is a mixture of local mythology and ritual and this never appeals to a stranger or outsider. Only a powerful poet, a talented sculptor or a mystic sage may be able to impart some understanding of it to one not born and nurtured in the tradition. But the macro-principles are usually understood, at least as an all-embracing framework, though not followed in its totality, because it speaks to man as man. It is a crisis of intellect that wants to adjudicate among the great religions of the world. What is important for the 21st century citizen is to come together and rediscover that this crisis of intellect can be resolved only by going back to the very ancient thoughts that have remained with us for more than twenty centuries now. The period of the first millenium BC is the most important period of history in this connection. That was the time when the axis of the world's thoughts shifted from a study of nature to the study of man's life and his inner aspirations. Then in India we had the Upanishadic Seers, Mahavira the Jina and Gautama the Buddha; in China we had

Lao Tse and Confucius; in Iran there was Zoroaster, in Israel there were the great prophets; and in Greece, Pythagoras, Socrates and Plato. That surge of activity and investigation and the profundity of thought of that period have never since been matched. They achieved so much with so little help from any gadgetry – which, by the way is what is helping us today to unravel further frontiers of knowledge. The philosophers of the first millenium BC achieved what they did by sheer rational thinking coupled with a certain unique intuition of their own. The test of significance of what they left for posterity is in the fact they have survived twenty centuries of war and peace, strife and hatred, and all the ups and downs of great empires and civilizations. It is extremely doubtful whether anything of what we call 20th century science and technology will survive as valid knowledge twenty centuries hence! The best guess is that not much of what we hold as science today will survive that long and even what we today call the scientific attitude may mean something entirely different in the year 4000 AD

QUESTION A-5: How may we, particularly non-resident Hindus, transmit the culture of Hindu worship to our next generation? How do we motivate them?

Just teach them how to say:

Om kesavAya namaH;
Om nArAyaNAya namaH; Om ShivAya namaH; Om durgAyai namaH;
Om subrahmanyAya namaH; and so on.

Just a few names of God, with *Om* in the beginning, with *namaH* at the end, and with the name of God in the dative case. Include only those names which you can relate to. If you don't know the meaning of a name, don't try to pass it on to the child. You must be able to explain something about the name, even if you don't know all the nuances of the Sanskrit name and its derivations. Include such standard names like Vinayaka or Ganesha or Ganapati, because He is the primal God to be worshipped; and Venkatachala-pati (the Lord of the Mount Venkata on the Tirupati hills), because there is no Hindu who does not believe in Him or His deity installed in the various temples overseas. Also include any other name which connotes your family deity or temple God which is very special to elders in your family. For instance one may say

Om vaideeSvarAya namaH

because LordVaideeSvara of Vaideesvarankoil in Tamilnadu may be the deity traditionally worshipped on all auspicious occasions in your family. Or you may say

Om vishvanAthAya namaH

because the Lord of the Varanasi temple is so important for Hinduism that it cannot be omitted. Or you may include

Om dattAtreyAya namaH

because you have never seen your father or grandfather doing religious ceremonies without invoking the Lord dattAtreya.

Thus all names which are subjectively very important to you or to your spouse, personally, should be included. But don't overdo it, either, for, more than fifteen to twenty names will be counter-productive as far as the passing on of the religious torch is concerned. Thus make a list of such names which is entirely your own. Don't worry about their small number. Worry only about the feeling you can generate in the name being worshipped. And most of all, when you expect the child to say these things, ensure that both the parents are also there to say the same thing.

The addition of *Om* at the beginning of every name is important even if you yourself do not understand much about it.

Om is the symbol of the Absolute Impersonal Godhead (the Ultimate Reality) of Hinduism; It is nameless but still the scriptures refer to it as *brahman*. Everything starts with it and everything ends with it.

At the end offer some fresh eatable to God, as a *naivedya*. Whatever you are going to eat may be offered, provided it is not a left-over. If there is no fresh cooked dish offer a fruit. Even a few raisins would do. And conclude everything with an *Arti,* with or without an *arti* song or prayer. In this way you would be following the hoary traditions of Hinduism but at the same time you would have cut your observances to the coat of your reduced availability of time. By giving this type of discipline instead of the conventional rote method of recitation of some stotras (which will be only mumbo-jumbo for the childen), we would be achieving the following:

- Each child will get a customised instruction, that befits the family and the particular environment and traditions in the family.

- The child would understand the meaning then and there. We are only paying a homage and obeisance to the particular deity named. The different names of god should be justified by appealing to the variety always inherent in Hinduism and the fact that the glories of God are innumerable and therefore also their names.

- The child has an infinite variety of possibilities of expanding this prayer routine into as long a one as anybody wants, as and when the child is ready for it. For, they have only to resort to various ashtottaras, sahasranamas and the like, which are abundantly available in the literature (even on the internet) – provided there is the motivation and the willingness to spare the time and the effort.

- By taking care to include Om at the beginning, and namaH at the end, of every one of the names of the divine, we have ensured (hopefully) the help of the Divine in the matter. So even long after we have disappeared from the scene, the 'child' would be ready for a spiritual maturity – just because of the Upanishadic saying: 'Those who worship That with the word 'namaH' would have their desires falling at their feet'.

⮞ The child would not have to murmur all sorts of unintelligible mumbo jumbo, which in any case would all vanish into nothingness when we of the previous generation are no more on the scene.

⮞ The child would have learnt the core of Hindu *bhakti*, which is very authentic, and this almost at no cost.

Of course, more fundamental than all the above, is the need for the present generation elders to believe in this, rather than simply make it a preacher's sermon. One should be able to teach by example rather than precept.

The only way to motivate them seems to be by ourselves living the Hindu way of life and believing in it. Without any effort to correct our own individual behaviour not only in temples and during special functions but in terms of our daily life all the 24 hours, we cannot expect to be able to transmit to the next generation any Hindu values of life by sheer word of mouth. Asking them to read V.S. while you yourself are watching a cricket match will not work.

If there is an altar in the house, – if there is not, the first thing is to create one – let us discipline ourselves to spend a few minutes (preferably half an hour, without compromising it to a minimum of at least 10 minutes) daily – every day at the same time, this is important – for both a silent meditation and a recitation of God's names.

It is important that all the members of the family be present together at this time of prayer. One should not hesitate on this score that back home in India one did not do such things. In the Christian world there is a commendable practice that when you sit together for meal you thank the Lord and pray together, at the beginning of the meal. The Hindu non-resident's substitute for this could be a common prayer at the altar either in the morning before one goes to work or in the evening time before all sit for dinner. This channelisation in cultural habits is a must if we want our children to imbibe something from the Hindu culture.

Any effort on our part to teach something which we do not ourselves do or understand will not be productive. It will actually turn out to be counter-productive.

QUESTION A-6: Very often we hear mystics and spiritual seekers reporting their so-called 'experiences' which are neither verifiable by scientific methods nor logical to our scientific ways of thinking. Are we to accept simply that there are things which we cannot explain?

The separation between Science and Spirituality is rather subtle and thin. When a mystic, religious or otherwise, reports his experience which from a scientific viewpoint and methodology is not amenable for verification, we should as true scientists be able to accept that, possibly, there could be things which are not explainable 'scientifically'. This is the humility which Science has all along been teaching us through its characteristic feature of raising more new unanswered problems every time we seemed to have answered an existing problem. Religion is not just rites, rituals and miracles, though these figure prominently in all popular practices of every religion. The thesis here is that though we may be apparently confronted with contradictions, if we look at the foundations or axioms from which the different conclusions of Science and Spirituality were arrived at, they can be seen to belong to two independent frameworks and as such are not comparable. The question of a logical contradiction does not arise.

Here is an example from Mathematics which shows that what appears to be two contradictory statements may both be true in their own setting, provided the hypothesis of that setting is granted. This may look like stating the obvious, but there is more in it. Look at the following statement where we are not being told where it is coming from:

$$5 + 3 = 1 = 5 \times 3 \tag{*}$$

Obviously this is an invalid statement, This is the conclusion we must arrive at if we were not given more data. Thus there is a contradiction between (*) and the ordinary arithmetic. This contradiction, however, will be resolved if we know under what hypothesis we made the statement (*). It was made under the hypothesis that every number would be treated as equivalent to the remainder it produces after a division by 7. Once this hypothesis is granted, we see that 8 is equivalent to its remainder 1, and 15 is equivalent to its remainder 1. Thus (*) is a true valid statement under the hypothesis made. It is certainly 'contrary' to the ordinary arithmetic where the statement would be

$$5 + 3 = 8, 5 \times 3 = 15 \text{ and } 15 \text{ is not equal to } 8 \qquad (**)$$

The two 'contrary' statements, (*) and (**) however, are both 'true' in their respective worlds that follow from the hypothesis made for them. One might say at this point that the new hypothesis made regarding casting off multiples of 7 and taking only the remainder is rather bizarre and seems to have been cooked up just to make a point. This is not so. It is not as bizarre as it looks. Ask any electronics student!

Nor am I giving bizarre meanings to the ordinary numbers 5 and 3 to get my statement (*). We are giving them the same ordinary meanings but we are putting them through a new process – the process of taking remainders after division by 7 – which we did not conceive of earlier. Once one understands the process, or we may say, this algebra, then 5 plus 3 and 5 times 3 could give the same answer though ordinarily they don't.

In general, when a scientist hesitates to accept the axiom of spirituality being the essence of Man and the validity of certain mystic intuitive experiences, he falls into the very superstition which he has been warning his fellow beings for centuries. He cannot contend that because the concept of the Inner Self appears to contradict his scientific rationale, it must be invalid. This is only similar to the attitude taken by sixteenth century priests towards Copernicus. Just because the propositions of Copernicus contradicted their religious beliefs and practices, they were considered to be wrong! The subject of the Inner Self is not in the field of Science; it is the field of *Vedanta*. Thus when a scientist hears a mystic talking about the Inner Self, he has no grounds for asserting that the mystic is talking about something that is non-existent. It is a different 'algebra' that the mystic is talking about. He is talking about a different process to be applied to the same body, same senses and the same mind and this results, according to him, in a different perception of one's own self. In the world of the seekers for Spirituality there are stories and stories of how each one comes to this conclusion from his own experience.

What is then the rational proof of the metaphysical statements of *Veda*nta? Where does the proof come from? The answer to this question is the grandest feature of Religion in general, and Hinduism in particular. It explains why Hinduism does not depend, for establishing its truth, on some event or the life history of some person or persons; why the progress of Science can never be inimical to the principles and pursuit of Hinduism which holds that its essential truths can be experienced by one's own intuition. Once you have disciplined yourself spiritually and experienced Divine Communion you can tune yourself to remain in that state even though you go about your worldly activities, playing your part in society. In this sense Hinduism gives you the privilege of 'seeing' for yourself what the scriptures are talking about. There is no better proof than seeing for yourself.

In Science, on the other hand, if you do not have expensive equipment, you may have to trust the printed report that such and such a result was noted in such and such an experiment conducted with that equipment. In the field of *Veda*nta the equipment is yourself and everything is in your individual power and effort. So every statement that others may make regarding the Inner Self is verifiable by yourself. In this respect *Veda*nta is like Mathematics. Mathematics is perhaps the only science in which the confirmation of every statement you make is one hundred per cent in your hands, because even though you use other people's results or theorems you can reconstruct for yourself in your own mind all the steps in the proof of those results and theorems.

This is what all sound mathematicians do. On the other hand, in other sciences, much of the confirmation of statements that even a great scientist makes may depend upon experiments which he himself cannot perform or has not ever performed. Thus Vedanta is more 'scientific' than the sciences. It is the science of the Inner Self. It starts from different axioms, but its methodology is the same – experiment, observation, conjecture, further experiment, observation, inference, dovetailing with the already established theory so that contradictions are explained or justified and so on.

Saint Thyagaraja, the great carnatic music music composer, in his song *'RAmabhakti-sAmrAjyam'* mentions how spiritual experience cannot be described in words, it can be only realised by self-experience (*svAnubhUti*).

QUESTION A-7: Why did the 'Perfect' God create this 'imperfect' world? Does it not throw a doubt of inconsistency in Sanatana Dharma?

The first part is probably a question which a child would ask. Even then there are variations of this question from the adult world also. 'What is the purpose of creation?' or 'Why at all is there a creation?' First let us answer the question of consistency. In fact Sanatana Dharma is the most consistent of all branches of knowledge. The most logical science, namely Mathematics, itself lacks a proof of its own consistency. Actually what has been proved is that the consistency of Mathematics cannot be proved. There are undecidable problems in Formal Logic. So one need not wonder when a Sanatanist says that the question of 'Why Creation' cannot be answered and has not been answered even in the scriptures. Of course there are schools of philosophy which subscribe to the idea that creation is a kind of sport for God. According to me this answer is a childish answer to the childish question 'Why Creation'. On the other hand, when we compare the Vedanta philosophy with all the sciences including Mathematics, it is Sanatana Dharma that is most consistent, the consistency being verifiable by one's own effort.. Because, in sciences like Physics and Biology expensive equipments are necessary for us to verify the truth of what other scientists say.

In Mathematics on the other hand, you can yourself go through the proofs of what others say provided you learn the background necessary for that proof. But even in Mathematics nowadays there are proofs of theorems only by a complicated computation in the computers and so not always accessible to all. It is only in Sanatana Dharma you can yourself arrive at Self-Realisation of what the great Rishis have said. In other words you have access to check the great truths by yourself, if you discipline yourself and follow the path. In spite of all this, even the vedas don't give an answer to the question: 'Why Creation?'. Maybe once you reach the *JIva*nmukta stage, maybe you will know, maybe you will not!

QUESTION A-8: Could B.G. be an interpolation in the M.B., by a later author?

I lean on the book 'Lore of Mahabharata' (1992) by Amalesh Bhattacharya, translated from original Bengali by Kalyan Kumar Chaudhuri, for the answer to this question originally posed by Bankim Chandra Chatterjee (1838-1894) in his Rachanavali. But most of the scholars including Shri Aurobindo have not accepted it. The entire M.B., including the B.G., was written many years after the war, which began in 3101 B.C. Veda Vyasa began the M.B. in 3041 B.C. and it took him three years to complete it. (Adi parva, 62/52). That the M.B. was not written before the war, but will be written after, in future, and spread over all the world – was an assurance Veda Vyasa gave to Dhritarashtra:

ahaM to kIrtiM eteshhAM kurUNAM bharatarshhabha.
pANDavAnAM ca sarveshhAM prathayishhyAmi mA shucaH.
(Bhishma Parva 2/13).

Further if you look at the manner in which the B.G. has impenetrated into M.B. in words and expressions enlivening it, you cannot countenance the thought that someone else wrote it and interpolated it in the book. There exists such a relation in feeling, poetic expression, spiritual insight that to imagine the M.B. and the Gita having been written by two separate poets is nothing but a travesty of imagination. 'The evidence for such a supposition, intrinsic or internal, is totally scanty and insufficient', says Aurobindo in his Essays on the Gita.

Sri Aurobindo has also spoken of "the four historical events. The siege of Troy, the birth of Christ and his crucifixion, the whisking away in exile, as it were, to Vrindavan, of Sri Krishna, and the dialogue of Sri Krishna and Arjuna on the battlfield of Kurukshetra. The siege of Troy was a creation of Greek civilisation, Krishna's domicile in Vrindavan was due to the cult of devotion (previously there were only meditation and rites of worship), Christ from the Cross brought into Europe the cult of human mercy and the dialogue at Kurukshetra will yet liberate mankind. Yet it is affirmed that none of these four events did at all occur." (Aurobindo's 'Thoughts and Glimpses' p.8). "If there were no Vrindavan anywhere then Bhagavat would never have been written" (ibid. p.7). In like manner it can be said that if the dialogue between Sri Krishna and Arjuna did not take place then no M.B. would have been written.

Tilak in his Gita Rahasya has said "That the M.B. and the Gita have been written by one hand, cannot be gainsaid… Gita has been put in the M.B. for the right reason and the right place, not interpolated. This conclusion remains at the end." (Gita Rahasya, p.447).

QUESTION A-9: Is it not wrong to consider Ramanuja and Madhwa on par with Adi Sankara as three main gurus of Hinduism when the theories of these two gurus do not conform to the sources of Absolute truth?

This was a question in the social media by one who believed in advaita. Let me record my strong reservations to this question. Ordinary people like us, should not under-rate scriptural and spiritual giants and Vedanta-stalwarts like Shri Ramanuja and Sri Madhvacharya. Even, as an advaitin, if you don't believe in their philosophy, they should be respected as much as advaitins respect Shri Adi Shankara. Shri Shankara, Sri Ramanuja and Shri Madhva belong to the triumvirate of towering

Sanatanists through whose expositions of Upanishadic philosophy (and mostly through them) India's spiritual excellence became famous and continues to be so, throughout the world. In all parts of the world, the moment Hinduism is mentioned, almost simultaneously the concept of spirituality and presence of spiritual excellences come to the mind of even the foreigner – all this is because of the universality of propagation and illumination by the three Vedantic Lighthouses: Shankara, Ramanuja and Madhva.

It may be *apavarga*, or *vaikunTa-prApti* or *moksha*. The goal is the same: getting out of the cyclic existence of the *JIva*. There is only preference, no negation.

QUESTION A-10: Why is Sri Rama Rameti shloka eulogised so much by Lord Shiva in answer to a question from Parvati? How is it equivalent to the chanting of thousand names of Vishnu?

The answer goes back to what is known as *kaTapayA sankhyA* in Sanskrit. First let us explain the *kaTapayA sankhyA*. See the table below:

1	2	3	4	5	6	7	8	9	0
क	ख	ग	घ	ङ	च	छ	ज	झ	ञ
ट	ठ	ड	ढ	ण	त	थ	द	ध	न
प	फ	ब	भ	म					
य	र	ल	व	श					

*The **kaTapayA – sankhyA** of* Sanskrit literature has the following two rules for words when they are read as per *kaTapayA sankhyA*: 1. Always the words begin with the unit place in the numeration. 2. Vowels are totally ignored. Following these rules we see that the numeral 52 is indicated by the word 'rAma'; because 'ra' stands for the number 2 and 'ma' stands for the number 5. There are 7 places in the shloka where 'ra' is followed by 'ma'. So we have 7 times 52, which is 364. The number 7 comes because, the *ra* and *ma* combination occurs seven times as follows in the shloka *srIrAmarAmarAmeti*…

rAma; rAma; rAma; rame; rAme; (mano) rame; rAma;

Now if you repeat the above shloka three times, you have caused the 'ra' and 'ma' combination (in that order) to indicate 3 x 364 = 1092.. That is how the three-repetition-tradition of the shloka establishes the equivalence with the *sahasra-nAma,* wherein Lord Shiva says, it is equivalent to the 1000 names of Vishnu!

Some may explain it as follows: *"shri rAma rAma rAma iti*... Is the shloka. *Ra s*tands for 2 and *ma* stands for 5. Three times *rAma* occurs. Each time you multiply *ra* by ma that is, 2 x 5=10. So the three times *rAma* gives 10 x10 x10 which is 1000. And that is why the equivalence". But I don't agree with this explanation, because, in *kaTapayA sankhya* multiplication occurs only when two consonants are mixed up as one consonant. For example *mra,* will give 5 x 2 =10, not otherwise.

Some examples for becoming familiar with the *kaTapayA sankhyA:*

शवि will stand for the number 45 जय will stand for the number 18. (See Wikipedia for further information)

QUESTION A-11: I feel that an excess of religious faith coupled with high-flown spirituality may slip into the colossal error of a fanatic refusal to see any virtue in forms of worship other than one's own. Is this not a crisis of intellect that has to be weeded off?

Certainly, yes. From the land of Sri Ramakrishna, Swami Vivekananda and Mahatma Gandhi, we cannot but agree with you. None of the spiritual acquisitions of humanity can be set aside. Just as we appeal to those who think that science is the be-all and end-all of human endeavour and tell them that they have another side to see, so also we must appeal to ourselves as followers of different religions or of schools of religious philosophy that we should not waste our energies in discussing at an intellectual level as to who is right and who is wrong. It is only a misguided intellect that will discover a difference between one name of God and another and between one faith and another. True religious life must express itself in love and respect for all humanity and aim at the unity of mankind. Dr. S. Radhakrishnan quotes:

rudrAkshhaM tulasI kAshhTaM tripuNDraM bhasma-dhAraNaM.
yAtrAH snAnAni homAshca japo vA devadarshanam..
naite punanti manujAM yathA bhUtahite ratiH..

Neither bead necklaces, nor the holding of tulsi leaves, nor wearing the three-line mark, nor ashes, nor pilgrimage, nor holy bathing, nor ritual sacrifice, nor meditation, nor visiting temples, nor having beatific visions of the divine, – none of these can purify man ultimately as would love of humanity and being engrossed in the welfare of all beings! Certainly, pride in one's culture and nationality is legitimate. But we may have to agree with Huston Smith when he says:

"this pride should be an affirming pride born of a gratitude for the values he has gained and not a defensive pride whose only device for achieving the sense of superiority it pathetically needs is by grinding down others through invidious comparison. His roots in his family, his community, his civilization will be deep but in that very depth he will strike the water table of man's common humanity and thus nourished, will reach out in more active curiosity, more open vision to discover and understand what others have seen.!"

QUESTION B-1: WHAT are the mentions in Hindu scriptures similar to Adam and Eve of western literature?

Well, such questions do arise in the minds of people; they have to be answered. But let me tell you, the answers will not take you anywhere.

First, in the conception of ancient history by the western world, creation is only a one-time event. But it is not so in Hinduism. Creation in Sanatana Dharma is a recurring event in the unending infinite past and the never-ending infinite future. So what we have in scriptures (particularly Srimad Bhagavatam, which is representative, as far as this subject is concerned, of all other scriptures of Hinduism) is the story of Creation in this day of BrahmA the Creator (whose one 'day' is 4.32 billion human years! (Already I can see several eyebrows have been raised in total disbelief – that is why I said: the answers will take you nowhere!). Well, on every morning of HIS day, BrahmA creates. As per the Vedas He creates it exactly as it was on the previous 'day' of His! (Authority: *'sUryA chandramasau dhAta yathA pUrvamakalpayat'* from M.N.U.: 1.14, 2nd sentence). This goes on probably every one of His days.

Now for the question of 'Adam and Eve'. We go back to Bhagavatam: Creation on this particular day of BrahmA –(in which we are living: it is now about mid-day in His span of a day): I am now copying the exact extract from Bhagavatam III-Ch.12 shloka 52 onwards:

"While he (Brahma) was thinking thus and hoping that the Divine favour would come to his help (for Creation) his body got divided into two parts. The body is called *kAya* because '*kA*' means BrahmA. That which belongs to Him is *kAya*. The two parts into which his body was divided became a man and a woman. The man was SvAyambhuva Manu and the woman was ShatarUpA. From that time onwards, the increase of created beings was by the mating of the female and the male. SvAyambhuva Manu himself got five children by ShatarUpA. – Two males: Priyavrata and UttAnapAda and three females named AkUti, DevahUti, and PrasUti. Ruchi, Kardama and Daksha were like Brahma already created. They married respectively AkUti, DevahUti and PrasUti". The rest is biological history! Believe it or not!!!

QUESTION B-2: The daily practice of Hinduism allows and sustains prayers to God, particularly to the deities enshrined in the temples; for example, O God, if such and such a good thing happens to me I will come to your temple and offer worship, a neyvedya and a contrbution, and so on. Does not this practice smack of a commercial deal? WHY is it not being questioned?

There are two kinds of such prayers. One kind is when we go and offer what we want to offer to the deity or the temple and then pray that we should achieve the ambition in our mind. But the other kind is more commercial. It would not offer the offering until the object of the desire is fulfilled. This second kind is the one which is practised more often. In the case of the first kind at least our trust in God has some credibility. In the second case there is no difference between this deal with God and the deal with a partner in business. Prahlada calls it a barter with God and the devotee a merchant. Perhaps in reality one trusts the business partner more than one trusts God! It is only religious and spiritual evolution that can change these habits. But look at it from God's point of view, if there be one such. He created you, me and all and He is waiting there for us to come back to Him and ask Him for what He is always ready to give, namely the ultimate *moksha*. Instead, we go to Him and ask for all the petty things of the world. And the irony and agony of God is **He keeps on giving all the things we want so that ultimately we may want what He wants to give us!**

QUESTION B-3: We are told that there have been so many avatars of God on earth in the various past. Then why have all the problems of the suffering world not been solved? If God has come down on earth, why does He allow the suffering to continue? why do we fight before His eyes?

This is a question which occurs to all thinking individuals at some time or other. But we forget that we think of this question only when we discuss the presence of the *avatara* of God. Why is it that the same question is not asked in respect of the all-knowing omnipresent Divinity, irrespective of whether He comes down on earth as an *avatara* or not? Even when Divinity is 'in its own heaven', it should be aware of all the sufferings man is subject to. So why does it not remove our sufferings by a stroke of its magic wand? The question thus posed seems childish, but there is none in whom this question did not arise in the course of his mental evolution especially in the darkest moments of his life.. The descent of Divinity on earth is to establish Faith in the existence of a higher reality and the truth of spiritual laws, so that we may have the strength to turn towards righteousness and steadfastly work for our salvation. If the Supreme Reality in the form of either the Omnipresent Supreme or an *avatara* solved all our problems of poverty and disease, do you think that will be the end of our problems? The cure of our bodily illnesses or of our poverty would still leave us at the same level of consciousness and spiritual evolution as before, so that, very soon, we would again be at one another's throat and the same chaotic world would continue. If God had really a purpose in descending on Earth, it could not be to solve our mundane problems of illness and poverty. It would be to clear the way for our spiritual growth. There might be great physical obstacles like Ravana or Kamsa who had to be destroyed for spirituality to grow, or there could be, as in modern times, a steep decline of all that is righteous and spiritual, not because of the gigantic presence of a Rakshasa or a giant-king, but because the entire humanity has degraded its own norms and standards. A Jesus did this by Himself suffering and making the supreme sacrifice for the cause of humanity. A Shankara did this by his intellectual analysis and preaching of devotion with an attitude of renunciation. A Ramanuja did this by the unceasing war against intellectual, religious arrogance and snobbery. A Ramakrishna did it by inspiring people to serve humanity unselfishly and see God in all forms. A Shankaracharya and a Ramana Maharshi did it by living the exemplary life of a saint. Our modern culture in general has gone overboard in testing how far we can go with sexuality, promiscuity, pornography, acquisitiveness, selfishness, aggression and violence. To turn this culture spiritually inward, and to make us look Godward, even an *avatAra* might find it difficult. That may be why perhaps the Almighty decided that we should experience a Pandemic!

QUESTION B-4: HOW does one know what one's *dharma* is? WHAT exactly is *dharma*?

This is a tricky question and difficult to answer. The literal word meaning of the sanskrit word '*dharma*' is 'that which sustains'. If you look into Manu-smriti which is one of the earliest expositions of *dharma*, it will get into the concept of *varNa-Ashrama-dharma*, which will give you answers that are academic and scriptural. In Hinduism all questions depend on the evolution of the questioner and the context in which the question has been raised. An answer to the present question, if it were from a child below ten, could be as a follows. The *dharma* of a doctor is to heal; the *dharma* of a teacher is to teach. Generally *dharma* connotes a man's role in life and so what is harmonious conduct for one (say, a soldier) may not be so for another (say, a priest). The *dharma* of a thing is by definition, the prime nature by which it is identified as *the* thing and by the loss of which it would cease to be *the* thing. The *dharma* of a student is to study. If he neglects his study and begins acting like a hoodlum he is falling into another's *dharma* and so departing from his sva*dharma*. Different people may react differently while facing the same set of circumstances. Just let us have a classical example from the M.B..

There were only three men – Arjuna, Balarama (Krishna's elder brother) and Rukmi (brother of Krishna's consort Rukmini) – who resisted the launching of the Great War in the M.B.. Balarama and Arjuna both wanted to take the path of renunciation; one the satvic way and the other the rajasic way. Balarama pursued his decision but Arjuna raised it too late and Krishna put him wise. But Rukmi's reason for not joining the war was egoistic, because, first he went to the Pandavas and offered them help. When they refused him he went to the Kauravas on the plea that he had an earlier ignominious defeat from Krishna before Rukmini's marriage, and they said: 'Why did you not come to us first?' and refused him. Thus he was left in the cold.

T.U.. has an everlasting summary of what to do and what not to do. 'Let your mother be a god to you; let your father be treated like a god; let your preceptor receive divine honour; let your guests receive hospitality like a god. Those acts that are irreproachable alone are to be performed and not the contrary ones'. The Yogavasishta lays down that what is not consistent with reason should not be accepted even if Brahma were to tell it. No human being is absolutely and perpetually blemishless. Love or admiration of one's exemplar should not prompt us to copy his imperfections. One should remember Parasurama's obedience to his father and not his slaying of his mother.

Dharma denotes the righteous ways of living while pursuing anything whatsoever in life. It is the principle and practice of righteousness. Devoid of *dharma*, one will miss the goal of fulfillment. Certain aspects of *dharma* change from individual to individual and also from stage to stage. But Sanatana *Dharma* recognises also the individual's freedom and concern. Krishna provided abundant clarity and enlightenment to Arjuna. But at the end of it all, he says: Reflect upon what you have known and then act the way you feel like.

Locate the Supreme as present in all. It is only a transformation of yourself. Make the mind godly, once for all. Feel you are for Him. Let everything you do be an extension of your offering to Him. Get fused into that wholesome Oneness. This will free you from all dependence, doubts and fears. Sanatsujata lists (in a lecture to Dhritarashtra) twelve facets of *dharma*: Knowledge, Truth, Self-control, scholarship, absence of intolerance, shamefulness for wrong-doing, patience, absence of jealousy, sacrificial ritual, giving, courage and calmness. If you still want to have a quick short list of what *dharma* is, here is a list of five for you!: Purity, Self-control, Detachment, Truth and Non-violence!!!. Or, put another way, it is an amalgam of the following six: 1. Self-confidence, fearlessness, *abhaya;* 2. Self-mastery, *(dama)*; 3. Self-integration, Arjavam, i.e, candour, straightforwardness, transparency; 4. Humility and modesty: *hrIh* (= Feeling of a shame in doing wrong); 5. Purity, cleanlinliness of body, mind, intellect and speech; 6. Compassion (*bhUteshu dayA*).

QUESTION B-5: What is Purity, according to Sanatana dharma?

(From 'The Great Hindu Tradition' by Sri Sarma Sastrigal, 6th edn. 2015):

Natural absolute purity according to the Shastras is unquestionably with the following: Fire; The feet of a *brahman*a; The hind part of a cow and the face of a goat or a horse; Puja articles even if bought commercially; A newborn; Mice, flies bees and their ilk, all amphibean creatures and things, elephants and horses; Water flowers and garlands, even if preserved in a refrigerator. Besides one should not question the purity of a child, a woman working in the kitchen or a person with a disease.

The M.B. answers, in numerous contexts, the question of purity of the human being,. The following is from 'The Mahabharata – An Inquiry into the human condition' by Chaturvedi Badrinath (2006):

Purity is of three kinds: of speech, of conduct and keeping one's body clean. To carry various external symbols like long hair, or to shave one's head, or wearing garments of tree or animal hide – all these are of no worth unless one's feelings are clean and unsullied. Whoever has 'purified' his body by fasting and other vows but has for his near ones no feelings of tenderness, destroys whatever he might have gained by fasting. Living a life-in-family with mind full of kind feelings for all beings is truly pure. The purity of heart is the true purity.

Bhishma says in Anushasana parva, purity is of four kinds: purity of the mind; purity that a pilgrimage gives, purity of conduct and purity born of knowledge. The last one is the highest. Those who do not dwell on the past, nor have a feeling of ownership in what is given in the present, nor are desirous of this and that, they alone are truly pure.

Krishna mentions five kinds of purity; of the heart; of the actions; of the lineage; of one's body and of one's speech. Of these the purity of the heart is most special.

QUESTION B-6: I have heard the statement: 'Man is the architect of his fate'. Does it mean we can alter our Fate? HOW?

Yes, in a sense. First of all let us be clear about what is Fate. The so-called *prArabdha is* whatever that is earmarked for this birth from the large bundle-load of consequences-to-be that we have acquired in all our past lives through our actions as well as thoughts. This *prArabdha* is our fate for the future. We cannot rewrite our past. It is a limitation, in our nature, our fate. But it is only our tendencies that are determined by our past (and the so-named fate). Our actions are not determined by our fate. Fate has nothing to do with it. Fate might have created the circumstances that led to our action, but the action is ours. Fate (*prArabdha*) might have contributed by shaping our tendencies which led to our action, but the action is still ours. It is our mind that dictates our action. All spiritual teaching pleads for the will of man to become stronger than the mind. It is not as if man is a helpless creature as a leaf in the storm or a feather in the wind. Man's will has a power which enables him to act in directions opposite even to his spontaneous bad tendency (*durvAsanA*). In this sense he is the 'architect of his fate'. Indeed this is the time when he should not slacken his self-effort. Ultimately, man's will must prove stronger than fate, because it is his own past will that created his presemt fate.

QUESTION B-7: What is your view on the folklore current among women particularly of South India that Goddesses Lakshmi & Saraswati being mother-in-law and daughter-in-law cannot co-exist in the same place and that is why they say, Money & Learning do not go together!?

Lakshmi is the consort of Vishnu, who created Brahma, whose consort is Saraswati. So Saraswati may be taken as the daughter-in-law of Lakshmi. That they could not get together is a myth, but very much current, of course. It is unsupported by any scriptural authority. The saying that Money and Learning do not go together is not true if you look at the modern civilised world of engineering, medical, technological and management professions. Saraswati & Lakshmi do coexist and actually thrive only when they are together!

In this connection it is interesting to note that it is Macaulay's English-based educational system which also contributed to such misconceptions. What did we do in olden days on Vijayadashami (tenth day of Navaratri) day? We taught our children the basic alphabets of the mother-tongue and of Sanskrit on that day devoted to Saraswati and continued with that training. After we adopted the English system of education we changed our style and put children in schooling on that day so that they will be taught English alphabets and continue to rise in western standards of education which had the only objective (for a whole century and more, from 1800 to 1950) of training the children to grow up as clerks and officers for the English-oriented Government. It is this education which came to be inconsistent with the prospering of Lakshmi the Goddess of Wealth. On the other hand if we identify Goddess Saraswati with the pure scientific and intellect-oriented spirit that is undoubtedly imbedded in our Vedas and Vedanta and Oriental style of Education, and identify Lakshmi with the applied science of all the Vedangas thereby identifying it with the growing modern areas of professional education this would have given us a better educational integration that we had been missing for one and a half centuries. The Saraswati of the East, which represents Pure Science and Abstract Knowledge and Lakshmi of the West which revels in Applied Science and Knowledge should have to come together!

QUESTION B-8: Confessions in Christianity gives an opportunity to redeem oneself from being a sinner for life by seeking forgiveness. Whereas Hinduism believes in *karma* and all the sins are carried forward to next birth. In today's world "To err is human" and "Forget and Forgive" are the order of the day. What is the reason, that Hinduism as a religion does not allow the person to redeem himself in the same birth? The same question has also been asked from a different perspective: WHY is *karma* not settled in one birth? Would it not promote honesty and justice in all? Why there's a carry forward system like in accounting?

My two cents: 'To err is human' and ' Forget and Forgive' are from living humans to living humans. Suppose in our Constitution of India, if we had said 'To err is human' and 'Forget and forgive' among our Directive Principles of State Policy, do you think the nation's judicial system can function? Same thing with the shastras and scriptures. They advise you to be tolerant, to be soft towards other's bad behaviour to you and so on. But the bad behaviour of those 'others' cannot be excused 'as a rule' by the shastras. So the shastras have made rules and rules.

Another very important observation. In modern days (in non-pandemic times) in many educational institutions, there is what is called a 'make-up' examination for those who could not for legitimate reasons, take up the main examination. It is only in Hinduism (of all religions) that you can 'make-up' for your own lapses. You are given another birth to change and and still another birth to change further,... ad infinitum. In all other religions, if you die with so many faulty actions in your life, you have to wait as a dead soul until the redemption (maybe punishment for sins committed!) comes, – God knows when!. In Hinduism you are given several births to gradually change, ultimately, even to a spiritual height. It is a succession of spiritual opportunities, says Dr. S. Radhakrishnan.

In fact this 'make-up' concept of explaining this was given to me by my late friend and respected colleague Dr. S. Venkateswaran (who was later, Director of BITS) because he had used it in one of his lectures on Hinduism in the University of London, when a question similar to our current question was raised after his address!

QUESTION B-9: Yudhishtira's question and his own answer after the other four Pandavas answered:

In the M.B., Shanti parva (Ch.167) there is a dramatic debate among the five Pandavas in the presence of Vidura about which way our living must proceed in practice. Yudhishtira raises the question. "In all men the three things *dharma, artha* and *kAma* are more or less active. Which is the best, which mediocre and which inferior?" Vidura answers first: 'The problem has to be viewed from a higher level. The quality of *dharma* is highest, *artha* comes next and *kAma* the lowest". Arjuna answers next: "This earth is the field of action and the aim of all action is to acquire Artha, for without it neither *dharma* nor *kAma*, i.e., enjoyment, can be satisfied". Nakula and Sahadeva together replied: "*artha* is very precious and rarely acquired. The pious one, if he is poor, his life is a total waste. But if an impious one became rich he is a thing to be afraid of. When *dharma* becomes one with *artha*, their coming together is like nectar. Their union is a triple enjoyment." Bhima says: "Craving for things is the best of the three objects of worldly existence. The entire world is moving impelled by desire. *dharma* and *artha* depend on desire, therefore, *kAma* (desire) should be considered the highest".

Yudhishtira now concludes: "In this sorrow-afflicted world man is bound by his own net of desires as a spider spins the web. Brahma himself has said man cannot be free, bound by desire for objects. It is not sin alone from which man suffers. Not only is man restlessly pursued by *artha* and *kAma* but d*harma* and virtue too are a sort of bond. One must rise not only above sin and adharma but also above d*harma* and virtue. When one is free from the blemish of good and evil the clod and gold become of equal value. Rising above d*harma*, *artha* and *kAma* one can achieve mastery over all three!"

QUESTION B-10: By saying that the Ultimate Supreme is the only Reality and by saying that everything else is transient and so not important, is not Hinduism under-rating the importance of daily worldly life and is this not the reason why India is behind many other nations in material prosperity in spite of its huge manpower resource?

Ultimate Supreme is the only reality, Yes. Everything else is transient, Yes. But the next statement is wrong. Hinduism does not say therefore the worldly life is not important. If they had said it is not important, the context means that they are not important for the ultimate objective of life, namely *moksha*. But there are three other objectives of life, namely *dharma*, *artha* and *kAma*. The pursuit of *artha* (material wealth & prosperity) or the pursuit of *kAma* (all desires, including the sensual ones) are both legitimate objectives of life, provided they are pursued in accordance with the first objective, namely dharma. The pursuit of artha & kAma in a way acceptable to dharma simply means that artha and kAma should be pursued as per scriptural injunctions in terms of self-discipline and societal discipline. The daily worldly life is considered so important in Hinduism that they have cared to lay down, in full elaboration and micro-detail, rules and injunctions starting from the morning ablutions and going all the way through the day upto the time that you go to bed. They invade even the privacy of your bedroom and lay down several do's and don'ts. These scriptural injunctions are there just to inculcate into you habits which you will never have to unlearn even when the time comes for you to look for something beyond the three objectives of dharma, artha and kAma.

Hinduism, with a paternalistic concern that it exhibits for your ultimate welfare, in all its scriptures, makes it clear to you, in no unmistakable terms, that your enjoyment of the driving and piloting of the real worldly life is not that important for you to exceed your speed limits, if you really have any ambition to look beyond! The father of saintliness in the Tamil world said this most succinctly, almost two thousand years ago. "Do all the good you can before the last hiccup deactivates your tongue" (Tirukkural No.335).

Some modern scientists make the mistake of thinking that they would find the truth of everything without first knowing themselves alright. But Hindu religion is clear that the more important thing is to know oneself right. How else do you prevent the misuse of science for war and terrorism? In the western world, philosophy and philosophical ideas are sometimes equated with exercises in futility, just because, philosophy was studied by looking for evidence for the validity of its ideas from everyday common experience of man and from the experience of his sense perception. How can this lead to the truth, when one has not recognised the primary ignorance about the divinity of man? Even the usefulness of intellect is limited because intellect itself starts with a primary ignorance about man's innate divinity.

QUESTION B-11: Is it not a crisis of orthodox intellect that arrogantly upheld some practices like sati?

As far as Sanatana dharma is concerned this kind of crisis of intellect expresses itself in so many other ways also. Since external exhibitions or expressions of dharma change from age to age, a dogmatic pursuit of such an expression beyond the times when it might have been valid can ultimately lead to a situation when the primary dharma of compassion and non-violence is jeopardized. The classic response of Vyasa, when asked to summarize the limitless scriptures that he had produced was; *'paropakAraH puNyAya pApAya parapIDanaM'* meaning: Merit (*puNya*) is what helps others and demerit (*pApa*) is what hurts others.

It is in this breed of arrogant upholding of the so-called *dharma* that practices like *sati* perhaps got generated without an eyebrow being raised. While it is true that Manu Smriti talks of woman having no independent status because, 'in her childhood she is dependent on the father, in her youth and middle ages she is dependent on the husband and in her old age she is dependent on the son' – the same Manu Smriti insists very emphatically that every man should act in such a way that not a single tear rolls down the cheek of a woman, for, if it does so, continues the Smriti, 'the person who caused that tear-drop will be destroyed with his whole clan'!. If the followers of Manu Smriti had only taken this seriously, women in Hindu society would have been put on the highest pedestal – which is what perhaps is indicated in the Indian habit of addressing or greeting every unrelated woman as 'Mother' or 'Sister'. But custom and tradition forced themselves away from the spirit of ancient times. They thrust humiliating and unfair norms on the woman of the household, particularly when she lost her husband, just as, at the social level, a caste-ridden arrogance created and sustained the practice of untouchability.

The touchstone of Hindu *dharma* is therefore the attitude with which one acts. One has to analyze oneself constantly. Whether it is a question of interpretation of caste rules, or a question of the meaning of the partnership between husband and wife, father and son, teacher and disciple, elder and younger – whatever it may be, the choice between what is *dharma* and what is *adharma* should be made only on the basis of absence or presence of an internal selfishness, (and of the presence or absence of a deep devotion to the Lord, as great religious masters like Ramanuja would say) irrespective of what the secondary scriptures, like Manu Smriti, have to say. Even if there is an iota of selfishness in what one is doing or saying, then there is the contamination of *adharma* in it. Selfishness may be of two kinds: one, which ultimately aims at a personal benefit of mundane return, or psychological satisfaction; and the other, of sense gratification. Only those actions, words and thoughts which are completely free of either type of selfishness are *dhArmic*. Pursuit of a *dharmic* principle as a dogma (for instance, irrespective of its social consequences) may ultimately end in nothing but self-gratification that one is upholding *dharma*. Any time the thought comes to you that you are the upholder of *dharma* and you are indispensable for the *dharma* to be nurtured, you may rest assured that egoism has set in and you have strayed from *dharma*. *dharma* is a very subtle concept. Even a divine incarnation like Rama who had every right to flaunt his observance of *dharma*, did not do so; he did not have the slightest egoistic pride that could lead him to proclaim that he was making the greatest sacrifice (of renouncing his right to be coronated as the prince of Ayodhya) for the sake of upholding *dharma*. His humility even prevented him from going beyond the simple statement, even in intense debates about the dilemma of right and wrong, that, 'Having been told by my mother and father to do what I am doing, how could I have done otherwise?'

QUESTION B-12: Have you ever witnessed or experienced, personally, a reasonably immediate effect of the power of any of the mantras of Sanatana Dharma?

This is actually a childish question. Throughout the history of Sanatana Dharma there are hundreds of instances of the power of Mantras having visible effect. Well, since the question has been asked, I shall answer it via a personal experience, which cannot be doubted in any way. The PuraNas have several passages where sure redress or healing is promised as the *phala* (fruit) of invoking, chanting or reciting or repeating a specific mantra. Experts will tell you what mantra or what stanza of a certain stotra should be invoked for what purpose, what disciplinary observances to follow and what should be offered to the deity formally. Hindu folklore and tradition abound with countless instances of the efficacy of mantras and the response of the divine to man's faith and dedication.

Decades ago, there was a railway station master, somewhere in erstwhile Andhra by name Narasiah to whom if a telegram is sent when someone is bitten by a snake, the poison will not intensify and when Narasiah did the incantation, or spell, the poison will be eradicated. He was nicknamed *"Pambu kadi Narasiah"* – 'pambu' is snake and 'kadi' is 'bite'. Such telegrams were allowed free of cost. The belief is that *maNi* (precious stone), *mantra* (incantation) or *aushada* (medicine). *Mani – Mantra – Aushada*, will cure illness.

However, lest we are misunderstood as revelling only in folklore and mythology, here is a dramatic instance of the efficacy of mantra even in the modern age, – to which I have been a participant and eye-witness.

The time was around 7-30 in the evening, during the nineteen-fifties, on one of the days of the Navaratri festival when the Mother Goddess is propitiated elaborately in all Hindu homes and temples with great zeal and devotion all over the country. The locale was the outermost corridor called ADi veedi, open to the sky, of the Minakshi temple at Madurai in Tamilnadu. Several thousands had gathered to listen to the daily lectures of Sengalipuram Anantarama Dikshidar, specially arranged as a nine-day series (*navAham*) during the festival. But as fate would have it, along with the people sitting on the Adi Veedi, several threatening dark clouds had also gathered in the sky, as if they also wanted to listen to the lectures of the renowned Dikshidar. Thunder boomed; the clouds seemed about to burst. Restlessness spread through the crowd and it seemed that, at any moment, they would decide to disperse, though reluctantly. Were the gods going to disturb the *navAham* and allow the clouds to burst? It certainly looked like it. There was no place in the covered portion of the temple to accommodate the thousands who had gathered in the open corridor.

Dikshidar came a little ahead of time, occupied his seat on the dais, and in his characteristic resounding voice urged the audience to repeat with him the following line from Lalita Sahasranama:

jwAlA-mAlinikA-kshipta-vahni-prAkAra-madhyagA

The chorus rang out and clear. Inspired by Dikshidar, the chanting took on a greater and greater intensity. The same line was repeated perhaps some twenty times. It was a thrilling scene to watch, participate and witness – the clouds dispersed and the sky became clear. The day's lecture was delivered as usual. The line from Lalita Sahasranama only meant: 'She (the Goddess) is seated amidst a massive fortress of fire called *jvAlA-MAlini*'. There are also other esoteric meanings of this half-verse, but, as we saw, it was not necessary to know the meaning to get the effect of the mantra, for except the Dikshidar and some learned members of the audience, the several thousands of the masses who joined in the chanting could not have known what it meant.

Well, sceptics might say, it was just a coincidence, nothing more! But read further:

In my personal experience, the same mantra was used by me for a similar purpose with the same effect. It was Shivaratri day, 25th February 1979. It was around 7-30 in the morning. A three-hour special Sai Bhajan was scheduled to start in another half hour in the open corridor of the Saraswati temple in Pilani, Rajasthan, India. A few friends and myself were setting up the place for the Bhajan, hanging pictures of gods, decorating them with flowers, spreading mats and durries, in short making all the preliminary arrangements for the gathering of devotees (mostly students of BITS), expected to number 100 to 150. From the morning, the sky had been clouded, but, as it was not a season for rain, nobody took any notice. But, as the final arrangements were being made, the clouds gathered in great strength and it was surely going to rain. In fact, a few drops were already on the ten or so volunteers who were working. It was suggested that they repeat the half verse starting *with jvAlA-mAlinikA*. The advice was taken by the others and each one, in his own individual way repeated the chanting of the line to himself. It did rain around five minutes to eight, but only for a minute or two. The clouds passed away and the bhajan went on uninterruptedly as scheduled. And, believe it or not, after the bhajan was over, in the afternoon of that day, it did rain and that too really hard.

QUESTION B-13: Is the idol or *vigraha* of a deity a deity?

Idol worship (worship of *a pratIka*) can probably be understood by the *incomplete example* of a flag of an army. An idol for a devotee is something like a flag for the army. **But the idol is more than a flag**. This is where the incompleteness of the example arises. An idol, by constant worship through *Mantras* culled from the scriptures, is actually the very deity which has been invoked into the physical frame of the idol, by *Mantra*-chanting. In Hinduism, the same question will have different answers to different levels of questioners. This is a point of difference between the philosophical process of Hindu thinking and the scientific process of human thought. From the point of view that there is only one absolute Truth and everything else is only a manifestation of that Truth, an idol is only a representation and not the 'real thing'. But from the point of view of a devotee who needs to worship Divinity in name and form, the images and idols which have been sanctified by the various *Mantras* and rituals are themselves the deities which have as much power as the Absolute. So a Balaji in Tirupati, a Nataraja in Chidambaram, a Meenakshi in Madurai, a reclining Ranganatha in Srirangam, a Visvesvara-linga in Kasi, a Jagannath in Puri, a Guruvayurappan in Guruvayoor, a Krishna in Udipi, a Varadaraja in Kanchi and a Venkateswara in Pittsburg and hosts of such sanctified 'images and idols' should not be cast into the role of just a 'representation' of the Absolute as a flag for the army. It is with this orientation that every devotee approaches a temple and worships the deity in the temple.

In the beginning his attitude is to assume that the Lord God is *in* the idol. But the Lord is certainly everywhere and so, in due time, the devotee, by the Lord's Grace, realises that his assumption that the Lord God is *in* the idol, is actually a truism. Thus what starts as an attitude or assumption, even though one may not have a belief, results in the realisation of the truth and this is far more than just belief or faith. This is **the esoteric significance of idol worship.** The millions of devotees who have benefited by such worship over several millenia both in their personal homes and in public temples constitute the unique testimony for the validity of this significance.

One more observation. Any worship for that matter introduces a duality between the worshipper and the worshipped and so is a comedown from the unique mental cognition of the Divinity inherent in oneself. Hinduism is therefore human enough to admit within its fold even those ordinary mortals who cannot rise, in their understanding, above the grossly concrete representations of God. In fact the religion goes even one step further. It says, in essence, each individual can worship God in whatever form that suits his competence, taste, and stage of spiritual evolution. (B.G. 7-21) This principle is in fact a recognition of the weakness of Man. If the grossest manifestation is the only thing that suits one's taste, mood, psychological make-up or intellect, one is free to worship God in that form. Even the same person may worship an idol at one time and at another time may meditate and attempt to merge in the transcendental Reality which is the basic chip that we are all made of, if we care to look within ourselves. One may choose one's favourite deity (*ishta-devatA*, in Sanskrit) and worship that as if it were the Ultimate. To be free to find expression to one's search for a personal God and seek His Grace for the purification of one's mind is a prerogative which every Hindu enjoys. This is the reason why the definition of a Hindu cannot be pigeon-holed into any grid that the western mind is familiar with. It is an extension of this thought that makes Hinduism a very tolerant religion. It is this train of thought in the Hindu mind that makes it live with different *Puranas* extolling different deities. The Shiva *Purana* may say that Shiva is the greatest God, every other God is subordinate to it. The Vishnu *Purana* may say the same thing of Vishnu. *There is no contradiction meant, implied or slurred over.* Such is the eclecticism of the religion. Here we certainly invite the criticism that Hinduism is too tolerant. But, *is there something like too rich a man or too beautiful a woman?*

The bottomline is as follows.. Since the permanent residence of God is in one's own heart, (Gita 18 – 61) every time a Hindu worships outwardly, he creates an idol (vigraha) or a picture for the God of his choice, or the God that suits the occasion, invokes God in that vigraha or picture from his heart and worships it in all the external forms he likes. This method of Puja (worship) is recommended to give devotion a concrete focus. Mark that it is God that is worshipped in the form of the vigraha and not the vigraha or idol as God. So long as you think it is an idol you have not got it. People who do not believe in God find excuses to find fault with the worship of God through idols and appear to be 'more loyal' than the religious, by propagating the argument that God is formless and so should not be worshipped through idols. God can take any form and so the form of the idol is good enough for us to worship God. It is the Infinite Absolute *brahman*, the all-knowing all-permanent Soul of our souls that is invoked into the form of the vigraha that is before us. *'Him the Sun cannot light, nor the moon, nor the stars, nor lightning, nor what we call fire; through Him all of them shine, and through His expression, everything is expressed'* (Mu. U. II-2-10). This Upanishadic passage is one among the many that are recited at Arti time, at the conclusion of a Puja performed in the vedic tradition.

QUESTION B-14: When one goes through the various Puranas, why don't we find a single uniform hierarchy of all these deities?,

It is very common in Hindu scriptures to glorify different divinities in different contexts. Each time a divinity is glorified they talk about it as the highest Transcendental Supreme; not only that, the other divinities without exception are said to be subservient to the divinity under consideration. It is difficult for a newcomer to Hindu thought to subscribe to this because he thinks of it as a confused hierarchy. Naturally he may misunderstand the whole presentation and think it is partisan. There is only one hypothesis by which one can clear oneself of this misunderstanding. And that is the hypothesis which Hinduism declares from the mountain tops every time it has an opportunity: **There is only one Godhead whatsoever.** There is no hierarchy in the worldly sense of the word. Each manifestation or presentation of that Godhead, as per the context, is to be considered supreme, for the period of that context. It may be Vinayaka who is considered supreme or it may be Su*brahmany*a in another Purana or Upanishad, and in another, Mother Goddess may be considered the supreme Godhead. Mother Goddess as the Gayatri is the *ParA-shakti*, non-different from the absolute *Brahman*. She is the UmA of Kena.U. She is the *devaatma-shakti* of Sv.U.. She is the *ParA-prakRti* of B.G.. In another context, say the Ramayana, Lord Rama may be considered as the Absolute *Brahman*. The right understanding would be to consider all divinities to be so many presentations of the same one Godhead about which the entire gamut of scriptures talk in so many varied ways.

For several centuries there existed an internal dissension (which is happily disappearing now amidst the modern onslaught of anti-religious attitudes) within Hinduism, particularly among the orthodox wing, about which name or what God is ultimate – **Shiva or Vishnu**. The vedic literature does not distinguish between the worship of Shiva or Vishnu. If we carefully go through the rituals which are totally veda-based, the names Vishnu and Shiva would occur almost indiscriminately without any connotation of the differences we attribute to the forms denoted by the two names today. Whether it is Shiva or Vishnu it refers only to the Supreme God – this is the intent of the vedas. '*He is BrahmA, He is Shiva, He is Vishnu, He is Indra, He is the Imperishable, He is the Transcendental Supreme*', says the M.N.U. This teaching of non-difference is important for the proper understanding of Hinduism. So long as you think it is Shiva or Vishnu and not the Transcendental Supreme you have not got the purport of the vedas. References to this identity among the literature composed by devotees of Shiva are innumerable; but this is not surprising since most of the devotees of Shiva also appreciate the non-dualist philosophy. But references to the identity of all names of God are also available in Vaishnava literature; here is a sample. Nammalvar, the Tamil Saint-poet, who is the foremost of the twelve Alvars and whose contribution of 1352 '*prabandhams*' (songs, stanzas) to the four thousand *prabandhams* of Vaishnava canon is considered as the Tamil Veda, writes:

Even if we scrutinise hard and discuss it further, the concepts of BrahmA, Vishnu and Shiva – after all the verbal exchanges, are tantamount to only one God of which these three are the names.

(Tamil: tiruvAymozhi 1-1-5.).

Thus God is One, in spite of His many names and forms. Many youngsters who have been influenced by the organization of religions in the western world constantly express doubts about the rationale of the multiplicity of gods and goddesses in the Hindu religious ethos. It is only when there is multiplicity, diversity and variety there is life, there is challenge, there is enjoyment. The challenge may be demanding but Hinduism has not only perfected it but also enjoys it as is evident from the endless festivals and colourful celebrations with a convenient mixture of devotion and extravagance, connected with the temples all over India. The many names and forms of God suit the multifarious tastes of people and their different levels of spiritual evolution. Multiplicity leads to enjoyment and the one-ness at the back, at the base, at the bottom, stands for Peace. **While oneness is primary, its manifested plurality is secondary.** The one-ness is *in spite of* the visible external multiplicity. When a Hindu worships the Sun as the Sun-God, what he is worshipping is not the physical star called the sun, but the Absolute supreme in its manifestation as the Sun.

The stories and complex mythology all go to show that it is the Ultimate Divine that is being talked about, though in terms of its manifestations, names and forms. When we worship the Sun as Sun-God what we are worshipping is the Absolute Supreme. A Shiva Purana may extol Shiva as the highest Transcendental Supreme and a Vishnu Purana may say the same thing about Vishnu. The Rama Sahasranama says that He is worshipped by Shiva and all other deities. The Shiva Sahasranama says that Rama is His devotee. There is no contradiction meant, implied or slurred over. When Hinduism says that all names and forms are those of God it means it. It is this catholicity of the culture and tradition of Hinduism that welcomes other religions as so many varied paths to God and consequently does not find anything contradictory or harmful in the coexistence of several Faiths. The external multiplicity is only an expression of the underlying truth of advaitic (non-dualistic) unity.

QUESTION B-15: WHY is rajo-guNa, inspite of its being the most dynamic (of the three *Gunas: sattva, rajas* and *tamas*) not acceptable?

Rajo-guNa is made up of desire, attraction and repulsion, likes and dislikes, enriched by attachment to the objects of one's desire. It is dynamic, certainly. But dynamism is not all that positive, as management experts may want us to believe. Dynamism, in the macro-sense, includes excitement, reaction to action, a constant distraction in terms of work and therefore an antithesis to peace and calm. The rajasic doer is eagerly attached to the work, passionately desirous of fruit, greedy, impure, often violent, sometimes cruel and brutal in the means he uses, full of joy in success and of grief in failure. (B.G. 18-27). He works from impulse and passion, seeking profit, rude and bold to be always one up. These do not warrant acceptability.

QUESTION B-16: When the Vedas prescribe costly and difficult sacrifices for man's salvation, how can mere praise of the Lord, or just repetition of His names, which costs no money, substitute for them? How can mere words and repetition of words have so much power?

The very ease with which one can practise *nAma-sankIrtana* is a factor in its favour. It is highly recommended by every Hindu scripture for many reasons. It is the only mode open to all, irrespective of caste, creed, sex, status of enlightenment, state of mind or any other distinction. It does no harm to others. It is not conditioned by time or place; any time is good enough. And there is no rule which says, you have to do kirtana only here and not there. There is no ritualistic requirement. The recitation of names can purify you both internally and externally and take you to the highest level of attainment, namely, *moksha* itself.

Mere words and repetitions of words do have great power. Those who rely totally on the limited laws of science and reason may argue that words are, after all, just sound and cannot be expected to cleanse or correct the mind of man. But a word is not just a sound. Kalidasa, in the very first shloka of his Raghuvamsam, very expressively brings out the identity between *vAk* (word uttered) and *artha* (its meaning, significance) by comparing it to the intertwining between the male and female forms in the *ardha-nArIshvara* representation of Shiva. When we say 'table' the four-legged piece of furniture instantaneously appears as mental picture. You cannot think of one without the other. People are sitting quietly in, say, a meeting. Somebody calls, 'Snake!'. Will the calm continue? Just the word 'snake' magically destroys it. One might be sitting before a plateful of delicacies, but if somebody nearby speaks of something dirty or disgusting, one is repelled by the food. The mere sound of words creates so strong a reaction.

Sri Sathya Sai Baba narrates an unforgettable story that illustrates this. A certain officer was inspecting the work of a teacher in a school. The officer who had a hearty contempt for 'mere talk' asked the teacher, "How can you ever hope to transform the nature of these children by the words you utter? Show them by deeds: act, don't speak!" The teacher protested and argued that words do have a profound effect on the mind. The argument continued for some time and the teacher was desperately looking for some way of carrying home his point. At last he resolved on a plan. He said to one of his pupils: 'Look here, catch hold of this officer by the neck and push him out of the room.' Hearing this, the inspector flew into a rage and started berating the teacher. The teacher said, 'Sir, I only made some sounds shaped into a few words. No one pushed you or hit you or even touched you. It was all mere sound. But see how it has enraged you. It was all mere sound. Words, sir, do help in modifying character and shaping nature. They have vast power.'

And Sathya Sai Baba continues to explain: "When words referring to worldly situations have such an electric transforming effect on the mind of man, certainly words conveying spiritual and elevated meaning will help in cleansing and correcting the mind of man. When we filter the air with harshness, we become harsh in nature, when we fill the atmosphere with hatred, we too have perforce to breathe that air and we are hated in return. When we saturate the air with sounds full of reverence, humilty, love, courage, self-confidence and tolerance, we benefit from those qualities ourselves. The heart is the film and the mind is the lens. Turn the lens toward the world and a worldly picture will fall on the heart. Turn it towards God and it will transmit pictures of the Divine".

There is another explanation, an esoteric one, for the efficacy of *nAma-sankIrtana*. It is a natural outpouring of sentiments from the heart and leads to a communion between God and Man. During *nAma-sankIrtanas* a charmed circle of sound is produced and a strange sense of the greatness of God and the essential unity of man creeps into the soul. With the successive awakening of each of the six yogic *chakras* in the human body, there are corresponding changes in one's body, emotions, mind and degree of consciousness. The progressive expansion of consciousness yields an increase of knowledge about oneself and a deepening awareness of the self-luminous Resident of the body, namely, the Atman.

The *Kundalini shakti*, which sleeps as it were at the *MUlAdhAra chakra* can be made by yoga practices to wake up, evolve and travel upwards through the *sushumnA nADi*. While it does so it is imperceptible to the senses. But every day it expresses itself, in every one of us, in all our activities. Particularly the expression of it in the form of the human voice is known as the manifestation of *nAda-brahman*, the Sound Absolute. Thus in the perfection of the human voice the primeval energy comes to prominence through the words, sentences, and mantras we utter. We do not realise, in our ignorance, that it is the Absolute Supreme that is expressing itself through our voice and that the satisfaction we derive in saying whatever we say is only an iota of that Infinite Bliss which is in us. If only we could recite the names of God unendingly, it would take us towards an identity with the *nAda brahman* at every step. A bhajan of the several names of the Infinite Being (like the Hare Krishna mantra or theBhajan mantras of Brindavan) creates the necessary vibrations, starting from the *MUlAdhAra-chakra*. An unceasing *nAma-sankIrtan* cleanses the crust of *vAsanAs* that has accumulated over several births, and thus paves the way for the stored-up Kundalini energy to get tuned to the frequency of the Infinite Energy in the Cosmos.

The recitation of the names should come from the heart, not just from the lips or the tongue. It must be a spontaneous manifestation of inner conviction and ecstasy. Such intense yearning for God purifies oneself as well as those around. Life is full of sorrow, beset with fear and despair. The only way one strengthens oneself to meet hard times is to contact the source of all strength and bliss, namely the Infinite God. This is the way to overcome the evil in us, lay low the *'pashu'* (beast) in us and instal the *'pashu-pati'* (Lord of all beings) in our hearts.

In reciting the names, however, one should not be guilty of offences to the Name. Such offences will more than offset the benefits of *nAma-smaraNa*. One should not insult or speak ill of others, since every one is divine. No distinction should be made between different names or forms of God, though one may have some tastes in the matter – which, mostly is because of one's background of evolution, not only in this birth, but in all previous births. The Divine Name should be looked upon as supreme truth and not as mere eulogy.

Also there is a popular verse which is very favourable to those who don't understand the grammar of Sanskrit:

> *apaNDito vadati vishhNAya paNDito vadati vishhNave/*
> *ubhayostu phalaM tulyaM bhAvagrAhI janArdanaH//*

The non-knower of Sanskrit language may say *'vishhNAya'* rather than the correct word *'vishhNave'* to convey the meaning: "To Lord VishhNu". But VishhNu the Lord takes only the attitude (*bhAva*) and so blesses both in the same way. Recall also B.G.9-26. Recall the Tamil devotee Kannappa Nayanar's story. Even in modern practice of law, it is the intention that matters and not the act.

It is true that the repetition of God's names will absolve one of all sins, but on that account one should not use the name as a cloak for the commission of sins. The cultivation of the five basic virtues, namely, Purity, Self-Control, Detachment, Truth and Non-violence, should not be neglected. One should not behave in a way which is devoid of love; one should not be governed by the conceits of 'I' and 'Mine'. The fundamental principle of *nAma-smaraNa* and *nAma-sankIrtana* is *shraddhA* (faith and conviction). Love of, and exclusive devotion to, the Lord, is necessary. When one does such a *nAma-smaraNa* it becomes a *yajna* in itself. The Lord Himself says in B.G. 10-25: 'Of all *yajnas* I am the *japa-yajna*'. The theme of *nAma-smaraNa* or a *bhajan* or a *japa* should be that the one Supreme Almighty, who is spoken of by different names, is the subtlest of things ever experienced, though hard to analyse or apprehend by ordinary commonsense and, therefore, every name of His should take us to Him, if we realise the intrinsic value thereof.

QUESTION B-17: Is it not true that our Puranas and Itihasas speak of meat-eating even by the Brahmins of that society?

We do have records of such traditions. Because of these traditions historians have tended (wrongly) to think of vegetarianism as a later interpolation into Hinduism. The fundamental thing to be remembered here is that **attitudes are important**. Gita (Ch.17: 16) calls this *'BhAva-samshuddhiH'*. Rituals and rites will mean the right way only if one's attitude is tuned properly. Let me tell you two stories.

One day Guru Nanak was lying flat on the floor of a temple with his feet extended towards the sanctum sanctorum. Every one thought he was committing the greatest act of disrespect to the deity enshrined in the temple. 'Why don't you turn your feet away from God?' someone asked. His quick retort was 'Show me a direction in which God is not there!'. The moral of the story is that it is the attitude that matters and not what you do. Incidentally this story demonstrates the truth of the maxim: 'Never attempt to do what great men, saints and avataras have done; on the other hand, listen to them and do what they ask you to do'. You can never imitate a personality like Nanak or Shankara and do what they did. Vyasa says at the end of his description of Rasa Krida that if you think you can do Rasa Krida just as Krishna did, it is like your imitating Lord Shiva's drinking the poison that came out of the milk-ocean. Nanak can extend his feet in the direction of the idol that is considered by everybody as God, because for him God is everywhere and he lives in that identity. For you and me, so long as we miss that feeling of identity of the feeling of the presence of God everywhere and in every being, we have to conform to the standard norms of discipline and tradition, because it is a ritual which trains us in the controlling of our natural *vAsanA* to do what the mind likes to do. Great men, on the other hand, are not bound by rules and regulations because it is they who make the rules – not that they sit down and concoct them for us but what they say becomes the rule because they say it.

Here is the other story. A great Guru (one version of this story names this Guru as Adi Shankara) while walking through a street of Varanasi with a disciple, got hold of a bottle of wine and drank it. The disciple thought that the Guru has shown him the way and that he could do the same. So he took the opportunity to drink wine too. But the Guru, further ahead, took molten lead in the cup of his hand and drank it with equal comfort. The disciple was nonplussed and immediately realized his error. Again it was the attitude that mattered, not the physical act. If you can see no difference between molten lead and any other prohibited article like wine then the ordinary restriction not to drink wine would not bind you. But so long as you are in the plane of the ordinary disciple who would still drink wine only to gratify his senses, the natural rules and regulations of Sanatana Dharma would apply and they have to be obeyed.

It would now be clear how, in the matter of the question raised concerning Brahmins eating meat in ancient times, while vegetarianism is considered a virtue in Hinduism, the crucial point is that it is the attitude that matters. When they are said to have consumed meat, the story says it was not to gratify their senses but to follow certain prescriptions of a ritual in which they put such faith that the animal which they killed would merge in the infinite. We moderns neither believe in that ritual nor do we have the self-control to stay away from meat except for the purpose of that ritual which they followed. In these circumstances it is no use quoting actions of great men for purposes of extrapolating to us, common mortals, the privilege of freedom to act in the same way.

QUESTION B-18: WHAT is a tAraka mantra? Is '*rAma*' a tAraka mantra?

'TAraka mantra' means a mantra which can ferry you across the cycle of births and deaths, namely the ocean of samsara.. There are only two *mantras*, in the whole of Hindu religious tradition, which get the epithet '*tAraka*' and these are the syllable *OM*, and the name *RAma*. This single fact epitomises the importance associated with RAma, the name as well as the Godhead, in the entire Hindu cultural milieu.

The derivation of words from their root syllables each of which is the root of a verb signifying an action, is, in the Sanskrit language, a very instructive excercise. Hindu religious literature is replete with such derivations for almost every word that it uses. Each of the names of God like Rama, Krishna, *Shiva*, Narayana, etc. – in fact, each one of the names of God in the various lists of thousand names of God (= *sahasra-*

nAmas) has been assigned several derivations from their root syllables. 'The one in whose memory yogis revel in the bliss of *Brahman*' – is the meaning of the word Rama– according to the declaration (*ramante yogino-nante brahmAnande chidAtmani*) in the Padma-*purANa* and in Rama-tApanI Upanishad. '*Ramante*' (they revel, enjoy) is the action which forms the root verb for 'Rama'. *anante brahmAnande cidAtmani* means in the infinite bliss of *brahman* which is itself the Consciousness (*cit*) Supreme as the Atman.

The greatness of the word 'Rama' is not just because what the son of Dasaratha did what he did. Preceptor Vasishta hit upon the name for the child of Dasaratha because he knew that it was already a '*tAraka-mantra*'. And that is why the name Rama has been isolated and earmarked to be equivalent to the whole of V.S.

The sage Valmiki before he became a *MahaRshi*, recited the name of Rama, several thousands of years and attained the status of a *mahaRshi*. The syllable '*ra*' comes from the eight-lettered *mantra* of Narayana and the syllable '*ma*' comes from the five lettered *mantra* of *Shiva*. Both are the life-giving letters (*JIva-aksharas*) of the respective *mantras*; because without them the two *mantras* become a curse. Without the letter '*ra*', the *mantra narAyanAya* becomes *na ayanAya* – meaning, not for good. Without the letter '*ma*', *namas-shivAya* becomes *na shivAya* – meaning, again, not for good. Thus the word Rama combines in itself the life-giving letters of the two most important *mantras* of the Hindu religion. The syllable '*ra*' the moment it comes out of the tongue is said to purify you from all the sins by the very fact that it comes from the *mantra* of the protector, *nArAyaNa*. *It expels everything which is not pure inside.* On the other hand, the syllable '*ma*' burns all the sins by the very fact that it comes from the *mantra* of *Shiva*, the destroyer. *It prevents anything from entering and soiling the receptacle which has become pure.* This is therefore the King of all *mantras*, the holy jewel of *mantras*, as is rightly sung by Saint Thiagaraja, who is one of the most famous recent historical examples of persons who attained the *JIvan-mukti* stage – the released stage even while alive, by the sheer incessant repetition of the Rama name.

QUESTION B-19: Praying to God, chanting stotras etc all purify the mind; this is obvious; Are there any other things which can purify the mind?

Yes, there are. I am borrowing from Indhu Dharmam (in Tamil) by Cho (pub. By Alliance 1996), which is again a summary of the teachings of MahA Periava of 20ᵗʰ century. In olden days, these small small things were observed from generation to generation and they helped the poor and at the same time elevated those who gave. For instance, when a poor man was conducting a marriage of his daughter, all visitors, relatives or otherwise, presented fives and tens – which considered isolatedly, is of course a small amount, but when it reaches the poor householder from several people, becomes a substantial help for him financially. This way the giver and the receiver were both benefitted – the former, spiritually, by the act of giving, and the latter by the eradication of his financial stringency. Nowadays all this has changed. People spend lots and lots of money in marriages, birthdays and what not and elaborate feasts are served to highlevel relatives and friends. The sorrowful part of the whole thing is: the host has some untold expectation in feeding the well-to-do friends, because he expects something back from them in the form of either a professional or financial help; and the receiver-guest at the party knows fully well that the whole thing has a purpose and so goes back after saying a formal thanks that comes only from the lips!. As such both the giver and the receiver are insincere to each other.

This situation has to change. Even small acts of social service, like weeding off unwanted growth from small pathways inside or outside developed localities, would itself be of great spiritual value that will clear the cobweb of dirt in one's mind and purify it.

QUESTION B-20: Your writings show you are an advaitin and you extol advaita-bhakti. Don't you have any appreciation of other kinds of bhakti, like, for example, the visishtadvaita model of Bhakti?

I notice the implied mild criticism in the question. Certainly I have great appreciation for all kinds of bhakti. The seeds of the concept of *bhakti* go back to even the vedas. The plant of *bhakti* sprouts in the Upanishads; becomes a full-fledged plant in the *itihAsas*, particularly the M.B., blossoms in the *PurANAs*, and flowers in the *Aagamas* both of the Saivite and VaishNavite varieties. The AlvArs and nAyanmArs bring out the fruits which ripen in the age of the AcAryas for all posterity to consume, enjoy and attain beatitude. The personal God with all His superlative attributes is worshipped mainly in six forms – *Shiva, Vishnu, Shakti, SUrya, GaNapati* and *Subrahmanya*.

Among the various non-Absolutist conceptions of God Shri Ramanuja's is the most well known, has the largest following and has the claim to the longest tradition. It conceives of a Personal God with infinite divine attributes and infinite varieties of auspicious forms. He, however, is the single Conscious Entity that has all matter and all the souls as His body. He has infinite compassion for the souls and so He is greatly concerned about their salvation. The soul has to comprehend this Inner Reality, rid itself of the three-fold miseries of life and merge in the infinite bliss of the eternal sanctity of God. This is *moksha.* This is a communion with God, not a realization of complete identity. Those who desire this, should practise a seven-fold discipline – namely, the discretion of consuming only the right type of pure food; dispassion; the attitude of living in the presence of the Absolute; the action of the five daily rituals (*yajnas*), the ethics of a *dhArmic* life, absence of frustration and, finally, the absence of delusion caused by affluence and material happiness. Such a one does his duties as the dictates of the Lord and in total dedication to Him. This leads first to internal purity and in due time blesses one with the insight of Yoga wherein one can visualise the Spirit. That leads to the awareness of the Soul of all Souls. Love of God pours forth spontaneously now. It is a self-forgetting Love that continues uninterruptedly like the pouring out of oil. This is *the bhakti.* The Lord may be conceived of as your guide, your master, your friend, your child, your beloved. Each one of these perfects the devotional attitude and ends up by creating the irresistible urge to see Him in person. Recall #63 in Alavandar Stotram: *pitA tvam mAtAtvaM*...... Meaning,

'To me and to all the worlds Thou art the Father, mother, beloved son, dear friend, well-wisher, teacher and the goal. I for my part am Thine – Thy servant, Thy attendant and a refugee at Thy feet. Having offered whole-hearted surrender to Thee, I remain, now, Thy sole responsibility'.

This is one of the innumerable verses in the ocean of bhakti literature replete with the depiction of the attitude of total surrender to God. That is the stage of *bhakti par excellence*. And when that vision of the Supreme Person sparks then is the stage of Supreme Enlightenment. Thereafter there is no return to the mundane living. The Lord then frees you from the bodily prison and takes you to His abode to live in fellowship with Him. The thing that makes this happen is only the Grace of the Lord and nothing else. That is why the Lord is said to be both the ultimate goal (*upeyaM*) as well as the path (*upAya*) to that goal. Such a faith ends up in the action of surrender to the Lord. Swami Desika lists eight kinds of devotion which epitomise the concept of spiritual love in a masterly fashion:

Feeling at home in the company of devotees;
Enjoying the worship of the Lord;
An unsatiated eagerness to listen to the stories of God;
Horripilation and choking of voice when hearing about Him,
talking to Him and remembering Him;
Performing of ritual pujA to the deities;
Not showing off in one's service to God;
Meditation of Him and Him only; and
Praying to Him, never for mundane trivialities.

QUESTION B-21: In B.G. Ch.6 Shlokas 37, 38 Arjuna asks two questions about what happens to a sincere yogi whose life ends before he sees any fruits of his *yoga-sAdhanA*. Krishna is supposed to have given him a monumental answer about further births where the yogi will continue his *sAdhanA* from where he left. I am not

convinced of this answer. The further birth and all seems to be only in the distant unknown future. Can you help me with something better?

You want me to be one up against the divine Krishna.? I am only human though boasting the name of Krishna. Well, I can see your stress in your question. It is all because you are too impatient, to see the fruits of your work rightaway. That means you are still not convinced about the whole teaching of the Gita. Instead of trying to answer you myself, I shall take the help of Prof. B. Mahadevan's book, The following is a verbatim quotation from his book 'TIMELESS GITA – ENDLESS BLISS' (2019) and I think this exactly answers your question.

"Most of us suffer from the thought that we must see the results of our efforts at the end of the day. This is the major source of mental stress that we experience. In matters pertaining to self-evolution and inner development the problem is even more acute as we do not know the results that we need to look for. This induces impatience and needless speed in doing things, all the time looking for results and looking for signals all around.

"What are we to learn from the assurances of Sri Krishna (in shlokas 6-41,42)? If we bring an element of faith (*shraddhA*) into this matter, it will relieve us of great pressure that we may face in terms of what if I don't succeed before I die? We will totally stop wasting our time looking around for positive signals, even when some of them may indeed be there. We will also reduce our efforts in running from one Godman to the other to find out if the inner development is indeed happening to us and what more needs to be done to accelerate the process. There will be no desire to compare and contrast ourselves with others who we think are making much better progress in self-evolution. We will feel no need for benchmarking ourselves against someone else.

"With thoughts taken away from many such distracting issues in our life, the possibility of progressing will only improve even more. The charm of the message of Shri Krishna in His shlokas (40 to 45 of Ch.6) lies precisely here".

QUESTION B-22: According to Sanatana Dharma, when was the original creation and what was the first creation? Or, to ask a similar question, As per karma theory, it is said birth of a *jIva* follows its *karma* in its earlier birth. Now, what came first? *karma* or birth?

The Vedantic tradition holds the view that creation is without a beginning. So the question of first creation does not arise. Creation and Dissolution alternate like day and night. The relation beteen creation and dissolution is like the relation between the seed and the sprout. So *JIvas* have always had a previous existence and must have done good and bad deeds according to their likes and dislikes. Taking into consideration the accumulated stock of merit and demerit of the *JIvas* the Lord dispenses justice and ensures that the *JIvas* receive the rewards of their actions. That the world of empirical existence is beginningless (*anAdi)* is brought out by the scriptural statement "The Lord created the Sun and the Moon **as before**" (*sUryA-candramasau dhAtA* **yathA pUrvam** *akalpayat* – M.N.U.) Therefore it is impossible to think of the predicament of the *JIva* without prior *karma* and also it is impossible to think of *karma* without the *JIva*.

QUESTION B-23: India has miracle stories in all its temple-cities. Can you guide us to any one of them which has an undeniable historical importance?

Certainly. Let me tell you about the miraculous recovery of the lost Tevaram hymns from the Chidambaram temple:

The great temple-builder King Raja-Raja I (985-1014 A.D.) had also a desire to unearth the *tevAram* hymns believed to be lost or hidden somewhere except the few that professional singers in some temples remembered. Once he heard about nambi-ANDAr-nambi, a little boy of a village near Chidambaram, whose devotion was considered so great, it was said that the *vinAyaka* idol of the place yielded to his request to eat a dish of rice offered by him. The King had this boy located and asked him about the whereabouts of the lost hymns of the Shaiva-samyAchAryAs. Back came the reply that the hymns lay in a locked room in the western *prAkAra* (corridor for perambulation) of the Chidambaram Nataraja temple under the seals of the hymnists themselves. The King used his authority as well as some imagination to recover the hymns at the place indicated but the whole thing was a heap of palmyra leaves under a mound of ants. At that time there was heard an aereal voice declaring that whatever was recoverable should be enough for this era.

What was recovered was probably 384 out of a supposed 10,000 hymns of Sambandar, 312 out of 49000 of Appar, 100 out of 37000 hymns of Sundarar, totalling 796 *TevAram* hymns made up of 8284 stanzas.

This is how the now well-known *tevAram* hymns were discovered. Raja Raja I had thus made the greatest contribution to the growth of Tamil literature. From that time onwards the hymns are being sung in all Shiva temples of Tamil origin by professionals trained for this purpose under benefactions made by successive generations of kings and philanthropists.

QUESTION B-24: HOW does one exhaust one's sin?

There are three kinds of sins – *mAnasaM* (done by the mind), *vAchikaM* (done by the speech) and *kAyikaM* (done by any organ of action). The first kind of sins leads to a lower level of evolution in transmigration. The second one is the cause of being born as animals and birds *(jangama),* which do not have the capacity to speak like the humans. The third one ends up in becoming an inert object *(sthAvara)* like what happened to Ahalya and Nalakubara. One can understand now why Devi Bhagavatam has in its prayer-sequence, the words '*namas-tasyai*' three times – one each for each type of sins one might have committed!

Bodhayana dharma sUtra has the following shloka on *the exhausting of sins*:

kRRitvA pApaM hi santapya tasmAt pApAt pramucyate/
naivaM kuryAM punariti nivRRityA pUyate tu sah//

shoceta manasA nityaM dushhkRRitAny-anucintayan/
tapasvI cApramAdI ca tataH pApAt pramucyate//

Regretting the sin done is the way to atone for the sin done. By taking the decision that it will not be done again is what purifies it. Every day one has to keep thinking about it and regretting it. Whether one is a tapas–performing yogi, or whether one is a defaulter this is what releases him from the sin. It is to be noted there are no unforgiveable sins in *sanAtana dharma*. Does all this mean that every sin is forgiven? No. Not everybody follows the rule of life-long atonement for one's sins; naturally he experiences the consequences of his sin in either in this life or in future lives. Also note that the two kinds of karma, *puNya* and *pApa* do not cancel each other; there is no double-entry system as in accounting practice. Sanatsujata reminds King Dhritarashtra on this very emphatically..

QUESTION B-25: Why does Hinduism extol the action of Rama in implicitly obeying his father and step-mother to go to the forest? How do we tell this to modern children who do not seem to appreciate the logic behind this?

This question actually arose from an NRI, in one of my expositions on the Ramayana. The reply given by me then as reproduced below (with some elaboration) will perhaps shake up some ultra-modern young minds. The entire scriptural literature with all its *PurANas*, legends and stories are one on this point that a father's word is law for the son. In ancient times this was so much of a truism that nobody even wanted a justification for this. Indeed when Bharata and all his elders and courtiers went to the Chitrakuta hermitage to bring back Rama to Ayodhya and when there was a long plea by Bharata to Rama that the latter should simply come back, because every one wants him back and Bharata would even substitute for him in the forest, Rama begins by saying only one sentence which seals the conversation for the day, even though all the great ministers, counsellors and rishis were present there. This one sentence is a half verse in V.R. and runs thus (2-104-22.) *mAtA-pitRbhyAm-ukto'ham katham-anyat samAcare?* This means: *When I have been told so by my mother and father, how can I do otherwise?* Nobody had any reply to this powerful statement. They all dispersed for the day. The conversation resumed the next morning with Bharata opening up new angles of approach. In current usage we may call it 'following the precedent' provided it is dharmic. Following the words of father and mother was the foremost dharma practiced.

For our purpose we should only note here how electrical the effect of that single statement was on that august assemblage of scholars, elders and experts. In order to tell our present day kids why every one in the Hindu cultural milieu considers this obedience to father and mother so natural and important, let us go to *Manu smRti* for the relevant portion which stipulates, demands and justifies this universal requirement of Hindu dharma. If there is anything in Hindu scriptures which may be considered to be as powerful and as emphatic and precise as the Ten Commandments of Christendom, it is this portion of the Manu *smRti*. We quote just six *Shloka*s: (*Manu SmRti*, Ch.2: 227 to230, 235, 237):

yam mAtA pitarau kleshaM sahete sambhave nRNAM/
na tasya nishkRtis-shakyA kartuM varsha-shatair-api//

tayor-nityaM priyaM kuryAt AcAryasya ca sarvadA/
teshveva trishu tushTeshu tapas-sarvaM samApyate//

teshAM trayANAM shushrUshA paramaM tapa ucyate/
na tair-abhyananunujnAto dharmam-anyaM samAcaret//

ta eva hi trayo lokA ta eva traya AshramAH/
ta eva hi trayo vedAH ta evoktAs-trayo-guNAH//

yAvat-trayaste jIveyuH tAvan-nAnyaM samAcaret/
teshveva nityaM shushrUshAM kuryAt priya-hite rataH//

trish-vetesh-viti kRtyaM hi purushasya samApyate/
esha dharmaH paras-sAkshAt upa-dharmo'nya ucyate//

'There is nothing in the three worlds which can compensate for the pains and sufferings that the parents, mother and father, have gone through in bringing up the son both at the time of birth and after. Even in one hundred years one cannot repay the debt which one owes them. To the two of them and to the guru, one should always do what is pleasing to them. If these three are satisfied, all dharma, penances and obligations stand fulfilled. The service to these three is the summum bonum of all penances. Without their permission no other dharma should be observed. They are the three worlds (bhur, bhuvaH, suvaH); they are the three Ashramas (brahmacarya, gRhasta, vAna-prastha); they are the three vedas (Rg, Yajur, Sama); and they are the three sacred Fires (gArhapatyAgni, the AhavanIya, and the dakshinAgni) of the Vedic tradition. As long as these three are living one should not have to observe any other dharma or penance. Anyone who is interested in his well being should serve daily these three most sincerely. A man's entire obligation for life is fulfilled if these three are taken care of. This is the supreme-most dharma. Everything else is only a secondary dharma.'

Because of the abundance of *smRtis*, and all of them are man-made, differences that may exist between them need to be reconciled. These have been done from time to time according to the age in which we live. The people in Maharashtra follow the *'dharma sindhu'* by Kasi Nath Upadhyaya. In South India the book *'Vaidyanatha dIkshitIyam'* authored by Vaidyanatha Dikshidar is followed. Both the books have been there for more than two centuries. These two compilers have boldly reconciled all the seeming contradictions in the various *smRtis*. And finally they always say: Wherever there appears to be an unresolved contradiction, follow the tradition of elders in your family. It is this culture of importance to family tradition that is one of the roots of the universal respect given to age and to elders in the Hindu milieu. There is also another compilation called '*nirNaya sindhu*'. All these compilations are taken from Manu, Yajnavalkhya, Apastamba and others, and are based on both Veda and VedAnta.

QUESTION B-26: The multiplicities of temples, the varieties of worship and the differences in the manifestation of deities all through the length and breadth of India, baffles even a resident Indian, not to speak of the visitor from abroad. Is there any rationale for the how and why of these temples and their variety?

To answer your comprehensive question, a whole book has to be written on Temples of India. I shall try to give some brief remarks as a rationale that you seem to want.

First of all, let us remember that everyone does not have the same taste. The variety of godhoods in *sanAtana dharma* provides an opportunity for one to 'choose' his *Ishta devatA* (favourite deity), depending upon his own ideas and tradition. The concept of *"kula devatA"* (family deity) is also relevant here and all devotees do not have the same '*kula devatA*'. However, all deities are only different forms of the one and only Brahman.

Between the second century B.C.E. and the 18th century C.E. India has continuously built a **multitude of temples** throughout the length and breadth of the country. The varied Indian architecture provides the art lover and the historian a feast that is fantastic in its quality and educative in its purpose. One finds oneself in the presence of something rich and spiritually satisfying. A multiplicity of forms, an exuberance of sculpture, the calm tenderness of frescoes, ceilings covered with paintings – everything adds up to the glory of the heritage. Every one of these bears witness to the collective faith and fervour of an anonymous collection of stonemasons and sculptors.

Though the physical environs of these large temples have been built in historic times by historical personages, the deity enshrined in each sanctum sanctorum very often goes back in origin to prehistoric (what the west would like to call 'mythological') times when that deity really appeared as a manifestation for a specific purpose. This is another reason why different gods and goddesses are worshipped by the Hindus as different manifestations of the same Supreme Almighty. Every one of these manifestations had a name and a form and that particular representation of the nameless Divinity had caught the imagination of people at one time and they have been worshipped ever since. Every temple of olden times has risen like this. There is probably no other culture in the world whose literature as well as history is so fully replete with a myriad of such manifestations of divinity and the exploits of that Supreme Almighty for the benefit of His devotees. This is not to say that Indians are the best devotees of God. It is only to say that India's past goes beyond the few millenia into which history dares peep into. The **ancientness of the country** goes back into such a distant past that the events recorded in the form of deities enshrined in various temples have been discarded by history as belonging to so-called 'mythology'. For instance, the deity, Nataraja of Chidambaram cannot be dated historically. Carbon dating and other scientific methods can apply only to the physical matter connected with the temple structure. It can in no way affect the concept enshrined in the temple that motivated the building of the temple. The concept is older than anything that history may attempt to speak of.

The **temple is the centre around which the whole of Hindu life revolves**; at least it was so till one hundred years ago. In most of the villages, there will be a Vaishnava temple at one end of the village and a Shiva temple at the other end. If it is not a small temple, one passes through a number of enclosures before one is face to face with the main deity of the temple. The statue of the god or goddess to be worshipped must have been made strictly according to the rules of iconometry, prescribed by the relevant *Agamas*. The *Agamas* form the source book of all ritualistic material, particularly relevant to the construction of temples and worship at home. The statue may be of gold, silver, bronze, marble, granite, wood or terra cota. The officiating priest is the only person authorised to enter the sanctum sanctorum. When the priest has finished the ritual puja and waved the flaming camphor before the deity, he comes out and shows the flaming camphor to the devotees almost one by one individually if possible. The devotees pass their palms over the flaming camphor and touch their eyes and forehead in reverence. The priest also offers the '*prasadam*' that is, a little lustral water taken in the hollow of the right palm and swallowed immediately with all reverence. The devotee makes a certain number of perambulations around the sanctuary reciting his prayers or *Mantra*, makes his prostrations to the Lord and leaves spiritually satisfied and enriched.

There are often elaborate **public ceremonies associated with each temple.** There are *car festivals* when the deities are profusely decorated and posited in a gigantic structure called a *ratham* with huge wooden wheels and the *ratham* being dragged manually by hundreds of people through the outermost path around the temple. Every temple will have such a *car festival* at least once a year. The richer the temple, the more elaborate are these. But despite these temples, their ceremonies and festivals, worship is essentially not congregational. Rather it is an individual matter to be carried on privately, when and in whatever fashion the worshipper may choose. **Religious observance** may take place not only at home but also in connection with work. Behind the machines in a factory there will be puja places created by the workers themselves. The Indian craftsman conceives of his art not as his own nor as the accumulated skill of the ages, but as originating in the divine skill of his god and revealed by Him. Every hospital and every commercial establishment will have a place, small or big set aside for worship and prayer with idols and/or pictures of gods. Every business concern would certainly have pictures of gods right at the place of money handling, with incense burning almost all the time. Every equipment that is installed, including a computer, would most probably be sanctified by appropriate worship of the Almighty before installation. The debut of a young professional dancer is essentially a religious ceremony – a consecration of the dancer to her art which itself is religious in its themes and motivation.

QUESTION B-27: 'I will never let down my devotee' says Krishna in the Gita. But this does not seem to be true. We see many devotees – some of them are really true devotees – suffer either hunger or poverty or disease or failure in their endeavours. In fact very often we see that a person who has no faith in God not only gets along well but seems to prosper more. How do you explain this?

This is the million-dollar question that baffles all non-believers, who use this argument to try to smash the faith of believers! The second observation (in the question above) however is cynical and requires no explanation in view of the universality of the theory of Karma.

The elementary answer to the main question is that God tests them to gauge the intensity of their belief and devotion. This answer is indeed given by many exponents of Hinduism and is also mentioned in some contexts in the Puranas. But experts in the scriptures (like Krishna Premi Swamigal) do not accept this answer. The elementary answer only underestimates the omniscience of God. He has no necessity to test us, ordinary mortals. He clearly knows we will fail in such tests!. But then this theory of God testing His devotees is certainly true in the case of confirmed intense devotees of the Lord. In such cases, He tests them – like a Bhadracala Ramadas or a Kannappar or a Tukaram or a Ramalinga Adigalar – just to show to the rest of the world how intense and effective is their devotion and how far a devotee's faith can carry him. He knows that they won't fail His test. In our ordinary cases, the theory that God tests us is not acceptable. We suffer because of our Karma. And we have to suffer it. Sanatana dharma is very clear on this point. In fact even in the case of leading devotees they could not avoid the suffering they had to endure. But their lives show how when the

Lord's Grace descended on them, the most intense suffering could be either transformed into intense delight, or, more often than not, God's Grace, instead of wiping out their suffering provided an insulation of faith that enabled them to be oblivious of the suffering underneath.

There is another subtle reason.. The Lord takes care of our welfare, no doubt. But this does not mean that we will have everything we want. He knows what our needs should be and what should be satisfied. We should not fault Him for missing our commuter train, for not getting the professional raise we were expecting, for the dissatisfactions in our expectations from our spouse, and for all the illnesses we are suffering from. And on these accounts we cannot also take the words *Yoga-kshhemaM vahAmy-ahaM'* (B.G. 9-22) as just a comforting statement said mostly to console us and no more. No. His declaration is really a serious declaration. He is talking of our long-lasting welfare,' namely a spiritual welfare', rather than petty mundane welfare. **When He says 'My devotee perishes not!' (in 9-31) what is meant is that we will not go down the spiritual ladder any more.** But in the process of His granting our spiritual welfare and Ultimate Happiness, if there also pours (it would, surely) a rain of mundane happiness, we should take it more as a bonus than as a satisfaction of a demand that we made on Him!

QUESTION B-28: In Ch.16, 17 of B.G., Krishna talks of both divine qualities and also evil traits. Why did God have to create evil in the world and make it difficult for us to overcome them?

God did not create evil and did not have to create evil. There is no Satan-concept in Sanatana Dharma. It is all man's doing. When man goes after his desires endlessly, he spoils himself and that is where evil arises. Krishna has epitomised all evil in six characteritics of man in Ch.16 of B.G. Ostentation-cum-hypocrisy (*dambhaH*), arrogance (*darpaH*), pride (*abhimAnaH*), hatred and anger (*krodhaH*), cruelty or harshness (*pArushhyaM*), ignorance and delusion (*ajnAnaM*) – these, in short are the fundamentals of all evil. It is the Desire that is at the root of it all. It is the human being that originates his desire out of one or more of these six demonish qualities and nourishes it. These demonic properties are not the innate nature of a human being. Due to wrong worldly beliefs they are mistakenly inculcated and are superimposed on the innate nature. Such a man is never free of unfulfilled desires.

It is worthwhile to quote here from Dr. S. Radhakrishnan's "The Brahma Sutras – The Philosophy of Spiritual Life" (1960). "If God had desired to create a world of automata, there would have been no evil. Evil is there because we sometimes (why, many times) abuse free will. If the world is a machine, then the human individual has no meaning. Man is not free until he is capable of creative activity. Note that there is no animal delinquency. Evil is not passivity but activity. God permits evil because he does not interfere with human choice. Man is subject to different sets of laws, like gravitation and other biological laws which he cannot violate. These laws he shares with all animals but there is one law which he does not share with animals, a law which he can disobey if he so chooses. It is the law of dharma, right and wrong."

FOLLOW-UP QUESTION: You say "Evil is there because we sometimes or many times abuse free will". Isn't the "free will" controlled by the three *Gunas* that make up the tendencies of a human? A human can of course strive for sattva guna with his will and karma but until then he will be bound by present tendencies and will perform karma according to those tendencies. That's the reason our tendencies don't change instantly after studying Vedanta. It takes time and lot of effort to get rid of ignorance, *tamas*. So the question is "is free will really a free will or it is limited by three *Gunas*?"

Gunas are your own. They are your tendencies latent in you. They constitute the ingredients of your free will. Free will does not come from outside. It is the work of the mind and intellect. And these latter are soaked in your three *Gunas*. So we cannot talk of the three *Gunas* and of freewill as if they are two separate independent things. Freewill and a consequent thought or action generate your future *Gunas* and the existing three *Gunas* influence your free will to act or think in a particular way.

QUESTION B-29: Why can't we reognise God or the Self by our senses? Do the Upanishads say so?

parAnchi khAni vyatRRiNat-svayambhUH,
tasmAt parAng pashyati nAntarAtman/
kashcid-dhIraH pratyagAtmAnam-aikshhat
AvRRittacakshhuH amRRitatvam ichhan.

This is a quote from Katha. U. II – 1 – 1. The Self-existent Lord made the senses turn outward. Incidentally the verb that the Upanishad uses here for 'made' is *'vyatRRiNat'* which means also 'punished', thus giving a beautiful meaning that the senses were 'punished' not to be able to look inward. Accordingly man looks towards what is outside and sees not what is within; it is the rare brave soul, who, longing for Immortality shuts his eyes to what is without and beholds the Self within.

The I.U. in its verse 4 refers to this inability of the senses to look within and dramatises it: "It (the Atman) never moves; yet it is too swift for the mind. The senses cannot reach it. It is ever beyond their grasp. Remaining still, it outstrips all activity. Yet in it rests the breath of all that moves". Sv.U. says: "Without feet it runs; without eyes it sees; without ears it hears'. Thus even though the Atman never moves (because it is beyond time and space) it is too swift, including also for the mind. Remaining still it beats the senses. The senses themselves cannot reach it, because it is not material. The natural function of the senses is to be extrovert. The mind also cannot reach it, because it is not the object of contemplation.

QUESTION B-30: In B.G. Ch.8 shloka 5 the Lord says: "Whoever leaves his body and departs remembering Me, 'even' at his time of end, comes to my *bhAva* (Purushottama); there is no doubt of that". And Swami Tapasyananda comments on the word 'even' (*ca*, in Sanskrit): "It is only if the thought of God has been the dominant idea of one's life and has been occupying one's mind all through

one's life the thought of Him will come to the mind at the last moment". Is this ever possible?

Pardon me please, readers, in answer to this question, I shall have to describe my own father's departure from this world in the following long article: I apologise for the length of the answer.

My father Sri R. Visvanatha Sastri (1882-1956) was always a picture of *karma-bhakti-jnAna* in action. On his big table in the office, (Sub-Court Sheristadar, Cuddalore) any office paper that needed his attention or signature would be disposed off then and there, leaving the table free for his vedantic books and non-stop writing. His elaborate puja at home never stopped even for a single day. You would be surprised to know that in one of his travels by train from Madras to Calcutta, his train stopped at a major station on the banks of the Godavari and it appears he had a quick bath in the river, came back to the platform, spread out his puja paraphernalia, finished his puja and got back into the same train in which he was travelling. His advaita knowledge and pursuit of advaita was so convincing from his behaviour as well as his reactions to events. He would take everything as God's will – good or bad, honour or dishonour, praise or blame, pain or pleasure, blame or insult, success or failure, small or big. I have seen it day by day, hour by hour. I have learnt most of my advaita more by observing him than from scriptures. His writings tell me now that all the time he was 'experiencing advaita'. I cannot describe it because it was his experience. But I can 'feel' his experience even now, long after he left me!

His last moments were so remarkable that as one who went through the unique blessed experience of watching how a noble soul should leave the body fully resonating with the shlokas 5 to 14 of B.G. Ch.8. I cannot but record it here for the sake of posterity to understand what Lord Krishna meant by these shlokas and to know what great traditions dominated this land from time immemorial.

It was January 8, 1956. My father was living in Madurai (Tamilnadu, South India) with me, my wife and three children of ours. Generally he was in perfect health, doing his daily religious routines which start with a bath in the early morning, sometimes in the river, but mostly as his age advanced, in the home. Every day he went through a routine of pUjA for possibly one or two hours. Then throughout the day he would keep himself busy reading and writing. He is the author of several manuscripts of advaita character. I have heard several of his religious expositions. Naturally as every Hindu expositor would do, if the context demanded, he would refer to these slokas of the Gita in these expositions. And when he expounds on the name and glory of Narayana, he used to say that one should cry out 'Narayana' so loud, that it is heard even in distant VaikunTha, the abode of Vishnu. Whenever as a teenager I heard these statements from him, I used to treat them as just rhetoric, but I did not realise he was really serious about it, until he showed me how one must die.

One month before his demise, he fell ill for a few days, even lost consciousness, but recovered very soon. Thereafter he even exhibited signs of double vigour. He resumed his river bath, and visits to the temple for darshan and so on. One day he called the pundits, (it was a solar eclipse day, Dec.14, 1955), performed some rituals (which later I understood was a *prAyashcitta* ritual), performed an actual *go-dAn* (gift of a cow), and so on. Since he was generally religious and of a most saintly type, we took these things for granted and did not realise that he was gradually preparing for his final exit from this world. December-January corresponds to the Tamil month of Margazhi (Recall: *mAsAnAm mArgasIrsho'ham* – B.G. 10-35) which corresponds in the divine reckoning, to their early morning time: 4 to 6. During this month throughout the Hindu world, morning pujas will be performed certainly in all temples, but also in most families of the traditional kind. My father used to do this early morning puja (called *ushat-kAla-pUja*, which would be in addition to the daily puja which came later in the morning at the usual time of 8 or 9). His routine for the early mornings during December-January was to get up at four, heat water for his bath and have his bath. The previous night itself my wife would have kept ready the firewood and the pot of water that was necessary. He would himself light the firewood and heat the water. After bath he would sit for the puja. Simultaneously, he would also light the small charcoal oven (known as *kumutti* in Tamil) and put on it a small vessel containing water and moong dhal and rice with a few spices, for making Pongal, for the *naivedya* to the Lord after Puja. The necessary materials would all have been kept ready for him by my wife the previous night itself. He would finish the Puja about 5-45 or so, and just before the Arti time the rest of the family (myself, my wife and children) would wake up and have darshan of the Arti.

This routine was going on every day of that month. But on the 8th January 1956, early morning, around 4-15 or so, he called me aloud and woke me up. I got up and noted that something was strange that morning. He said that he had just taken a quick bath, and was about to begin the puja, but he felt not quite well. 'Go brush your teeth and come quickly' he said. My wife also got up and both of us were ready for him in a few minutes. He asked me to bring a shawl and cover him up. I saw he was shivering. He sat opposite the puja altar where all the puja materials had already been arranged as usual the previous night itself. He asked me to open the vessel containing Ganges water (which had earlier been opened on the day of the eclipse mentioned earlier) and give a few drops to him. He took up the rudraksha mAla from the puja materials and wore it. Also he wore the vibhuti as well as the usual Urdhva-pundram on his forehead. He spoke only a few words to get the things done as he wanted. My mind began to find meanings for the instruction he had given me a few days earlier that I should read aloud the Gajendra *Moksha*m chapter from the Bhagavatam. daily while he would be doing the early morning Puja – which I had been following, though not on all days.

This day he made me sit near him and asked me to go get the book and read '*ambhasya pAre*'. This refers to the first chapter of the M.N.U.. which follows the three chapters of the T.U.. in the taittirIya *brahmana* of K.Y.V. It is a long paragraph going over to four pages. I have heard him say on many occasions that this particular *anuvAka* (paragraph) contains all the great mantras. Long ago, even as a boy I had been taught by himelf the vedic chanting of this Upanishad. I picked up the book from his bookshelf and started reading and chanting it. By that time I realised the gravity of the situation because when I noted that he was not starting his puja, but just asked me to sit and read this portion from the veda, and remembering the instruction about the Gajendra *Moksha*m regimen of the past few days, I knew he was preparing himself for the final journey. Naturally I faltered in my reading, both because of the excitement and also because I had not been keeping myself in touch with the reading of these passages due to my worldly activities and professional obligations. When I faltered, he told me, 'See, you have not been reciting it regularly and now you are faltering'. And then he started shouting the name 'Narayana', 'Narayana'. His crying out the name of 'Narayana' repeatedly became so loud in the next few minutes, that later in the day my friends who lived a furlong away from me were going to report to me that they heard the shouts of 'Narayana' in the early morning several times. He must have cried aloud the name 'Narayana, probably more than a hundred times that morning. I became fully aware of what was going on, from his point of view; so, I did not disturb him. But he signalled to me and put his head on my right lap while all the time crying out 'Narayana'. The recitation of the Narayana name did not stop at all.

My wife in her anxiety called a neighbour, who called another neighbour who was a doctor. The doctor came, examined, gave a coromin injection and went away. But all the while my father, though fully conscious, did not respond to any of the mundane conversation that either the doctor or my wife generated. The children (ages 8, 5 and 3) came and watched the drama that the grandfather seemed to be enacting. He just signalled to them to sit. My wife offered some black coffee (there was no milk in the house at that time) which he did not refuse. He allowed it to go through his throat. He was lying on my lap and the nArAyana mantra was going on still aloud. It was clear that he had already bade good-bye to this body and its mundane associations.

I had now finished the chant of *ambhasya pAre,* and not knowing what to do further and not getting any further instruction from him, (because he was now not allowing himself to be distracted even a little from his loud nArAyaNa recitation) I started reciting the *purusha sUkta* which I happened to know by heart. As soon as I started it, he signalled to me by a shake of his head that that was OK. The decibel level of the narAyana recitation was going down now. My wife got panicky and went out to call the same doctor once again. She returned in just a few minutes with the doctor. By this time he had stopped reciting Narayana and appeared to be sleeping, still on my lap. The time was 5-40 AM. The doctor came and pronounced him dead.

yoginaM vishvanaathAkhyaM asmat-tAta-svarUpiNam.
AtmalaabhAt-paraM lAbhaM vaktAraM na kadAcana../
gItArtha-grantha-kartAraM shrIguruM praNamAmyaham.
yo.antaH pravishya me vAcaM dhRRiitiM buddhiM pracodayAt..//

I bow to my revered Guru, in the form of my own father, the Yogi known by the name of Visvanatha, who never ever thought of anything as a gain other than the regaining of the Self and who composed the meanings of the Gita in a book of his own. May he be immanent in me and prompt my speech, fortitude and intellect.

Here is a picture of Sri R. Visvanatha Sastri:

PART C

QUESTIONS ON MIND & VEDANTA

QUESTION C-1: Every one in the world is after happiness in one's life. When this is so how can we, particularly the younger ones, accept the teaching of Vedanta that happiness is not outside?

Everyone is certainly after happiness and all our activities are motivated by the pursuit of happiness. But the debate-cum-discussion is about what is happiness. Try to understand the logic of the scriptures. They say that happiness is not to be sought outside. The Upanishads are never tired of declaring that happiness is one's natural state of being. If you start chasing it you become unhappy. The moment you think happiness is outside you, you have implanted the seeds of unhappiness in your mind. The unhappiness is not in the absence of things, but it is in our wanting them and searching for it. This is not a cynical way of looking at things, but it is a positive assertion. Looking for pleasure in the material sense as an end-in-itself leads to real unhappiness. Happiness, pleasure, bliss are always with us in the initial state.

Some elementary analogies: The natural characteristic of water is its coldness as well as liquidity. If water is hot, we naturally ask: Why is it hot? The very fact that the hotness is questioned shows that hotness is not the natural characteristic of water.

Whenever we are unhappy, others question why we are unhappy, But when one is happy most others (even when they meet you on a walk) don't ask you why you are happy. This is because happiness is our natural state!

Whenever we want something, we move from this initial state. When our want is fulfilled, we go back to our initial state. Therefore happiness is not what was given to us by the thing we thought we obtained, but it is our natural state. Unhappiness arises out of grief, fear or delusion or unattained desire. Grief is always about a happening in the past. We are unhappy of something which we had and which we have now lost; it could be money, possessions, kith and kin, peace, anything. We think we had it; actually it was not ours, it was His. This misplaced vision makes us grieve about our past. Sometimes we are unhappy because we are fearful of the future. What will happen if I lose what I have now? What will happen if nobody comes to my rescue? What will happen if I die? – all this is fear about the future. In between the past (which creates grief) and the future (which creates fear) there is the present in which we are deluded by our present attachments and desires. The delusion caused by attachment is the reason for the dilemmas into which we always land ourselves: whether we take this alternative or that, both being important for us because each is interlinked with something in which we have placed our attachment. We are attached to the present. We do not want (desire) the present happiness to become the past. That is delusion, for it cannot be so. Present happiness will surely pass and become the past. On the other hand, we think sometimes that the present unhappiness will continue in the future; and that is also a delusion. The happiness given by the senses carries along with it the bitterness of disappointment when the pleasure does not continue, the satiety of fulfilment because we know the pleasure will cave down the next moment, and sometimes also a disgust born out of the satiety. The flimsy happiness obtained by sense-indulgence, arising out of changing appetites of the flesh and the mind, is a fleeting joy, whereas the joy arising out of an inner self-control and a sense of perfection is permanent. One's sleep also looks like happiness. But it is born out of inertia and ignorance. This happiness is totally oblivious to the higher calls of Man. The only happiness that is not transient is the state of being the Self. It is pure and unsullied. We are told by the Seers that the state of *samAdhi* (= yogic trance) is like this.

The Gita has a beautiful delineation of happiness and pleasure in terms of three kinds: SAtvic, Rajasic and Tamasic in shlokas 37,38, 39 of its 18ᵗʰ chapter: That in which one rejoices by self-discipline and which puts an end to pain, (at first is poison but in the end is nectar), that pleasure is *sAtvik*. That which is born from the contact of the senses with their objects, which at first is nectar (*agre amritopamam*) but in the end is like poison that pleasure is known as *rAjasik*. That pleasure, which at first as well as in the sequel deludes the Self, arising from sleep, indolence and heedlessness is known as *tAmasik*.

QUESTION C-2: Why do we fear death? What is the remedy?

Every one has the fear of death some time or other. But that becomes ineffective. A temporary dispassion that follows such fear of death usually vanishes after a further experience of life's goodies. On the other hand those with a high sense of values do not forget the fear and they look for antidotes for it.

For men steeped in ignorance and worldly *mAyA* to rise to salvation, the miseries of worldly life themselves are steps. When a person is dreaming during sleep, so long as the dream experiences are pleasurable, he does not wake up. Only miserable events in the dream wake him up. So also, in worldly life, so long as things appear pleasant, the worldly man does not wake up from the mAyic world to realise the Truth. The miseries of *samsAra*, the fear of death — these kinds of feelings are the ones that direct him to the goal. We know death is sure to come. But so long as it does not confront you, you don't realise the severity of that fear. Therefore it is the knowledge that comes out of experience that life is full of miseries, that turns your path towards one of *nivRtti* (cessation of activity). Rarely a blessed one in a million turns to *jnAna*-path the moment he becomes aware even mentally of death. Such are the Buddha and Bhagavan Ramana.

When the mind thus turns to *nivRtti* path, that soul gets into the Grace of deathless, birthless Lord. That Grace makes him look inward and takes him on to the Supreme. That is when the Ego of 'I' gets extinguished along with *vAsanas* of all kinds of bondage. What remains is the deathless Atman.

What is this Ego? It is the false conviction that the body is the Atman. So long as that remains, the impending death of the body will be considered as one's own death. When the Ego is extinguished the very concept of death is uprooted.

Ramana Maharshi's explanation: All know that they must die some time or other; but they do not think deeply of the matter. All have a fear of death: such fear is momentary. Why fear death? Because of the 'I-am the-body' idea. All are fully aware of the death of the body and its cremation. That the body is lost in death is well-known. Owing to the I-am-the-body notion, death is feared as being the loss of Oneself. Birth and death pertain to the body only; but they are superimposed on the Self, giving rise to the delusion that birth and death relate to the Self. In the effort to overcome birth and death man looks up to the Supreme Being to save him. Thus are born faith and devotion to the Lord. How to worship Him? The creature is powerless and the Creator is All-powerful. How to approach Him? To entrust oneself to His care is the only thing left for him; total surrender is the only way. Therefore he surrenders himself to God. Surrender consists in giving up oneself and one's possessions to the Lord of Mercy. Then what is left over for the man? Nothing-neither himself nor his possessions. The body liable to be born and to die having been made over to the Lord, the man need no longer worry about it. Then birth and death cannot strike terror. The cause of fear was the body; it is no longer his; why should he fear now? Or where is the identity of the individual to be frightened? Thus the Self is realised and Bliss results.

QUESTION C-3: It is often said that one's ultimate aim in life should be attaining of *moksha* or liberation or self-realization? Kindly explain.

Ultimate Godhead is one, though it has many names and forms. Upanishads call it *brahman* and declare it is the final cause of the universe, as an all-pervading, self-luminous, eternal spirit. You may think of it as a vast boundless ocean of which the universe is just a wave. You and I are fragments of that wave. The divine state of man is his natural stte. In order to discover this divinity in one's own self, we have to have selfless love of humanity, worship of the divine, control of the mind and of the senses and finally the pursuit of truth. This is the foundation of Sanatana Dharma. But Man has generally two attitudes – one self-centred and selfish and the other which motivates him to sacrifice and love. The latter is the divine instinct which is pronounced to be our natural instinct. The animal instinct in us is what we have ourselves cultivated in the journey of our several lives. We have to consciously pursue the divine instinct. This pursuit is what is called spirituality. As a Hindu you may go up the spiritual ladder at your own pace. If you want earthly pleasures (called *artha* and *kAma)* you can pursue them. Dharma and *moksha* are the other two pursuits possible. There is nothing wrong in pursuing one or more of these four. But in the long run, you will be tired of pursuing *artha* and *kAma* and also *dharma* (which relates to social and moral behaviour). How long can one be a playboy?. How long does one seek wealth? How much fame does one go after? In the long run (which may be several lives), one will want something beyond the three goals of *artha, kAma* and *dharma*. Hinduism strongly believes and recommends to you that there is a fourth goal *moksha*. This *moksha* is ultimate eternal happiness.

Even to be a perfect do-gooder to society, the inner strength has to come from something beyond the first three objectives. Worldly happiness is not ultimate happiness. Many people, even those who have everything good in their material life, find it necessary to go to Swamis and scholars, complaining of an un-understandable non-fulfillment in their life – which has nothing to do with anything earthly or material. Any material pleasure is after all an intermediate experience between two moments of pain and vice-versa. Real permanent bliss comes from the Inner Self. The only thing that transcends the cycle of repeated births and deaths is the state of *moksha,* which is just the Realisation of the Inner Self as *Brahman* itself.

QUESTION C-4: What is the brain in relation to the mind?

Mind is made up of four constituents. The first is the receiving mind, which receives all impulses and impacts, from the external world. It just receives, like an antenna. What sifts these pieces of information and analyses them is the *buddhi,* the intellect, which is another part of the mind. It is the discerning function of the mind. Then there is the storage part of the mind, which is called chittam. The agent of all these activities is the *ahamkAra* (ego) part of the mind, which, by its very nature possesses authority over all actions of the other parts of the mind. These four parts are together called the mind, very often in the literature, without care being taken to distinguish the different functions. The physical framework through which all of them of work is of course the brain. Just as the body is the physical basis for the soul (*JIva*) which is a subtle entity 'residing' in it, so also the brain is only a physical basis for the mind. Mind is too subtle to be put into any physical framework.

QUESTION C-5: What is meant by the spiritual path?

When a living being dies it is only the body and external physical manifestations that die. The soul (*JIva*) does not die. It travels from one body to another new body. But all the while, the mind, which subtly clings on to the *JIva,* travels along with it. The mind, however, does not remember what it did in the previous body. (There could be extreme rare exceptions as in the story of JaDabharata in Bhagavatam). The mind and *JIva,* together individualized in this fashion, go on from body to body again and again. This is the unique principle of transmigration.

The mind, which is irrevocably 'attached' to the *jIva* actually carries with it the weight of all the experiences of each life. This weight is not the memory – memory was in the physical brain which died – but it is a heavy luggage of impressions (pure and impure) which it has collected in each of its sojourns in a body. The mind is like the wind which carries the smell of a rose garden through which it has blown, even long after it has left the garden. Like the wind which has passed through a filthy and stinking place, the mind carries the stink (good or bad) that it has collected in its previous births and lives into its succeeding births. Thus are born the tendencies and in-born nature of people. These tendencies are nothing but the aggregate of imprints left in the subconscious mind, of all the actions, thoughts and expressions constituting all the previous lives. They colour the nature and state of mind of the present life. They are the so-called *vAsanAs*. It is these *vAsanas* that abet the pentad of troubles (called *klesha-panchakam* in Sanskrit) that constantly bother us. These are: *avidyA* (Ignorance), *asmitA* (egoism); *rAga* (desire); *dveshha* (hate); and *abhinivesha* (fear of death).

Mind serves as the material that carries these *vAsanAs* or tendencies during its passage along with the *JIva*. In fact, in Upanishad metaphysics, 'mind' is not recognised as a separate existing entity on its own. It is only a flow of thoughts on the subtle bed of *vAsanAs*. It is only a bundle of desires. If there were no thoughts or desires, there would be no mind. These *vAsanAs* have been inherited. The accumulated tendencies are not all evil. There are two nobler ones, namely, *shraddhA*, that is FAITH; and *bhakti*, that is, DEVOTION-cum-DEDICATION. Faith is faith in the divinity of the Self within each one of us. Devotion to that Inner Self and Dedication to everything which represents that Divinity together constitute the *bhakti*. The scriptures say that this *bhakti* is in fact a natural tendency of all of us – except that the accumulated *vAsanAs* of the other kind (namely, the GANG OF THIRTEEN, consisting of **attachment, hate, desire or lust, anger, greed, delusion, arrogance, jealousy, the nasty feeling that 'all miseries are coming only to me', malice, show or vanity, pride and captain Ego of all these**) are so overpowering that the latent *bhakti* shows up only after great effort. The thirteen evil tendencies of the mind, – create obstacles for the expression of this devotion and dedication. Not only do they create obstacles but they pull us in exactly the opposite direction, away from the divinity that is inherent in us. It is therefore necessary to exercise our will (*icchA*, in Sanskrit) so that we may extricate our intellect from the clutches of the Ego and its subordinate gang of twelve. The will by nature is neutral. It is neither good nor bad. It has to be trained to recognize the EGO every time it rears its head and to say: 'Hey E-GO, you go!'

Before we proceed any further let us record here a rejoinder. When we say above that Faith *(shraddhA)* and Devotion-cum-Dedication *(bhakti)* are the only two noble tendencies of the mind we are not ignoring the many noble qualities of the mind like pity, compassion, honesty, humility, and a host of others. These latter are all consequences of Faith and Devotion. We are making a distinction between fundamental tendencies, that is, channels of the mind, and the feelings that arise when the thoughts of the mind flow into these channels. When compassion arises in the mind it is because already there is a faith-channel in the mind namely, the faith that the other being is equally a being like ours. When humility arises in the mind and in the actions triggered by it, it is because there is already a flow of thought in the mind along the channel of devotion-cum-dedication towards something that is held worthwhile to motivate that feeling of humility. Similarly a wrong feeling, say, that of revenge, is because there is already a thought-flow in an anger-channel or a hate-channel or both. Thus feelings are all consequences of the basic tendencies (channels caused by the *vAsanAs*) of the mind. These basic tendencies are only twelve *plus* one (ego) *plus* two (Faith and Devotion-cum-Dedication). It is the good and bad imprints that the mind carries from its previous lives that reflect themselves as the nature of a person in the present life. A mind which has in its previous lives helped the poor, has been sympathetic, compassionate and noble, shows up in the present life as one who is very noble and gentle almost from birth. The thought-flow of such a mind is already attuned along the channels of Faith and Devotion.

As far as each life is concerned man has to express himself through his free will and it is by the same free will that he has to conquer the thirteen undesirable *vAsanAs* that prod him on into unhealthy directions. This process is actually a perpetual internal fight in each person between the good and the bad. The challenge is to channel the mind away from its tendencies into the only two good ones. That is the task of each individual. If he does not embark upon this task it means he has not raised himself up from his animal status. God warns Man by turning his hair gray. In the animal world most of them do not develop gray hair. They behave like what they should, all the time. Only Man does not behave like Man; he needs the warning and he gets it; that is the latest time by which he should *will* his mind to turn to nobler tendencies. Still if he would not give credence to the extraordinary instead of the ordinary, still if he would not stop his rude and aggressive behaviour, still if he continues to be insensitive to others as if it were an affirmation of his independence – it is only because of the accumulated *vAsanAs* from all his previous lives and because he has not yet learnt in this life to use the discerning part (the intellect or the *buddhi*) of his mind. The power of this discerning part is the power of his will and is therefore called Will-power.

The mind is the meeting point of Science, Religion and Philosophy. It is the basic substratum for the development of spirituality. It is Man's mind that understands the scientific phenomena of nature and it is with this mind that one coordinates with nature to work out his 'conquests' of natural phenomena. It is in Man's mind that Religion is born when he needs internal solace and satisfaction. It is with the same mind that he is able to abstract the concrete world before him to go into speculations of either science or philosophy But with all this it is this mind itself that is man's greatest enemy. Man can never say with finality that he is in control of his mind. So *Veda*nta places a great emphasis on the need to control the mind and on the efforts and strategies for controlling the mind, even partially. The path prescribed by Vedanta for this control of the mind against the pulls of the thirteen undesirable channels is THE SPIRITUAL PATH. In fact it can even be defined through simpler concepts. If you perceive objects as a 'Vishaya' (meaning, objects in which you have *rAga* and/or *dvesha*), you are still an *ajnAni* on the material path. *RAga* is attachment and liking and *dvesha* is dislike and hate. On the other hand if you perceive them as '*padArthas*' that is, purely as an object in which you have neither *rAga* nor *dvesha,* you are already on the spiritual path of a *jnAni!*

QUESTION C-6: I am simply aghast at the multiplicity of sahasranamas of God which are everywhere in the scriptures. It is too massive to gather even one sahasranama and the meaning of the names into one's mind. Can you just give a tiny sample of this profundity of names of God and their meanings briefly?

Yes, Only a tiny-tiny microscopic sample. Each name of God that appears in various scriptures and stotras reverberate the cncept of Divinity, or Glory or an action or an attribute or quality of the Supreme manifested in this form as a saguNa *brahman.* We shall try to be brief in each case. In each case we give only one meaning though the same word has several meanings because of the richness of the Sanskrit language.

1. *AbAla-gopa-viditA:* She is known to all young & old

2. *Adi-devaH:* Most Ancient Lord

3. *anAdiH*: beginningless, because He is the cause of everything.

4. *anAtha-jana-rakshakaH*: He protects people who are rudderless

5. *anirdeshya-vapuH:* He cannot be indicated by this or that; that is his form

6. *anuttamaH:* Unexcelled; Nothing more supreme.

7. *aprameyaH*: The immeasurable

8. *Arta-trANa-parAyaNaH*: He is ready to come to the protection of the distressed

9. *AtmavAn*: the one who is His own Self

10. *Atma-yoniH*: Everything is born out of Him

11. *Aum:* The primeval word indicating *Brahman* and so everything in the Universe

12. *avijnAtA:* In the role of *JIva*, he does not know the Absolute Truth

13. *bahirmukha-sudurlabhA:* She is unattainable if you look outward

14. *bhakta-parAdhInaH*: He is subservient to the call of His devotees

15. *bhakti-priyA:* She is dear to devotees because of their devotion

16. *bhavishhyat-padma-sambhavaH:* He (Hanuman) is earmarked for the next Brahma's post

17. *bhUta-bhavya-bhavat-prabhuH*: He is the Lord of the past, present and future

18. *Chhinna-samshayaH*: He removes all our doubts by His mere look

19. *GahanaH*: He is so profound that He is unfathomable

20. *haripriyA:* She (Lakshmi) is the beloved of Hari

21. *hridayasthA:* She who is residing in our hearts

22. *hrIM:* Creative, sustaining and dissolving aspect all put together

23. *Krishna:* One who gives bliss, by his very existence

24. *kshIrAbdhi-tanayA*: (Lakshmi) is the offspring of the Ocean of Milk

25. *lakshanagamyA:* She is unattainable by any kind of definition

26. *mahAtejaH*: By His brilliance the Sun derives its brilliance

27. *Narayana*: He is both the means (for the Suprme) and the goal (Supreme)

28. *NiranjanA:* She is faultless

29. *nirbhavA*: one without birth or death

30. *nirlepA*: She is attachmentless

31. *padma-nAbhaH*: Transcendental Supreme that is the Ultimate source of Time

32. *Priyakrit:* Giver of all you want so that you may want what He wants to give you

33. *PurushaH*: The indweller in the body

34. *purushottamaH*: He is the supreme Purusha

35. *Rama:* One in whose memory men revel in joy and happiness.

36. *SanAtanaH*: Unborn, everlasting

37. *shAshvata-dharma-goptA*: Protector of the eternal dharma

38. *Shiva:* The most auspicious; therefore 'Love' itself

39. *Shiva-shaktyaika-rUpiNI*: She is a composite form of Shiva and Shakti

40. *smRita-sarvAgha-nAshanaH:* Destroyer of our sins by very remembrance of Him

41. *stavyaH:* He desrves to be praised by all

42. *svayam-jAtaH:* He brought forth the Universe out of his own prodding

43. *udbhavah:* the material cause for the origin of the Universe

44. *VAsudevaH:* The source of all divinities

45. *VasuretaH:* His Inner Light is the source of birth for his own manifestation.

46. *VatsalaH*: the supremely affectionate, who loves the devotees deeply.

47. *Veda-vedyA*: She is the One to be known by all the vedas

48. *Vishnu:* the all-pervading One, not conditioned by Space or Time

49. *Vishvam*: The whole universe in which he is immanent.

50. *vyaktAvyakta-svarUpiNI*: She has the form of both the Manifested and the Unmanifested

This list can go on really endlessly. Every sahsranama of every deity adds names of such kind. This is the profundity of names of God, unique to the traditions of Sanatana dharma, not found in any other religion of the world. And when the commentator himself is full of divine Grace, the names get further excellence through their variegated meanings. Just one example. Take the line *aNur-brihat-krishash-sthUlo guNabRRin-nirguNo-mahAn; adhRRitaH*…from V.S. On the face of it, the line means atomic, microcosmic, lean, fat, full of attributes, attributeless, great, supportless. Now Sage Parashara interprets them as describing the eight powers of yoga, namely, *aNimA, mahimA, laghumA, garimA, Ishitva, vashitva, prAkAmya* and *prApti* – meaning, the powers to become atomic, transcendent, light, heavy, the power to will anything, beyond any natural phenomenon, effortless attainment of anything, and omniscience coupled with omnipotence!

QUESTION C-7: We are told that our most sacred scripture consists of two parts – the Samhita part which is nothing but mantras and rituals and the second part called the Upanishads which are mainly about Atman, *Brahman* and renunciation of material objectives. We are told by every teacher and Guru that the Upanishad part is the important one. Why then is there such a conflicting division

into two parts? If the second one is the important one, what is the role of, and necessity for, the first part?

Very interesting and incisive question! You are asking about the Karma kanda part of the Vedas. Why is it there at all, is your question. I shall go to Adi Shankaracharya's Introduction to T.U. *bhashya* and use his own words to answer your question. Karmakanda is not there to be thrown away. To proceed to the second part, namely *jnAna kAnda*, one needs to have an almost total *chitta-shuddhi* (purification of mind). Without the observance of all the karmas and rituals either in this life or in previous lives, one does not get the mind-perfection to even want to aspire for *moksha*, which is given only by the Upanishad part. By pursuing all the rituals of karma kanda one will certainly go to heaven to enjoy heavenly bliss, but that bliss is time-bound. By a long-long pursuit of these material objectives (including heavenly bliss), over several lives one gets the readiness and urgency to look for an everlasting bliss of *moksha*. That is when he is influenced by the Upanishad part. It is the Karma-kAnda which chisels your mind to look for a spiritual hankering for the end of this transmigration. Pursuing material objectives is a necessary preliminary so that one gets satiated by them, if not in this life, definitely in a series of successive births!

QUESTION C-8: What is your own understanding of God?

How to describe God? Words cannot express Him. The eyes cannot see Him. The ears cannot hear Him. He cannot be indicated as this or that. He cannot be related to something as subject and object. He is taller than the tallest. He is shorter than the shortest. There is nothing greater; nothing smaller. He cannot be predicated as the doer of some action, because the undoing of that action is also His. He cannot be attributed as the possessor of something because He possesses also the opposite of that something. He cannot be thought of by the mind, because He is not the *object* of any thought-process. He cannot be gender-specified, therefore to call Him as a 'He' itself is a failure of words. For all you know 'He' can be a 'She'! So the Upanishads also refer to Him as IT. It is incomprehensible, unfettered, uncontaminated, unattached. It has no before, no after, no middle, no inner, no outer. It cannot be classified by category or by action or by quality or by relation. Because He thus transcends everything and also includes everything, He is called Vishnu which means He who overlaps everything that can be conceived. He is beyond everything. He is beyond time, beyond space, beyond causation. He is the grandest, ever. He is the supreme-most. He is therefore *purushottama* – which literally means the SUPREME PERSON. But here, 'person' does not simply mean a person in the ordinary sense of the word. The supremeness indicates that any *personification is itself transcended.* It indicates complete transcendence of everything. Our finite expressions can never do justice to the grandeur that is God. He is the Colossus, as it were, spanning everything. This is the **TRANSCENDENCE** aspect of God

He is immanent in everything. There is nothing in which He is not there. Whatever we see, whatever we hear. whatever we smell, whatever we touch, whatever we feel, is all full of that Divinity, that is He. The universe that is visible and can be also mentally visualised is the concrete expression of that self-luminous spirit that is He. He is therefore *vishvaM*, the Universe itself. Without Him there is nothing that exists. He is the substratum behind everything that is inanimate. He is the soul of everything that is animate. While He is infinitely higher than ourselves, He is also infinitely near to us. He is nearer to us than our hands and feet and mind. He is the soul of our souls. He is the Ultimate Reality behind everything that is tangible either to the senses or the mind. He is the Cause of every effect and so He is the Cause of all Causes. Not only does the Universe spring from Him but ultimately it dissolves in Him. So He is both the effective cause and the material cause. The nearest expression in 'name' and 'form' for this Immanent Absolute is the Shiva-*linga* which represents the Ultimate when the entire universe has merged into it. He is the One that survives in us from childhood to adulthood and through old age from birth, as the I that we talk of when we refer to ourselves. He dwells in us as the only permanent resident. He is the real, the inner 'I'. This 'I' never changes. If we list all that might be called 'mine', including one's physical possessions, one's relatives, one's own body and limbs, mind, mental opinions, all that can be classified as 'my…' and throw out all this, then what remains is "I". This 'I' is the self of the upanishads. It is that which we see beyond right and wrong, beyond effect and cause, beyond past and future. He is the soul of our very understanding though we may not understand Him. He is Consciousness itself. He controls our very intellect from within. He is the inner controller. He is the *antar-AtmA* of everything. This is the **IMMANENCE** aspect of God.

He is perfect. He is so perfect that we may not be able to visualise the perfection. This perfection, both in action and in peace, is symbolised by the Shiva-*naTarAja* icon in its famous dancing form. But God descends from this pedestal of perfection and assumes an imperfection in terms of a name and form so that we mortals may be guided from our extremities of imperfection onto the path towards perfection. This descent of the Divine from its divine pedestal is called an Avatara. The complete such Avatara is supposed to be Krishna. But in this Avatara God's mystic powers of *tirodhAna* (= illusion, deception) have been so much interwoven with His other functions that, for us, it is difficult to understand the perfection in Him. Maybe that is why the Avatara as Rama has been extolled as the model of perfection for us humans to follow and emulate. He is an Adarsha-purusha (Model for Emulation). In fact he is called a *suvrata* – one who has the best vows, the best character, the best behaviour. The word *vrata*, in Sanskrit, indicates a fundamental way of life from which one does not swerve. That His *vrata* is great, good, unexcelled, is what *suvrata* says. Rama's *vrata* was five-fold: To give protection to all those who sought his refuge; To abide strictly by the promised words of the father and mother; to be responsible, as a king, to the people of his kingdom even at the cost of his own personal comfort; to be totally unperturbed in the most adverse of circumstances; and never to flaunt his real (divine) stature which was always hidden behind his human exterior. This five-fold *vrata* was so excellently and so exemplarily pursued by him throughout his life that even after several millenia, his very name itself is Divinity personified in the entire Hindu world. This is the **PERFECTION** aspect of God.

Tramscendence, Immanence and Perfection – **TIP** – This is the tip of the Iceberg that is my understanding of God!

QUESTION C-9: Is there a logical argument, based on unrefutable reasoning, for the existence of God? As far as I can understand the Upanishads their so-called *mahAvAkyAs* seem to me to be only dogmatic presentations of personal opinions and views.

Probably there is no strictly logical argument. It is always a mixture of reason and faith. The faith part is like a funnel which is needed to pour oil into a minute holed container. Without the funnel you will never succeed in pouring any liquid into that container. The container is the reasoning rational mind which receives information or knowledge through its microscopic receiver-mechanisms.. The funnel of faith is a necessity for the pouring or transferring any knowledge content into the mind. Let us analyse this duo of Reason and Faith.

By depending solely on Faith in the scriptures, one tends to be dogmatic. By depending solely on Reason one falls into the trap of rationalising one's desire-dominated opinions. Such a person proves what he wants to prove. There is a third factor called Personal Experience. Even that can be deceptive, because one may be projecting one's own favourite ideas. So, the three have to be together in a symbiotic manner. Reason, Faith & Experience. Sanatana Dharma has the characteristic of an ideal mixture of variety, flexibility and tolerance. It says, if there is a God it has to be a creative force, an overall intelligence governing the universe and an all-pervading essence that binds together everything in the universe. So they say it is omnipotent, omniscient and omnipresent. You may say this is only a definition and does not prove the existence of God. For the present, give it a name: Universal Mind.

The beauty of Hindu philosophy, particularly, advaita vedanta, is not to question whether that Universal Mind really exists or not. On the other hand it starts with what is experienced at the human level and first explores the innermost recesses of the human mind.. This investigation leads to what constitutes the innermost essence of man. One finds that this innermost essence of man is the seeker himself, rid of all his tools of search. In fact, the mind itself is part of the luggage which has to be shed off. But the exploration of the innermost core of man is inextricably linked with what one may call the pre-conditioning of the mind (technically called *vAsanAs,*) left in the mind as a cumulative effect of all traces of experience in the memory bank. This varies from individual to individual and so the understanding of the innermost core also varies from person to person. This core reality within us is the subject of all experience. It is the eternal witness to everything that I do or think. Advaita Vedanta concludes that there is no God other than this eternal witness in oneself.

The question whether God exists or not is not relevant from the absolute point of view. The necessity or otherwise of a God, the existence or otherwise of a God with superlative attributes all arise only in the mundane world which is only relatively real. As far as the absolute truth is concerned only non-duality is the Truth. You may call it God but that God is not your God with superlative qualities; it is *Brahman* without name, form or any attributes.

Look at it in another way. Man is conscious of his limitations. He is capable of imagining or conceiving the infinite and in comparison he knows he has limitations that make him lack that infiniteness. The Advaita Vedanta says these limitations constitute his Ignorance (*avidyA*) and so long as he is subject to these limitations he cannot dispense with his religion or his belief in God. Reason is strongest when it accepts divine guidance. This divine guidance does not have to necessarily come from a personality called God. We should be able to think of it as something which makes us think. This is the consciousness within us. This is what guides us. This is divine guidance.

QUESTION C-10: Why is the word *'namaH'* important?

The word *namaH* means prostration. But it is not just that simple. There are two syllables there, namely, 'na' and 'ma'. The syllable '*na*' stands for a negative. The syllable '*ma*' stands for the word *mama* which means, 'my' or 'mine'. Together the word *namaH* says 'not mine'. So when we offer anything to the Lord, say, a flower in the form of an *arcanA*, we better recall to our mind that we are offering what is naturally His, to Himself. It is not as if something belongs to us and we are offering it to Him. The only thing that belongs to us is, probably, our mind. It is this that we should offer to Him so that He can use it, come and reside in it, and purify it as He thinks fit. (This is what Shankara says – on behalf of us all – in one of his famous shlokas (#43) in S.L.). Instead of doing that we are offering a flower, or sometimes an eatable, calling it *naivedya*, or sometimes some money, in the hope of getting a greater benefit.

The two syllables '*na*' and '*ma*' indicate therefore the attitude of '*na mamakAra*' — that is, I prostrate to you with that feeling of total detachment from what I call 'mine'. The T.U. says at one point, that those who worship Him with the word '*namaH*' on their lips (*taM nama ityupAsIta*) are so special that all desires will fall and bow at their feet (*namyante.asmai kAmAH*). The I.U., in its very last *mantra*, which therefore is the last *mantra* of the entire S.Y.V, says to the Fire-God Agni (the visible manifestation of the Ultimate Supreme) — 'we will make innumerable repetitions of *namaH* to You, please take us along the right path' (*agne naya supathA rAye, asmAn vishvAni deva vayunAni vidvAn, yuyodhyasmat juhurANameno bhUyishhTAnte nama uktiM vidhema*).

There is one more interesting truth about the word '*namaH*'. This is an observation from Sathya Sai Baba. It is about the T.U. quote of '*taM nama ityupAsIta*'. In T.U. right in the same passage, two more vedic declarations are there: "*tanmaha ityupAsIta / mahAn bhavati / tanmana ityupAsIta / mAnavAn bhavati*". – meaning, "Worship Him with the word '*mahaH*'; one becomes a '*mahAn*', a great person; Worship Him with the word '*manaH*'; one becomes a most respectable human".

Now Sathya Sai Baba observes: "Why did not humanity stick to the worship of the Almighty with the word '*mahaH*' or '*manaH*'? Why did it prefer to go with the word '*namaH*' only?" And Baba himself gives the reason: The two words '*mahaH* and '*manaH*' start with the syllable '*ma*', which immediately links with the word '*mama*' that smacks of *mamakAra* (='mine'ness). So Baba says, the human mind is so fickle and so unsteady that the very consonant '*ma*' with which a word begins brings back the ego into the play of the mind and so it is very difficult to discard the *ahaMkAra* with use of words that begin with 'ma'. On the other hand the word '*namaH*' begins with the negative 'na' and so the ego is first discardeed before the '*mamakAra*' symbol 'ma' comes into play; and that is why great seers have stuck to the word '*namaH*' for all worship! REMARKABLE INDEED!

QUESTION C-11: Between Mind (*manas*) and Intellect (*buddhi*) whose responsibility is greater, in our *sAdhana* for spiritual progress?

Well, this is a tricky question, because both have an almost equal share in carrying out the *sAdhanA*. Still there are arguments to establish the greater responsibility of the intellect, whether it is devotion (*bhakti*), or *dhyana* (Meditation) or Karma yoga (Methodology of doing actions) or JnAna yoga (the spiritual route to Self-Realisation).

Take just one example: Devotion. You are an young man of 20 or 25, Your father has told you to devote some time to prayer daily. And you are trying to follow it. You start your prayer with the intellect concentrating on the routine of chanting the prayers. Side by side the mind is revelling in the excitement of 'Pujara in the cricket match the other day with Australia when he stood like a rock defending one end of the wicket all through the match to secure India's victory'. The mind is not able to get over that excitement of just the other day. It is the intellect (buddhi) now which has to pull back the mind and remind oneself of the father's injunction about the chanting of prayers. That is why Gita itself (in confirmation of what all it has been saying throughout) at the very end, in 18-57, emphasizes; "*buddhiyogam upAshritya…*"

R. Visvanatha Sastri, in his GItAmrita-mahodadhi, (in Sanskrit, pub.2018) comments (p.140) on the importance of buddhiyoga and therefore of the intellect's importance over the mind:

"Ordinary people go by what they see; but knowers of Truth do otherwise. Whatever one gets by sense experience has to be examined by *buddhi*. All external perceptions have to be internally examined by the 'internal sight'. Cf. B.G.: '*buddhiyukto jahAtIha..*' (*2-50*), '*buddhyA yukto yayA pArtha..*' (*2-39*), '*dUreNa hyavaraM karma buddhiyogAt..*' (*2-49*); '*buddhiyogam-upAshritya..*' (*18-57*). '*tatra taM buddhisaMyogaM..*' (*6-43*). All this brings out the importance of '*buddhiyoga*' and the necessity to cognize implied truths by *buddhi*. The fact that one has the body has to be understood by the *buddhi* that this is only an appearance – 'I am not the body.'. So the *ashvatta* tree described in #s *1* and *2* (of Ch.15, B.G.) is to be seen by *buddhi* as that which should be cut asunder ('*chheditavyaH*') (*#3*) and the *brahma-svarUpa* hidden behind all the external experience has to be uncovered by '*buddhiyoga*'. That is why the GAyatrI mantra begins with the word '*tat*' as the only thing to be cognized and revered by means of the '*dhIH*' (intellect), – in the third line of the GAyatrI – that is, by *buddhiyoga*".

Swami Bhoomananda Tirtha in his Essential concepts in the B.G. vol.4, p.170 totally agrees on the importance given to *buddhi-yoga*, as above. "If the thoughts, responses and attitudes of the mind are to be refined, intelligence will have to intercept the course and give its own corrective and sublimating inputs. It is a grave mistake to think that mind and heart alone are involved in devotion. Mind merely subserves the intelligence which is the one to be properly refined and stabilized". That is why, he says, B.G. *2-49* is so emphatic about *buddhi-yoga*.

Let me conclude this discussion about manas and buddhi by referring to the vedantic concept of how the mind works. The eyes look at an object. What exactly is that object, what is its nature, the eyes do not know nor is it the business of the eyes. Mind follows the eyes towards the object. Now there happens a *mano-vritti* (modification of the mind); but this is only half the battle. The buddhi has to come in the picture. It is the buddhi that has consciousness, though a reflected one from the Supreme. It is this reflected consciousness that 'illuminates' the object. This illumination is called *phala-vyApti*. The *mano-vRitti* plus the *phala-vyApti* together spark the knowledge about the existence of that object in the mind. When either of the *vyApti*s is absent, mind does not recognise what there is.

Two examples. When the mind is seriously engaged in something, even if somebody stands in front, the mind does not notice him; this is because of the absence of *mano-vyApti* (though the *phala-vyApti* is there). Again when the mind is supposed to recognise the Atma within, the *manovyApti* is there but the illumination of the 'so-called object' by the buddhi is not there because, the buddhi with its finite power of illumination cannot illuminate the infinite Light within (of the Atman). So here the *phala-vyApti* is not there though the *mano-vyApti* is there!

QUESTION C-12: To claim that the appearance of the universe is an illusion, as the advaita philosophy says, does it not mean that the world is useless?

No. In fact, if anything can be useful, it is only the illusory! Illusory means neither real nor unreal. Utility implies duality, like means and end or agent and action, and so on. Utility has no relevance to *Brahman*, which is beyond all distinction. The unreal, like the lotus in the sky, can never be useful. For it is never perceived! Utility of the world has to be judged in terms of *moksha*. There are non-advaitins who consider the world as a real training ground for *moksha*. But advaita regards the world as illusory, and thus it actually invests the world with greater utility for *moksha*. You don't have to give up the world in order to follow advaita. By examining the world through the scriptural lens, the spirit of *vairAgaya* (dispassion) becomes more pronounced from the thought that the world is an illusion (MithyA) than when it comes from the idea that it is merely transitory! The boy-brahma-jnAni Dhruva says in Bhagavatam (Skanda 4, ch.12, shloka 15) that by realizing this world to be nothing more than a dream appearance caused by Ignorance, and by knowing it to be superimposd on the Self by avidyA (*'avidyA-racita-svapna-gandharva-nagaropamam'*) he has developed *vairAgya* towards it!.

QUESTION C-13: There is a flood of posts on social media from yoga enthusiasts, from scriptural expositors and even from others on the necessity for meditation. What exactly is the ultimate purpose of Meditation?

The art of Meditation recommended by both Yoga shAstra as well as scriptural expositions has a major inbuilt objective other than Salvation or *Moksha* or samAdhi.. This inbuilt objective has to do with the Ego in us. And handling the Ego is the most difficult part of the process. And this, again, has to happen, through the medium of the mind where Ego is in the prime seat. When we are in the dreaming state, *buddhi*, the intellect, the discriminating part of the mind, goes to sleep and so there is no discrimination. The mind draws its sources from its own memory indiscriminately and presents to us all sorts of funny situations and happenings, without any coordinates of time and space. When we are in the deep sleep state, even this part of the mind goes to sleep. So we don't think during sleep, but the ego part of the mind, namely the ego-sense, which being present before, during and after sleep, maintains continuity of the person's individuality from our pre-sleep condition to our post-sleep condition. But the main function of this ego in one's mind is to identify itself with all the thought waves that arise in the mind. This identification is the prime cause of all our ignorance and all our miseries. Every time a thought wave arises, the ego-sense comes in the forefront and claims that thought wave. One of the early purposes of meditation is to teach the ego-sense not to identify itself with the thought wave that arises in the mind but to make the mind external to it, 'something that you can observe,' according to the Mother (of Aurobindo Ashram), 'as you observe things occurring in the street'.

In other words, the thoughts of the mind should be discarded as not pertaining to the Self. The ego-sense itself should become subordinate to the presence of the Self. The thought of the Self should be dominant. When a meditating individual stands thus in himself, as a witness to the dances of the ego-mind, he will notice how the drunken revelry of the mind slowly quietens. To obtain this quietude of the mind is not such an easy affair. This psychological feat is the main purpose of Meditation.

QUESTION C-14: Is the *advaita* of Shankara the correct interpretation of the Upanishads or not? Is not the *viSishTAdvaita* explanation of Ramanuja the ultimate answer? Which of the three great Masters has the correct philosophy applicable to our daily life? To which of the statements in the Upanishads shall we give importance or dominance? To the statements that are obviously absolutist, as recommended by Shankara? Or to those that are obviously non-absolutist as recommended by Madhwa and Ramanuja?

Too many questions! This is a crisis of intellect as far as the ordinary busy intelligent educated layman of the modern world is concerned. What matters is not how the three Masters differ on the facets of difference and non-difference among the three entities: God, *JIva* and Universe; what matters is the non-difference in their teaching to humanity in regard to what one has to do in the daily world. It is interesting to note at this point that to whatever school a noted saint or devotee belongs, his prayers or compositions always include the thought that whatever birth he may have to take in the future, whatever number of times he may have to be born in the future, his only prayer is that he should not forget the name of God. The unity of Indian culture should be seen in such common characteristic prayers. Every saint would say that our needs and desires are endless and so in our prayers to God we must not seek anything except devotion to Him. In fact this is why Hindu religion is one in spite of all the differences in the interpretations of scriptures. Any attempt to sort out these differences at an intellectual level may become just an exercise in futility.

These questions usually arise after a casual acquaintance with the Hindu philosophies by occasional reading and listening. In a misguided self-reliance motivated by an exposure to western culture and in imitation of the thought process, associated with it, one thinks an arbitration is possible among the Great Masters. To boot, such questioners, look for an integration, at an academic level, of these philosophies through an intellectual debate and discussion. They do not realize that such an integration, would have ben already accomplished by the Masters themselves, if it had been possible. Great intellectual giants like a Vedanta-Desika (1269 – 1369) or an Appayya Dikshidar (1520 – 1593), who spent all their lives on these philosophies (not just on week-ends only!) with superlative achievements to their credit, should have given us such integration and synthesis, if at all one was needed and one was possible.

Well might one echo with Jagad*guru* ShankarAchArya of Shringeri: *'You cannot see the feet of the Lord, why do you waste time debating about the nature of His face?'* The very nature of the literature of the Upanishads does not allow one unique interpretation. The Upanishads, as we know, are collections of free candid and detailed discussions between teacher and disciple and it is for the reader to draw his or her own conclusion after assimilating the analysis thus presented and in the light of one's own spiritual experience. It is here that the great *AcAryas* help. Even to understand them one will need the physical presence of a *guru*. It is therefore not fair to expect the Upanishads to tell us whether this is right or that is worng. To follow one of these masters with single-minded faith and try to understand that master and his perception of what the Upanishads say might itself occupy a whole life-time.

The differences in interpretation have certainly generated a succession of philosophical literature by later thinkers and writers and the body of literature on both sides is nothing but voluminous. Instead of trying to arbitrate among the great Masters, we should only aim to understand one of them in as much fullness as possible. This one Master may be chosen, as per one's tradition, taste, attitudes and upbringing. In saying this we certainly invite the criticism that Hinduism is *too* tolerant. But, is there something like too rich a man or too beautiful a woman?

QUESTION C-15: Is Ramayana just a narration of a story or event or it has vedantic content? I hear many expositors praise the vedantic content in Ramayana, particularly the Aditya hridayam. Can you explain this?

Well, it is going to get longish. I shall try to be as brief as possible. (For a better elaboration you may go to the Adityahridayam chapter in my book: MEET THE ANCIENT SCRIPTURES OF HINDUISM')

VedaH pRAcedasAdAsIt sAkshAt RamayanatmanA, meaning, it was the Veda itself that manifested in the form of Ramayana by Valmiki – says one of the verses that precede the Ramayana recitation. *Vedaishca sarvairahameva vedyaH,* says Krishna in the Gita (XV – 15), i.e., I am the One to be known from all the Vedas. These two authentic quotes are enough to establish that the core principle in the Ramayana is nothing but the Absolute Itself. The word 'Ramayana' means it is the means to reach that Absolute Light that is Rama. To have an insight into that all-pervading effervescence that is Rama is what is meant by *Rama-darshanam* and this is the essence of Ramayana. The Gita also emphasizes this in the *shloka* (VI-30) '*yo mAm pashyati sarvatra…*' The Blissful Form that is the Lord is certainly known by various forms and names, but the Reality is One only'. Valmiki himself underscores this when he writes in the Ayodhya kAnDa (7 – 14): Whoever does not see Rama and whomsoever it is who is not seen by Rama, such a person is at the low end of the populace.:

V.R. II – 17-14:

yashca rAmaM na pashyettu yaMca rAmo na pashyati/
ninditaH sarvalokeshhu svAtmApyenaM vigarhate//

In fact at the end of the epic Valmiki declares that every one in Ramarajya attained this spiritual peak of seeing Rama as omnipresent. He waxes eloquent and says that the entire world became full of Rama (*Rama-mayaM*). Clearly this universal perception of the Absolute is the goal of the entire epic. In every one of our lives our own spiritual goal should be to discard everything that is sense-perceptible and become one with that Absolute The very Avatara of Rama is to propagate this *Dharma* path by His actions and behaviour and to establish the path of Wisdom by His name. (*dharma-mArgaM caritreNa jnana-mArgam ca nAmataH*). The key *mantra-shloka* of Ramayana 'dharmAtmA satyasandhashca rAmo dAsharathir yadi…also* incorporates this truth of Ramayana by the word 'dharmAtmA'. This Blissful Absolute is what is explained in the Aditya-hRRidaya-stotra. Its purpose is to propagate this for the welfare of the world; not that it was not known to Rama. What it explains is the multiplicity of manifestation of Absolute Reality. Rama Himself is the Absolute Reality. So, there is no point in explaining Rama-*svarUpa* to Rama Himself. But Rama had to play the role of a human being till the destruction of Ravana. So to respect and be true to that subtlety, Agastya used the artifice of the Sun-God to explain the various attributes of the attributed Absolute (*saguNa-Brahman*). This was the Aditya-hRRidaya-stotra which has, as its content, the glories of *Brahman*, the Absolute.

This stotra should not be mistaken or under-rated for an ordinary piece of divine praise. Recall the essence of Ramayana is the expatiation of that Blissful Ultimate Reality. We must try to understand this stotra from that viewpoint. What was the purpose of the Avatara of Rama? To vanquish Ravana. And who is Ravana? He is none but the *ahamkAra (=Ego)* in us which has taken root in us over several lives. By the attachment we have to so many varied things we have developed the possessive instinct in everything that is associated with our BMI. Recall from B.G. (Ch.16: *shloka*s 12, 13, 14, 15)

AshApAsha shatair baddhAH…, Idamadya mayA labhdhaM…,
asau mayA hataH shatruH…, ADhyobhijanavAnasmi…

Only by vanquishing this *ahaMkAra* can we realise the *AtmA* within us. To destroy this *ahaMkAra* so that the Self shines by its own glory is the intent of the story of Ramayana.

The Supreme Self is Rama. First He kills all the undesirable *vasanas* inherent in us; this is the destruction of tATakA the demoness. Once the bad *vasanas* are destroyed, mind has to be strung into a strict discipline. This is indicated by the breaking of Shiva's bow by Rama. From then on one has to get involved in the affairs of this material world. Without the association of *prakRRiti* one's life-journey itself is an impossibility. So Rama gets into wedlock with Sita, incarnation of *mAyA-shakti* (*PrakRRiti*) of Goddess Lakshmi. Even though this means involvement in every action of the material world, one has to be doing it without attachment – in other words, there is a renunciation involved in this involvement without attachment. (I.U. very first shloka). Rama exemplifies this renunciation by his marathon act of renouncing the very crown that was offered to him the previous day. This is the grand renunciation (*mahA-tyAga*) that is the key-point in the whole story. And thereon one gets into the forest of DanDaka – which, symbolically is nothing but the *samsAra* that we have to cross. The king of this forest of *samsAra* is the ten-headed Ravana – (i.e. *ahaMkAra*) ten heads indicate the ten senses by which we get involved in *samsAra*. But we are not able to encounter this *ahaMkAra* head-on; because his gang is far and wide. So we have to meet him slowly vanquishing his subordinates one by one. First the destruction of *kAma, krodha lobha* (*khara, dUshhaNa, trishiras*) – the three Rakshasas with whom Rama fights in the Dandaka forest. Then comes *moha* (delusion) in the form of Maricha. Then one has to destroy the non-discrimination (*aviveka*) in the form of VAli and make a lasting friendship with *viveka* (Sugriva) that is Discrimination.

And now we get the most trusted lieutenant, *bhakti*, in the form of Hanuman. He is the One who helps us to find our enemy and his headquarters. Once we resort to *bhakti,* Lanka that is our physical body, should now be burnt, even when alive, we should have nothing to do with this body or its goings-on. This is the *lankA-dahanam* of Ramayana. Then we can take the support of *utsAha* (Vibhishana), i.e. perseverance and zeal. We are about to cross the Ocean of Ignorance; before that we crown the zeal which is ours now. And we are ready to destroy the several associates of *ahaMkAra* – *mada* (arrogance) in the form of Kumbhakarna; jealousy (*mAtsarya*) in the form of Indrajit – and that takes us to face the root-enemy, *ahaMkAra* right face to face. It is no easy task, to destroy this *ahamkara* – which, in fact, is the greatest barrier to our knowing our true Self. Our own real nature is *jnAna*. The body is inert. So any aggressive attitude towards the body-mind-intellect is not called for. The strategy to quell the fierceness of the Ego is to propitiate this *jnAna* nature of ours which is nothing but *Brahman* itself; and that originates the Aditya-hRRidaya stotra.

So we come to the last stage of our confrontation with *ahamkAra*. Ravana was *ahamkAra* personified, and even for Rama it was no easy task. For this direct confrontation with *ahaMkAra* we need to be aware of our own real nature, *sat-cit-Ananda*, that is, *Brahman*. *Brahman*'s power can be spoken of in two ways. One is known as *parAshakti*; Its innate nature is jnAna. It is also known as *VidyA* (knowledge) and also as *cit-shakti* (Absolute Consciousness). The manifestation of this is the duo of *JIva* and *Ishvara*. B.G. calls it *Purushha* or *kshetrajna*. The other Power of *Brahman* is known as *aparA-shakti*. Its nature is inert. It has several other names such as, *PrakRRiti* (Cosmic Nature), *avyaktaM* (the unmanifest), *avidyA* (Ignorance) and *MAyA* (an untranslatable word). This is what gives rise to the five fundamental elements and therefrom the entire universe.

When this *avyaktaM* in its equilibrium stage where all the three *Gunas* are equally poised (*guNa-sAmyaM*) is one with *cit-shakti*, then there is no *vikAra* (transformation) of anything; that *citshakti is* known as the *para-rUpa* of *Brahman*. In other words, it is the *nirguNa Brahman*, to be realised and known. When the Absolute Consciousness is associated with the *Sattva*-dominated *avyaktaM*, that is called the *apara-rUp*a of

Brahman; also known as *saguNa-brahman*. This is the *Ishvara* with all infinite qualities (and also the God of all other religons) and is to be worshipped and meditated on. This is what shines in our *hRRiidayAkAsha* with the light of a thousand suns, so to say. This is the Aditya that we propitiate everyday

QUESTION C-16: We don't seem to have understood Nature 100%. But the Supreme Absolute is said to be beyond Nature. How then can we understand the Supreme?

You have the answer inbuilt into your question. Yes, Understanding Nature itself is still going on for the past 20 centuries and more. How are we to understand something beyond Nature? The logic is alright. Only by stopping the inquiry about Nature and by turning their mind to something that is beyond, the ancient sages of India succeeded in unravelling the truth about the Supreme which is beyond. Unless you also do the same thing, namely, ceasing to run after Nature and all its multifarious manifestations in the universe, you will never get to know even an iota of that which is beyond Nature. Want to try?

Yoga-rato vA bhoga-rato vA sanga-rato vA sanga-vihInaH/
Yasya brahmani ramate cittaM nandati nandati nandatyeva.//

Enjoy the sport of life transporting yourself into yoga; Be serene in silent solitude and noisy crowds; When the mind is dissolved in *Brahman* It is always blissful, playfully blissful!

QUESTION C-17: The philosophy of advaita has the fundamental assertion that the Supreme Absolute is *nirguNa* (attributeless). Then how is it that almost all followers of advaita have no reservation about the worship of the *saguNa* form of God while striving to comprehend the *nirguNa* concept of Godhead

This is a standard doubt in the minds of beginners in advaita. I consider two particular shlokas from Narayaneeyam as a remarkable answer to this question. The first one is no.10 of Dasakam No.99:

*avyaktaM te svarUpaM duradhigama-tamaM tattu shuddhaika-satvaM
vyaktaM cApy-etad-eva sphuTam-amRta-rasAmbhodhi-kallola-tulyaM/
sarv-otkRshTAm-abhIshTAm tad-iha guNa-rasen-aiva cittaM harantIM
mUrtiM te samSraye'haM pavanapura-pate pAhi mAM kRshNa rogAt//*

Tr. Thy nature as Absolute Being is not manifest to the senses or the intellect. It is therefore difficult to grasp or attain. But Thy Being manifest in *shuddha-satva* (spiritual purity) as Krishna is like the wavy surface of the ocean of Blissful Spirit, definite, clear and easy to grasp. Therefore I resort to the worship of this form of Thine which is superior to anything manifested and which is lovable and enchanting by its sweet beauty and other blessed attributes. Oh Krishna, Resident of Guruvayoor! Deign to free me from my ailments.

The philosophy of *advaita* has two facets. One is the '*kevala-advaitam*' and the other is '*bheda-abheda-advaitam*'. The former one will not even talk of any attribute-ful form, as a possibility in the absolute sense. In other words, even *Ishvara* belongs to a lower reality than the Absolute. And because, everything other than the Absolute is non-real, *Ishvara* has to be non-real. But the *bheda-abheda-advaitam* says that the wavy surface of the ocean even though it appears as if it can be distinguished from the ocean, IS the ocean. There is no distinction between them. If we have to make a distinction between them that distinction is one 'without a difference'. In other words, *bheda* (difference, distinction) appears 'without a real difference'. God is the highest being in devotional thought and He must therefore be Absolute also, even as the wavy surface and the ocean are one and the same in spite of the apparent difference. Bhattatiri's advaitic leanings are in this category. Bhattatiri, through this *shloka*, sets at nought all the nagging dilemmas of a doubting advaitin, in regard to worship of the Formful. The real Nature of the Absolute Godhead is '*duradhigama-tamaM*', that is, to reach out to it is most difficult, almost impossible. Recall: '*Greater is the trouble of those whose minds are set on the manifest; for the goal, the unmanifest, is very hard for the embodied to reach*'. (B.G. 12-5).

The second one is shloka no.3 of Daskam 91:

bhItir-nAma dvitIyAd-bhavati nanu manH kalpitaM ca dvitIyaM
tenaikyA-bhyAsa-shIlo hRdayam-iha yathAshakti buddhyA nirundhyAM/
mAyAviddhe tu tasmin punarapi na tathA bhAti mAyAdhi-nAthaM
tat-tvAM bhaktyA mahatyA satatam-anubhajan-nIsha bhItiM vijahyAM

Tr. Fear arises from the consciousness of a second (thing) different from oneself. This consciousness of (such) a second is indeed an imaginary super-imposition of the mind. Therefore I am trying my best through discrimination to discipline the mind in the consciousness of oneness. But when this power of discrimination is overpowered by Thy *mAyA*, no amount of effort is of any avail in getting established in Unitary Consciousness. Therefore Oh Lord, I am trying to overcome the fear of samsAra by constant and devoted worship of Thee, the Master of *mAyA*.

This is one of the key *shlokas* that trumpets the highest *advaita* concept,. The sentence '*manaH-kalpitam dvitIyaM*' (The consciousness of a second object is an imaginary superimposition of the mind) constitutes the '*brahma-sUtra*' of *advaita*. Bhattatiri clearly makes the point that the unity of the *JIva* with the supreme Spirit is the ultimate goal. But he hastens to add that the same is not reachable by any one directly but only through the love and service of Him and His Grace. It is only by God's Grace that non-dual consciousness is obtained. The devotee merges in His Being by His grace, The 'I' disappears in Him and 'He' is left. The becoming merges in the Being. It is not vice versa. This is what one might call Realistic *advaita*, to be subtly contrasted with '*kevala-advaita*'.

QUESTION C-18: All expositors on Sanatana Dharma and invariably all the books uniformly emphasize two things as sine qua non for success on the spiritual ascent. They are: 1. High percentage of sattva guNa and 2. Almost nil bad vAsanAs in our native character. Well, this is clear. What is not clear is the different ways in which we

can mould ourselves such that this happens. Can you give us a list of various possibilities?

I appreciate your anxiety, though yours is a tall order. I shall try. First let us understand some basic things about *VAsanAs*. The word *VAsanA* is used in Advaita in the sense of the sub-conscious or latent tendencies in one's nature, habitual impressions or preferences or tendencies. These are nothing but the ripples (*vrittis*) that always move in mind. The *VAsanAs* of previous births will be dormant inside. They travel with our subtle bodies to our next births. *Remembrance of God's names and glories incessantly for a long time is the only antidote. A vessel with filthy water with foul smell, if continuously filled with crystal clear pure water, That water will slowly remove the filth and smell and after some time the vessel will be itself crystal clear pure Water. *VAsanAs* are actually continuation of previous births. When a person's desires remain unfulfilled in life the same become his *VAsanAs* on rebirth – in other words, to attain the desires of the previous incarnations. Now the question is how to remove *VAsanA*? Sage Patanjali calls them as *aklishta vRittis* which can be removed by *klishta vRittis* (prayer, meditation, satsanga, bhajan, kirtan, etc). But there is the danger of *klishta vRitti* also becoming *VAsanA*. So the sage advises that first you remove all *akilshta vRittis* by using *klishta vRitti* and then throw away the *klishta vRitt*i also so that mind is pure and free without *VAsanA*. The *VAsanAs* hold a powerful hold over the seeker's mind, though he has studied the shAstras. Three types of *VAsanAs* obstruct Self-knowledge. When we fashion our lives according to the standards set up by society and when we want to earn others' appreciation and respect by imitating false and wrong habits, then it is called *loka VAsanA*. – worldly tendency. The first thing that we have to do is to stop living up to the Jones. A seeker has to learn to accept censure and praise alike. *ShAstra VAsanA* is revelling in the thoughts of the *shAstras*, being attracted by the intellectual thrill that this knowledge provides, without living this knowledge.. (Most of us seekers, do fall under this category). *ShAstras* are only pointers to the Truth. One has to renounce the pointer and turn in the direction indicated. The intellectual thrill one gets from the study of the shAstras is like mistaking the menu-card for the food. One should not become excessively preoccupied with the study of the shAstras. The Vedas, themselves, warn us seekers on this. The pre-occupation with studies could become an impediment to our spiritual progress. Thirdly, the clinging attachment to the body and sense pleasures is *deha VAsanA.* Whoever seeks to rediscover the Self, while devoting himself to fattening of the body, says Shankara, is like one who proceeds to cross a river on the back of a crocodile, mistaking it for a log of wood. The body is just a vehicle given to us for our spiritual journey, to reach the Supreme. The body has to be fed properly and kept perfectly fit, but the seeker has to give up living in the flesh as the flesh and recognise that he is much more than the body. So long as the seeker remains in these *VAsanAs,* bondage will continue to exist inspite of the intellectual conviction that the Self is of the nature of Satchidananda

Now let us talk about how to get rid of *VAsanAs* (particularly the wrong ones). Mostly this is answered by me in various books of mine, each time with a different emphasis. But I shall collect them here as a master list of eighteen suggestions.. The numbering below does not imply any priority order; I am listing them as they come to my mind: (Let me apologise in the beginning itself for the length of this answer)

1. The *VAsanAs* do not split themselves into three kinds, as karma does (stored ones called '*sanchita*', those called '*prArabdha*' which have started giving their consequences and '*AgAmi*', what is getting into the account by present actions). All our *VAsanAs* keep on influencing our minds in all our lives, because we are only hugging our perishable outside (*kshara purusha*) which is simply the aggregate of all past tendencies and attitudes). The only antidote therefore is B.G. 9-27 which focusses everything on devotion and dedication.

2. The great concept of yajna of the Gita. By doing every work as a yajna, you avoid *VAsanA* of the work sticking to you!

3. The strength and quantum of *VAsanAs* can be inferred from the intensity of difficulty in trying to concentrate when you sit for meditation. In every meditation through a japa or a mantra there is always a gap between two successive repetitions of the mantra. This gap is the 'state' of unthinkingness. The longer is the gap the better it is for the purification of the mind, through riddance of its *VAsanAs*.

4. Six factors of past experience (both in this life and in all previous lives) constitute the good or bad of one's *VAsanAs*. They are the colour of KNOWLEDGE, the kind of ACTION, the quality of the DOER, the texture of the INTELLECT, the temper of the FORTITUDE., and the nature of ATTITUDE TO HAPPINESS. So these six entities must be under your inspection and correction, if necessary, all the time.

5. *VAsanAs* are not in our control. Past is past. The only way to nullify the effect of bad *VAsanAs* is to chant the names of God incessantly

6. Develop a familiarity with, respect for and belief in, religious texts (ShAstras)

7. Listen to expositions by the spiritually knowledgeable and have interactions with them in the style of B.G.4-34. This is the famous Shravana discipline. In fact hearing vedic chants will help.

8. Associate mainly with sattva-oriented people and scholars, if possible by keeping the right role-model before you., Observe the basic tenets of Sanatana Dharma – particularly the habit of giving, helping the needy and also by a proper follow-up of the lessons of the Gita

9. MahA Periava of the last century in talking about shloka 61 of Sou.L. elaborated the necessity of a spiritual *prANAyAma* – inhaling by left nostril *(IdA nADi)* and exhaling by right nostril *(Pingala nADi)*. This will increase the sattva qualities.

10. The Sanatana Dharma tradition has its own way of passing some unusually good daily habits, (though they may appear to be odd, for a stranger) to the next generation. In that way, let me remind of you of two elementary-looking habits, which, if practised daily, will help you rid of many bad *VAsanAs*: (A). Keep a handful of the flowers *(nirmAlyam)* offered to the Lord the previous day and, as many times as possible, pass your palms over the flowers and touch your eyes and forehead in reverence, just like you do when the temple priest shows the flaming camphor on a plate before you; and (B): After you bathe either in the river or at home, first wipe off your back dry, so that the bad *VAsanAs* which have just left you during your bath will get back to your back and not to your front and chest (The traditionalists interpret this as Lakshmi & her unwelcome sister who may be vying with each other to invade (and reside in) the first-dried portion on your body after your bath!)

11. Anytime you see anybody elder to you of whatever caste or religion or sex, make a reverential bow (not like saying 'hi' like the American) to him or her, maybe by saying 'Namaskar'.

12. Self-discipline, through the process of control of senses, maybe by yoga practices

13. Prayers to the Lord for His Grace, through Pujas, stotras and chants

14. More than everything else, *bhagavan-nAma-smaraNaM* is a sure antidote for getting rid of bad *VAsanAs*.. The *VAsanAs* occupy your mental make-up and storage. The bad ones constitute a reservoir of unclean water. It is a reservoir which has no facility for being emptied or drained. The only remedy is to keep on pouring clean water into the reservoir (of mind) allowing it to overflow until all the unclean water loses its density of contamination. The names of God are purfiers. They fill up the mind with sattva guna.

15. If you cannot do full sahasranamas or stotras select a few shlokas which have only names of God in them and no pleading or asking

for redress of this or that grief or granting of desire. For instance, in Venkateshasuprabhatam, choose the shloka beginning with 'shri padmanabha'; in Nrisimha-karavalamaba stotram, the shloka beginning with lakshmipate kamalanAbha.. and similar ones full of only God's names in various stotras. Even while worshipping in temples, do not ask for anything. 'I surrender to you, Oh God' (*sharaNaM prapadye*) should be the only attitude of prayer. In fact I always recommend either or both of the shlokas 11-18, 11-38 of B.G. because, they have no contextual fixation and they don't ask for anything and they are applicable as a glorification of the Absolute anywhere, any time.

16. In routine conversation avoid the habit of using nonsensical trash words (mainly picked up by associations in this very life) as response to happenings, but use God's names instead, all the time.

17. Instead of dwelling on the sense objects as criticised in B.G. 2-62, dwell all the time, or for as much time as possible, on the attributes of the Absolute and all attempts of descriptions associated with *Brahman* – all-pervasiveness, the causeless cause of everything, transcendence, immanence and perfection, namelessness, formlessness, non-dual nature, blissfulness, unrelatableness to anything, undefinableness and everlasting quality; this process has the name of **non-interactional sAdhanA.** (Swami Bhoomananda Tirtha suggests this). The Sadhana will create a sanga with all good things, and eradicate the bad associations in the mind. *taccintanam* (thinking of That Supreme), *tat kathanaM* (talking about that Supreme) and *anyonyyam tat-prabodhanaM* (mutual conversations about that Supreme) – these three form the royal route to Spirituality. Practising them is like pounding the grain to separate the rice from the chaff. There is no limit on the number of times the grain is pounded. It is pounded until it is separated from the chaff!

18. Develop the four qualities of *MaitrI, Karuna, mudita* and *upeksha*. *Maitri* is sharing the happiness of some one who is happy and not

being jealous of him. *Karuna* is the *VAsanA* of sympathy with one who is unhappy. *Mudita* is the habit of ourselves being satisfied when the other person is happy. *Upeksha* is the habit of consoling by solace and counsel to someone who is unhappy though it is his bad karma which has created his unhappiness. Lalita sahasranama says (name no.570) these four *VAsanAs* will take you to the Goddess.

QUESTION C-19: What is the so-called 'beginningless ignorance' which all advaita books as well as expositors talk about?

Well, you have asked a very fundamental question. Advaita says you are not the BMI, you are not whatever you are thinking you are. It says 'You are other than whatever you think as yours, your mind, your body, your intellect, your possessions, your parentage, lineage, profession, in fact everything you may call yours. Then what remains? That is what they say: Whatever remains after discarding everything of yours, including your name – whatever remains, is YOU. This may be difficult to understand and accept, but that is what advaita holds. Then you may ask, 'Why don't I know this?'. That is where the glitch is. Who is this I now? Since you have discarded everything which you thought was yours, including your name, then what remains. Vedanta says 'That is the Self'; that is you!. At this point Vedanta says you are not able to recognise or understand it because of your 'age-old Ignorance'. This Ignorance is not in this birth only, it was there in your previous life, – in fact in all your lives. Your next doubt is: 'When did this ignorance start?'. The answer to this is: It is beginningless. This is exactly the crux of this question: What do you mean by beginningless?

Now sit back and think. Last night you had a dream, let us suppose. When did you wake up from the dream? You say, yes I know it exactly, something happened in the dream and before I could respond to it in either a positive or negative way, I woke up and I looked at my watch it was 11-10 PM. Now this means you are aware of the end of your dream. Now let me ask: WHEN DID YOUR DREAM START?. Can anybody answer (whenever they had a dream), when did that dream start? Every one can answer the question: When did your dream end? But nobody, not a single person in the world, from time immemorial, can answer the question: When exactly did your dream start?. Dream is a beginningless ignorance (of reality) which vanishes when you come back out of the dream.

This is true even about our sleep. We all sleep, sometimes in the daytime and always at night. Now we all know when we woke up from our sleep. And we all agree that we are ignorant during our sleep. Whether it is daytime or night time, you were awake and aware of things before the sleep started but cannot point when exactly you lost that awareness. So Sleep is also beginningless (that is, no cognition of a beginning) but has an end which is cognisable.

This is exactly the case of our BEGINNINGLESS IGNORANCE about our real existence as THE SELF. We are now in that Ignorance stage and that is what our Vedanta, our rishis, our gurus say. Our Ignorance is about the spiritual Reality, namely, 'I AM BRAHMA ASMI' just as during our ordinary dream (amidst daily sleep) we are ignorant of the 'material reality' of which we were aware before getting into the sleep mode.

So 'beginningless' means 'giving no cognition of beginning;. Thus a dream as well as sleep are beginningless. But just as these two however, are cognisable when they end, in other words, just as they have an end which is experiential, so also our 'beginningless Ignorance' will also have the end when Self-Realisation occurs.!

QUESTION C-20: What does it mean to say that the Self or God is free? Does He have free will? Free will implies multiple options and a freedom to exercise choice. Does He have several options? Why does He choose one of them? In that case is He so ignorant of the future to have to choose from his options? What governs His choice? Nature or *prakRti*? Is He a slave to His Nature? What desire makes

Him choose? If He is omniscient, omnipotent and omnipresent, why does He have to have options, choices, freedom to choose or not to choose? Why? why? why? Does it not all add up to saying that such a God is a bundle of contradictions?

Questions galore! To answer all these questions one has to dole out a vast material about the concept of Godhead in Hinduism. We shall just briefly give the punch line. Whatever you take the Ultimate Godhead to be, either Impersonal or Personal, what is important is that the Hindu description of Godhead is rather tricky because it simultaneously possesses 'contradictory' qualities. So it is difficult to think of a parallel in the finite world of ours. He has no desire, yet He has Will! He chooses and chooses not! He intervenes and He also never intervenes, only watches! He has options but each option is His own Will! He knows the future, yet He chooses to act! The future is what He makes of the present. Nature (= *prakRti*) is His slave, but He allows Nature to take its course. He is Personal, but not 'personal' in the worldly sense, because He is all-knowing. He is perfect, not in the sense of free from limitations, because limitations don't exist outside of His will! Yes, He is a bundle of contradictions, if you yourself don't have faith in your Self! *PrakRti*, the Nature of each being, is only the power of the Self within. It is this Self within, called the *purusha* that makes the *prakRti* work through the lower self. The B.G. makes an impassioned appeal for us to make this surrender to the Self within. After showing His cosmic form to Arjuna, Krishna declares: I have already conquered and vanquished all your enemies; be only an instrument of my action; go and fight. So the plea is for us to be the instrument of God's Will. We are supposed to be like the needle in a gramophone which only traces the channels already chalked out for it by the designer of the record.

WARNING! Such injunctions as 'Be the instrument of God's will' and associated ideas about the not-so-free free will are only for those who are already a few steps up in the spiritual ladder.

SUPPLEMENTARY QUESTION! How does then one know that one is up in the ladder?

Answer: Ask yourself, whether these injunctions make sense to you; if they do, then you are ready to rise further. If they do not, then your free will is still free!

QUESTION C-21: What if once we are supposed to attain *moksha*, that very realisation of Self is also an illusion (*MAyA*)?? How to confirm ourselves hundred per cent that this is not the absolute truth? What if *brahman* too is illusion? Why can't *mAyA* be more powerful than *brahman*?? I mean the same *mAyA* deluded supreme *Brahman* to such level that *brahman* (we are all) forget our true self and trapped inside *MAyA*jaal…isn't *MAyA* more Powerful than *Brahman*? What if *MAyA* is only absolute Reality and everything else including *brahman*, nature just a side effect of *MAyA*???

All these questions arise in the minds of those who think that rational sense is everything and who have little respect for anything that comes from so-called religious or spiritual people or literature. Such questions are only fantasy, a bundle of misunderstandings.. Let me ask them a question. Does the questioner (A, say) know his or her grandfather? The answer may be: Why not, I have seen him play with me. My next question: What about your great-grand-father? The answer may not be so emphatic as before, but it may be something like: Oh Yes, my father used to talk about him! I go further up and further in my questions. How do you know that your great-great-great-grandfather ever existed? It is only your confirmed belief that the descendents of that distant great-great-great-grand father – which includes the questioner also as a descendent – would not have ever been born but for the existence of that person whom you don't know, have not heard about, and have not seen any record of his. Can't you extend this logic to the existence of the supreme Master of this Universe, which the ancient Rishis are talking about?

In Swami Ranganathananda's words, doubt based on *shraddhA* is creative; such doubt is wholesome and necessary; but mere doubt, and too much of it, is bad. If too much of 'the will to believe' is bad, too much of 'the will to doubt and disbelieve' is equally bad. Many of our modern people have this 'will to disbelieve' to an unhealthy degree, as many of our traditionalists have this 'will to believe' to an unhealthy degree. The former is cynicism and the latter is gullibilility. Cynicism is a deadly mental disease. It spells the death of creativity, the impoverishment of the inner man. No new truth can such a one discover, no value can such a one experience in life; the very impulse to seek truth and meaning has been stifled in that individual; and this impulse to seek, and the spirit of *shraddhA* behind it, are the very life-blood of science and religion.

Secondly who told you that *mAyA* may be more powerful than *brahman*? Throughout the scriptures it is clearly and unambiguously proclaimed categorically that *mAyA* is the shakti of *brahman* and as such is used by Ishvara, the Saguna *brahman* who holds the power. (B.G. 7-14). The question "Why can't *mAyA* be more powerful than *brahman*??…isn't *MAyA* more Powerful than *Brahman*?" is totally sub judice and is absurd! You can't be building your own theory of Vedanta, without the sanction of any of the Upanishads or shastras. It is like building a new science without Newton's Laws of Motion!

"I mean the same *mAyA* deluded supreme *Brahman* to such level that *brahman* (we are all) forget our true self and trapped inside *MAyA*jaal" – This comment again is incorrect. For nothing deludes *brahman*. What is being deluded by *mAyA* is our intellect with which our *JIva* has wrongly identified itself. It is this intellect (and therefore the *JIva*) that is deluded. Once the *JIva* through the same intellect is cleared of its delusion by gradual spiritual ascent with knowledge and practice and final self-realisation, the whole drama is over – there is only *brahman* and nothing else.

QUESTION C-22: Which shall we take as the correct response when different teachers of Hinduism – why, the Vedas themselves – give differing answers to the same questions?

This is a legitimate question. Yes, Vedas themselves confuse us sometimes by their different answers at different places. In fact the Vedic tradition seems to be contradicting itself if you look at it as if they were written by successive generations. You will have passages in the Vedas which say that the universe was created by God in the way in which a carpenter creates or constructs a work of art from his mind. At other places the same Vedas will declare that the entire universe came just out of the will-power of God as a manifestation. At some other places questions will be asked by Vedas themselves, like, 'Who knows about this Creation?' Such writing, if at all, reflects only a questioning intellectual mind which tries to present the truth to several levels of understanding. If the levels of understanding are confused and permuted by us in terms of chronology we end up by saying that the Vedas are either a jumble of incoherencies or that they are mostly superstition except for the Upanishads. But even in the Upanishads we find theological discussions take place exactly as in the other parts of the Vedas. The only explanation for all these apparent inconsistencies is to accept that the Vedas keep talking at different levels of understanding all the time. In fact the Upanishads get the highest respect from us because some of the highest level of discussions are there.

Suppose the question is: When was God born? There could be three different answers at three different levels. One first answer is to say that God was born on such and such a day, implicitly assuming that the question is about Rama or Krishna. Another answer is to say that God is unborn, that is, never born, and so the question is ill-posed. A third answer is to say that God manifested himself at the beginning of creation and this manifestation may be spoken of as his 'birth'. The three answers given cater to three levels of understanding. Similarly every question about Hinduism has varied responses depending on the questioner's level of evolution and the framework in which we are supposed to answer the question. It is in this sense that the so-called contradictions arise in the Vedas. So when different teachers give different answers to the same question, one should find out the level of evolution of the questioner or the audience to which the answer is given out and in what context..

QUESTION C-23: 'Rope and Snake' analogy is everywhere in books of advaita. Are there other analogies to substantiate the truths of advaita?

Certainly. Vedanta books are full of analogies, Just as the 'rope-snake' analogy is so prevalent in advaita, equally prevalent is also the silver-nacre (*'shuktikA-rajata-nyAya*) analogy. Starting from the dream-sleep analogy, there are scores and scores of them. Here are some which are self-explanatory. Most of them have been picked up from the book 'Jnaneshvari', of the famoust saint JnAneshvar of Maharashtra. A well-known one from Jnaneshvari:

Whatever happens happens only to your shadow, not to YOU! In a forest, a monkey and a human being, scared of a lion which is chasing them, climb a tree and station themselves on the branches of the tree, safely away from the clutches of the lion. The lion keeps banging on the shadow of the monkey. Every time the lion hits the monkey's shadow, the monkey on the tree gives out a shriek, jumps from branch to branch and thus gets more and more excited. In its excitement, in due time, after its shadow has received a few beatings from the lion's paw, the monkey falls from the tree and duly becomes an easy prey for the lion. Now the lion starts beating the shadow of the man, but the man uses his discretion and is unperturbed by the lion's beating of his shadow. Finally, the lion gets tired, goes its way and the man is saved. *Now Jnaneshvar says, when experiences, good or bad happen to you, think that they are happening to your shadow; then you will not be affected either by happiness or by misery.* The Lord behaves like that in every one of His actions and so He is not touched by them!

Other analogies:

1. When the period of childhood vanishes, there is no more the dread of the child-hunter round the corner. So also the Realised sage has no consciousness of the world of matter.

2. When a log of wood catches fire, the whole log is on fire and thereafter there is no distinction between the burning wood and the fire that burns.

3. Stand on the seashore watching the waves of the ocean, the big ones swallowing the smaller ones. But to the ocean itself, everything is only water and there is neither big wave nor small wave, nor any swallowing of one by the other.

4. It is absurd to say that the Sun 'sees' darkness and destroys it!

5. Can fire burn fire? Can a dagger pierce itself? In the same way when one realises that there is nothing different from him, no action will attach itself to him.

6. The sea cannot distinguish which of its waters belong to which river.

7. Embracing one's own shadow cannot be spoken of.

8. The moon's reflection in water moves and dances; but that does not mean any dancing of the moon.

9. Once the jug of water kept in the sun breaks and all water is spilt, the reflection of the sun is lost, but not the Sun itself.

10. When a man wakes up from a dream, there is no action done, so also the Lord God resorts to Prakriti; but this is no action done by God.

11. The same mango is characterised by its taste by the tongue, by its colour by the eyes, by its smell by the nose, by its touch by the skin. So also knowledge has different facets of expression as *shabda, sparsha, rUpa, rAsa* and *gandha*. But knowledge is the same.

12. He who has not seen the Sun in the sky, is likely to mistake the Sun's reflection in a small pool of water as the Sun and will also think that when the pool dries up there is no more Sun!

13. We never know when our sleep actually begins. So also our Ignorance of our own Self has no beginning!

QUESTION C-24: The scathing criticism by Lord Krishna in the Gita shlokas 2-42 to 44 of Vedic rituals seems to be rather unparliamentary to the tradition of Sanatana Dharma. Can you explain this strange attitude in the very scripture which upholds Sanatana Dharma?

For a proper reply to this question, I shall lean, almost verbatim, on Swami Tapasyananda's book on the B.G. (Ramakrishna Mutt, 1984), p. 78.

The criticism offered here is intended to draw the distinction between the outlook of Krishna's teaching and that of the Vedic fundamentalists who hold the Purva-mimamsa system of thought. They think that the purpose of the Veda is to induce man to perform rituals and fire sacrifices, which will give heavenly felicity. But once the *JIva* has enjoyed and exhausted the enjoyment of that felicity, it has to come back to the earth to do more karma and go through the same rounds again and again. Such an outlook therefore multiplies man's desires and ambitions. Their mind becomes 'many branched' or 'divided' by all kinds of passing desires. They are just like wanderers in the expansive field of life and miss the ultimate destiny of man. Those who have a spiritual world-view are free from desires, and they follow the single goal of the realisation of man's spiritual nature.

QUESTION C-25: If Faith is the bottom line of Religion, why all the posture of logic, philosophy and rationale? Also, What is the good of mere belief without an actual experience of God?

The highest level of Bhakti or Faith has an example in the story of Kannappa Nayanar, who is considered as a model by Adi Shankara himself. At that *tIvra-tIvra* level (=most intense level) of Faith even the distinction of 'you' *(tvam)* and 'That *(tat)* – recall the *mahAvAkya* 'tat-tvam-asi'* – vanishes. Man's greatest enemy is the ego. This is actually a superimposition by our Ignorance on the Self which resides within. There are two kinds of this superimposition (incidentally note that, without the language and content of philosophy, nothing can be explained fully in Sanatana Dharma). The two kinds are *'tAdAtmya adhyAsa'* and *'samsarga adhyAsa'*. The first one is our attachment to the lower self, namely, the BMI. The second one is an attachment to everything that one calls 'mine'. Both kinds of superimposition (= *adhyAsa*) have to be eradicated in order to reach the identity of the individual *JIva* with the ParamAtmA. When the forest-dweller Kannappar's faith takes him on to the stage where he places his sandal-covered foot on the forehead of the Lord (Shiva-linga decorated with eyes, nose etc.), all distinctions of 'me' and 'mine' had vanished for him. Otherwise he would not have done what he did. This is ultimate experience of oneness with God!. It is the stage, not the experience, described as the goal of Bhakti and JnAna. That is why Shankara says this devotee is a model. This ultimate stage is the same whether you approach it by means of Bhakti or by Jnana. In fact, that you start with Faith, go through an intellectual pursuit and then end up with a feeling of oneness with God – is the answer to the question: What is the good of mere belief without an actual experience of God?!!!

QUESTION C-26: B.G. seems to say: "I have the right only to Action and I should not hanker for the fruit of the Action; the thought that 'I am the doer' is the ego. The wise man knows he is neither the doer nor the experiencer". Tell me, then who is the doer-experiencer?

The straight answer is: The doer-experiencer is the one who has identified with the BMI. But immediately a follow-up question will arise, namely, Who is that who has identified with the BMI? This requires explanatiom.

The BMI is your outer personality. The inner personality is the Self. But we all make the mistake of thinking that the BMI is the Self. So we have two things called 'the Self'. One is the Real Self and the other is the false self which we have created for ourselves. Who is the 'we' here? It is the *JIva*, the spark of the Supreme, (wrongly translated as the soul) which is what makes us living. The false self is called the perishable Self *(kshara purusha* in Sanskrit). This is actually the result of identification with the BMI. Who makes this identification? The *JIva*. The real Self has no identification with the BMI. So it is neither the doer nor the experiencer. But if you, the perishable Self, also do not make the identification with the BMI, then you are also neither the doer nor the experiencer. That is why the entire Vedanta and certainly the Gita, says, do not be the perishable Self, identify yourself as the Imperishable Self *(akshara-purusha)*

Because the *JIva* has wrongly identified with the BMI (and has thus created a *kshara purusha)*, all the happiness and miseries of the BMI are also experiences of the *JIva*. If on the other hand the *JIva* identifies itself with the *akshara purusha* inside, then already it is out of samsAra. When we ordinarily say 'I' or 'we' we mean only the false Self. But if we consciously train our mind to think in terms of our being the Real Self, then there is no samsAra. It is therefore the mind which has to do this job of releasing itself from the wrong identification with the BMI. Mind itself has only a borrowed consciousness *(cidAbhAsa* i.e. reflection of the Absolute Consciousness); but it is with that borrowed consciousness the mind has to wake up to the real Truth, namely, '*ahaM brahma asmi'*.

So what is the answer to the question: Who is the doer-experiencer? It is the one who has identified with the BMI. In other words, as my father used to say in his lectures, the doer-experiencer is the one who thinks he is the doer-experiencer. 'nAhaM kartA, nAhaM bhoktA' is the battle-cry of Advaita.

QUESTION: C – 27: WHAT IS NIRGUNA-DHYANAM?

A spiritual seeker-friend asked me the above question. First I told him that this is a serious question and should be asked only of great scholars.

Still I thought I will attempt to answer. First of all there cannot be any *dhyAnam* (meditation or even continuous thinking) of something which has no attributes. For instance V.S. (and other stotras also) uses contradictory names both applicable to the Lord – like *'eko naikaH'*, *'ajaH'* and *sambhavaH;* All this is because he is *nirguNaH*. *'nirguna'* means something which has no attributes, no name, no form, no characteristics, no qualifications – nothing to specify it. So how do you think of it or about it? That is why all our teachers like Maha Periava, or Ramana Maharshi or any of the known great expositors tell us to meditate on a saguna object, like a divine form by means of a mantra or shloka, and **they assure us** that this will ultimately lead us onto the realization of the nirguna specification implicit in the Mahavakya: 'AHAM BRAHMA ASMI'. The conviction of *'aham brahma asmi'* turning into a realization *'aham brahma asmi'* is the *nidhidhyasana* that scriptures talk about.

In my opinion, the concentrated (*nididhyasana*-type) churning in one's mind of the content of shlokas like the following (of Shankara in his *Brahma-jnAnAvaLImAlA)* may help.

tApatraya-vinurmukto dehatraya vilakshanaH/
avasthAtraya-sAkshyusmi cAhamevAham-avyayaH//

dRRig-dRRishyau dvau padArthAu sthaH paraspara-vilakshanau/
dRRig-brahma dRRishyaM mAyeti sarva-vedAnta-DiNDimaH//

I am free from the three kinds of afflictions – namely, those within the body (*AdhyAtmika*), those from external factors or beings (*Adhibhautika*) and those caused by higher powers (*Adhidaivika*). I am other than the gross, subtle or causal bodies; in other words, I am none of these. THEN WHAT AM I? I am the witness of the three states of waking, dreaming and deep sleep. I am the very Self, indestructible and changeless. There are two things which are always different and mutually distinguished from each other. One is the seer and the other is the seen. The seer is *Brahman* and the seen is *mAyA*. This is the high proclamation of all Vedanta.

The beauty of these shlokas is that they summarise the whole of Vedanta in just a few words. The real *'aham'* is nirguna – it is the Absolute itself. By repeating the mantra *'aham brahma asmi'* one cannot become *brahman*. The realization has to come when every 'I' sense and 'my' sense vanish. But this can happen only by *saguna dhyAnam*, and we are told authoritatively, that continuous *saguna dhyanam* will alone eradicate the 'I' feeling and the 'my' feeling, purely by God's Grace and by nothing else. So *'nirguna dhyAnam'* is only an academic expression. *'saguna dhyAnam'* is the cure for getting out of this cycle of samsara.

QUESTION C-28: Which is the correct path – renunciation or the path of action?'

Vedanta does not have answers to such binary questions. Krishna Himself naturally extols both the paths and delineates the types of people and the paths which will suit them. One who is in the initial stages of spiritual evolution, one who is a householder, one who is still engrossed in the pursuit of his worldly desires and aspirations, one who is restless and dynamic – for such people the path of action is prescribed. But, for the same person, when he is at a stage where he is established in equanimity, for one who has been able to disentangle himself from the spiralling coils of desires and ever-increasing aspirations, for one who has traversed a long way in the practice of meditation, for one whose tendencies have settled down to a state of calm and quiet – for such people the path of renunciation is prescribed. Action and non-action are opposites, but a proper understanding of both is necessary for the efficient practice of karma yoga.

QUESTION C-29: Compared to semetic religions Sanatana Dharma seems to be too vast and complicated. Can you suggest two or three simple wholesome ideas of Hinduism which every ordinary Hindu can keep as a motto and life elevator? Also what may be just

five key take aways from B.G. that are empirical to a normal human being?

Certainly. There are just three pillars of Sanaatana Dharma, great purifiers, to which if one holds on, one is almost done! 'Every action whether religious or not does create bondage when you do it with attachment and a longing for the result of the action. But if you do it the karma yoga way (*'yajnArthAt'* – B.G. 3-9), there is no bondage. The three purificatory actions which should be done without slipping are: *yajna* (sacrifice, worship and stipulated ritual), gift-giving (*dAna*) and askesis *(tapas* – accepting suffering or difficulty of penance for a noble cause or spiritual uplift). No excuses for these three are allowed. *yajna'* is the totality of all your duties and obligations – either in your public life or your private life. '*daana'*, the art and habit of giving, covers your attitude and response to the rest of the universe other than you. And, finally, '*tapas'* covers your responsibility for the uplift of your own individual Self by yourself. But even these three (B.G. 18-6) must be done in the karma yoga way, namely, with detachment and without desires for the fruits of the actions

Regarding five takeaways from the B.G. for the normal human being, I am glad you asked this question. They are

1. *Indriya-nigraham* (sense-control) through *yoga-sAdhanA*.

2. Equanimous view of the universe or *brahma-bhAva*.

3. A *sAtvic* devotion to to the One non-dual Absolute.

4. The observance of *svadharma* without any expectation or attachment to the fruits thereof.

5. A total self-negating surrender to that Absolute Reality.

That these exhaust the teachings of the Gita is borne out by Shankara himself in his *bhAshya* of verse XI-55:

matkarma-kRn matparamo mad-bhaktas-sanga-varjitaH/
nirvairas-sarva-bhUteshhu yas-sa mAm eti pANDava//

Be a doer of my works, accept Me as the supreme being and object, become my devotee, be free from attachment and have no enmity to any living being. For, such a man comes to Me, Oh Pandava. In his introductory words to this shloka Adi Shankaracharya says that this verse contains, at one place, in an integrated manner, the essential teaching (for our *mokshha*) of the entire Gita for the purpose of our implementing it in practice.

In fact, these five take-aways plus the three pillars mentioned above constitute a capsule-vedanta lesson for every one.

QUESTION C-30: Advaita-bhakti – Is it not a contradiction in terms?

Listen to the golden words of the Maha-Periava of the 20th century. There is no pleasure in life if we cannot exhibit Love or Prema. It is a common experience that there is no greater delight than Love. But the fact is, in whatever object or person we place our love, one day or other we get separated from the object of our love because either something happens to us or something happens to the object of our love. And from that moment what was once a source of happiness becomes a source of sorrow. The only object which will never get separated from us is God. If only we can make Him the object of our Love! Then there will be no end to the happiness we can gain. The happiness will be everlasting. When this love matures into Supreme Love of God, we can see the entire world as Himself! Love towards one object and for the same reason Hate towards another object – this pattern will give place to an Infinite Love which sees no high and low, no distinction of duality. It is this Bhakti that helps us to avoid the pitfall of a wasteful loveless human life. **Love of God maturing into the insight of seeing the entire world as Himself is Advaita Bhakti.** God is our only true Love. Until we learn to place ourselves unreservedly into His hands and see the world as Himself, our trust wherever else we give will be betrayed again and again. If we are intelligent we learn the lessons after one or two such betrayals.

The million-dollar question is: Can we ever rise up to these levels? Yes, we can. Just for the sake of clarity take the concept of idol worship. Is there a God within the idol or is it simply an inert matter? Hinduism first prescribes to you: Have an attitude of belief that God is in it; start with that attitude. It is a *bhAvanA* (mental conception, fancy) of course. But there is a logic here. God is everywhere; and so He should certainly be also in that inert matter called 'idol'. This is the truth. But this truth does not appeal to us in the beginning, because we expect the indwelling God to somehow express Itself so as to be visible to our perception. So the only thing we can do is to have an attitude of belief, a *bhAvanA*. If we go on practising this *bhAvanA*, it means Truth is being practised as a *bhAvanA*. In due time the false belief that idols of God are only idols, will disappear and it will gradually lead one to the realisation that it is in truth not a *bhAvanA*. In fact one will reach the *bhAvanAtIta* stage where one does not have to have any *bhAvanA* any more, because what has been taken as true is indeed true! **This is the esoteric basis of not only idol worship, but of saguna-brahma worship also (Worship of a form with attributes). In short, advaitabhakti is on understanding the Reality as it is, while the bhakti of the other schools is belief-centric.**

Between JnAna (Knowledge of the Absolute) and Bhakti (Devotion) there is this interdependence. For a devotee the accompaniment of jnAna is an indispensable crutch, without which he is blind. For the man (JnAni) of Knowledge, bhakti (devotion) or prema (divine compassion) is the only way in which he can express himself.

QUESTION C-31: It appears the concepts 'shravaNa, manana and nididhyasana' which are talked about as the royal road to the consummation of advaitic wisdom and realisation, are not as such mentioned anywhere in B.G. Am I right?

I am afraid you are not right. You may be right so far as the three words 'shravaNa, manana and nididhyAsana' are concerned as words. But the concepts are certainly there in Ch.4 – 34. The words '*praNipAta, pariprashna* and *sevA*' take the roles of '*shravaNa, manana* and *nididhyAsana*' in an esoteric manner. Let me explain. My source is Dr. Radhakrishnan's B.G.

Here the prostration (*praNipAta*) stands for the *sAdhanA*, namely, '*shravana*' (hearing & listening) of spiritual talks and advice from knowledgeable scholars & practitioners of sanAtana dharma. It is not just hearing. One has to receive it in the heart & hold on to it.

The word *pariprashnena* indicates the *sAdhanA* of *manana*, i.e., chewing by the mind what has been learnt, by a process of churning the logic and the sequence of ideas by repetitions, questioning and analysis. The sages and scholars whom you approach for such a spiritual guidance, would be able to answer your questions like: 'Who am I? How and why am I under bondage? By what means shall I be freed? What is Ignorance? What is Knowledge?,' and the like. These questions are not theoretical or academic questions. They will invariably arise some time in every one's life – if not in this life, in succeeding lives. We must combine devotion to the Guru with the most unrestricted right of free examination and inquiry or *jijnAsa*.

The word '*sevayA*' stands for a *sAdhanA* of *sushrUshhA*, namely service. It means 'to long to practise what is heard'. To do what is told one needs a lot of humility. Once the quality of humility is there a natural desire will arise to do service to him before whom we are humble. By the quality of service and self-effacement we knock down the obstructing prejudices and let the wisdom in us shine. To quote Dr. Radhakrishnan, 'Truth achieved is different from Truth imparted. Ultimately what is revealed in the scriptures (*pranipAta-shravana*), what is thought out by the mind (*pariprashna-manana*) and what is realized by the spirit through service and meditation (*seva-nididhyasana*) must agree'.

QUESTION C-32: The thing that bothers my intelligence when studying advaita is the claim by advaita that there is a Pure

Consciousness which does not need to have any content to be conscious of. Is there an explanation possible? Is it not illogical to talk about a contentless consciousness?

No there is no loss of logic. The Absolute Consciousness that advaita talks about is like Pure Light that does not have to light anything in order to be Light!. We shall borrow a remarkable illustration used by the author of the book 'Advaita Vedanta' by Prof. M.K. Venkatrama Iyer.

From architecture to sculpture, from sculpture to painting, from painting to poetry, from poetry to music, there is a gradual transition from a situation of content-domination to one of form-domination. In architecture brick and mortar occupy the dominant content. This dominance recedes into the background when the sculptor with his chisel produces a whole saga out of just one piece of stone. In painting there is very little physical content, but there is a substantial amount of form that predominates. In poetry by mere words one brings out a whole bundle of meanings, emotions and expressions. Here matter or content is at its lowest and form takes over almost fully. But when we move over to music, there are not even words. By the mere form of music one is enraptured into whatever emotion the composer has designed for you. Music is pure form with no material physical content. If this can happen in art, it can also happen in the description of reality behind the universe where, as we advance in spiritual evolution we pass to higher and higher states of consciousness. Starting from the waking state of consciousness in which we are so full of content that even the consciousness behind it is hidden, we go step by step until we reach the stage where there is no matter but only pure spirit, pure consciousness. Twentieth century Physics tells us that our consciousness is in some intricate way mixed up with the external world. Vedanta declares that there is no mixing up, in the sense that there is only consciousness. There is not even a subject and an object

QUESTION C-33: This is about a contradiction which I sense between Katha U. and B.G. In the Upanishad it says "*manasaivedam AptavyaM*" (Only by mind, *Brahman* has to be attained) and in the B.G. (C-43) it says "*buddheH paraM buddhvA*" (Knowing It as beyond buddhi, the intellect). If it is beyond buddhi, how can it be attained by mind, which is the same as buddhi in this context?

There is no contradiction. However, this is a very legitimate question. Intellect has to be used all the way until the intellect itself understands that the Supreme is beyond the intellect. Because the Supreme *brahman* is not an object to be understood by the intellect. Intellect has the knowing ability only because it has a reflected Consciousness from the *brahman* itself which is Absolute Consciousness. This reflected consciousness is like the reflected light from a mirror (on which sunlight is falling) and this reflected light may illumine a dark room, but cannot illumine the Sun itself. So also buddhi with its reflected consciousness cannot illuminate *brahman*. Buddhi has itself to realise this. This is what one means by saying *brahman* is 'beyond' buddhi.

We shall have another analogy. There is what is called a *shAkhA-chandra nyAya* in Vedanta. You want to see the third day moon (which is only a small arc on the third day of the bright fortnight). You are not able to see it. Your guru says: "Look at the tree nearby. Look at those branches. Get to this particular branch right above you. There are leaves in it. See the two leaves at the end of the branch. At the end of the two leaves you have a small space through which you can look at the yonder sky. Now see, that is where the moon's arc is visible". Yes, that is right and the moon is visible now. Now, the moon is far far beyond the tree and its branches. But they helped you to locate the moon. Once you have located the moon's arc, the tree and its branches etc. are all of no significance. They are only pointers. In the same way your buddhi has to be used to look beyond the buddhi, far beyond the buddhi to perceive the presence of *brahman*. And thereafter, once you have realised that *brahman* is not anywhere, it is you yourself, the presence of buddhi or mind is of no significance. Buddhi and the mind were only pointers.

The same thing with the logic that advaita uses. All the way when you go upward in the ascent of learning advaita, there is a systematic use of very accurate logic.. But after a certain level, logic will fail to guide you, because *Brahman* is beyond logical reasoning. Just as we discard the leaves and branches of the nearby tree to perceive the distant moon or star, so also we should discard the buddhi and logic at that last stage. Still '*brahman* is attained only by the mind' means it is now the mind which has to realise its ignorance. Remember whenever the mind 'perceives' something, there are two things happening. (Refer Last two paragraphs of Answer to Question C-10). There is vritti (modification) of the mind in terms of the object (this is called *vRitti-vyApti)* and there is an illumination by the *cidAbhAsa* (reflected consciousness in the mind) of the object that is to be perceived (this is called *phala-vyApti*). In the case of *brahman*, the cidAbhasa cannot light it (because finite torch cannot illuminate the Sun), and only the *vritti* of the mind happens. But now there is no object (only *brahman* is there) which is being lighted. So the mind-*vritti* is only the recognition of its own Ignorance because the connecting light namely *cidAbhAsa* which is what connects the mind with its 'object' of perception is unable to 'illuminate'. In other words, *'phala-vyApti'* is not there. So it is not the mind which is perceiving *brahman*, but the mind along with its buddhi have become one with *brahman*; there is only *brahman* now, no mind no buddhi! They have themselves become *brahman*. (Those who can understand Tamil can also refer to verse No.169 of *kaivalya-navaneetam* by TANDavarAya Swamigal) on this topic.

QUESTION C-34: I do find some technical words in advaita books which are sometimes left undefined. Two examples are '*svarupa-lakshana*' and '*taTastha-lakshana*'. Can you help?

First let us understand the word '*lakshana*'. The word means: sign, characteristic, quality, attribute or mark. There are many more meanings, but these are what are relevant now. In the present context, we may take '*lakshana*' to mean 'definition'. If the essential character is used in the definition, it is called '*svarupa-lakshana*'. If only an accidental or indicative character is focussed in the definition, it is called '*taTastha-lakshana*'. H_2O is a *svarupa-lakshana* of water; Water cannot be other than H_2O. Sugar is sweet; sweetness is a necessary qualification of sugar. But blueness is a qualification of the sky, though not a neessary qualification, because the sky may not also be blue. Such adjectives (like blueness of the sky) are called *viseshanas*. *Viseshanas* are not *lakshanas*; they are only qualifications. When what appears to be *viseshanas* happen to be both necessary and sufficient, they become *svarupa-lakshanas*. On the other hand, instead of directly pointing out to *brahman* which is a tall order even for the Vedas, we look at the created universe and infer the Almighty behind. We cannot see Him through ordinary perception but it is He that is the ultimate reservoir and source of everything. This kind of description or definition of God is called *taTastha-lakshana*.

The word *taTastha*-requires an explanation. *taTa* means 'shore'. A visitor comes to a village for the first time. He asks a resident, 'Is there a river nearby? Where is it?'. And the resident replies: 'You see that yonder cluster of a line of trees.. They are on the shore of the river. That is the river'. Here the shore ('*taTa*' in Sanskrit) is used to indicate the location of the river which is not visible. This is how the name '*taTastha-lakshana*' arose for an indicative definition, which is however not a complete definition. Another example of a '*taTastha-lakshana*' would be telling someone that the house they are referring to in the street ahead is the one with a crow on the chimney. The crow on the chimney is *taTastha lakshana* of the house that is being sought. The fact that the Almighty is the Father of the Universe is *taTasha-lakshana* for the Almighty. The *svarupa-lakshana* of *brahman* is '*satyam-jnAnam-anantam*' given in T.U.

QUESTION C-35: In the Gita Krishna takes the stand that He is the sovereign Lord of the Universe, namely Ishvara. In what way is this

Ishvara different from *Brahman* the Absolute Reality? According to advaita, are we ultimately *Brahman* or Ishvara?

This actually is not one question; it encompasses several lessons on advaita. However, briefly we can summarize the interrelationships of *brahman, Ishvara* and *JIva* as follows:

Brahman is *nirguNa*, attributeless; is not the predicate of anything, cannot be pointed at, is neither this nor that – and thus it goes on.

So there is no way of 'worshipping' it. No, we cannot even talk about that except by giving it a name, though not a form. Therefore Upanishads give it a name '*tat*', just for purposes of referring to it and to say that '*tat*' has no attributes. But our intellect wants to do something with the Almighty Supreme. A worship, a prayer, a meditation, an offering or whatever. All these involve a duality of the worshipper and the worshipped. The moment we think of *Brahman* as an object of worship or prayer or meditation, immediately, the concept of *brahman* is automatically jeopardized. Thus the intellect has created *brahman* with attributes – a saguna *brahman*. The very fact that our intellect has come in the picture implies that *mAyA* has done its job. It is *mAyA*'s effect that there is an intellect and we begin to think of objects through our intellect. Thus *Brahman*, with the *upAdhi* (impact, coating, influence, superposition, covering, conditioning,... – choose your word) of *mAyA*, is called *saguNa brahman*. You can go on debating now whether we (through our intellect) created the *saguna brahman* or whether it is somewhere there, if not an object, as a subject. That question is neither relevant, nor will it take us anywhere.

That *saguNa brahman* is the *Ishvara*. Now *Ishvara* has all the superlative qualities that any religion associates with Almighty God. But *mAyA* did not create *Ishvara*. It is *Ishvara* who has *MAyA* in His control. It is like a snake having poison but is never affected by its own poison. *Ishvara* is not affected by His *mAyA*.

However, the spark of *brahman* which is the core essence of beings, ('*JIva-bhUtAM*') is the creation of *mAyA*. So all *JIvas* are under the influence of *mAyA*. To get out of this *mAyA* we need the Grace of that *Ishvara*, who, by His infinitude of powers (which will operate when you surrender to Him exclusively (cf. B.G. 7-14) can take us out of the grip of *mAyA*.

Thus *Brahman* and *Ishvara* are the same, except for the way we look at them. If we don't look for *brahman*, but knowing we are *brahman*, if we 'are' *brahman*, then there is nothing more to say or do. 'aham brahma asmi'. Period.

On the other hand, if we want to look 'at' *brahman* in some way or other, already we have made *brahman* an object and thus it is already only the *saguna-brahman* that we are talking about. So we can 'look at' it, meditate on it, aspire to 'reach' it and all that sort of thing.

JIva on the other hand, so long as it is in the grip of *mAyA*, is separate from *brahman* and also separate from other *JIvas*. Once it transcends *mAyA*, it is *brahman*. This is the *JIva-brahma aikyam* that advaita keeps trumpeting to us. When *JIva* identifies itself with *brahman* there is no need to bring in an *Ishvara* now; because the very identification of *JIva* with *brahman* already includes the identification of *brahman* and *Ishvara* – because the identification itself is something that transcends *mAyA*. So the *upAdhi* of *mAyA* is gone from both *JIva* and *Ishvara*.

QUESTION C-36: According to the Vedas, Upanishads or the Puranas, the main aim of life is to attain *Moksha*, Liberation or Enlightenment. So much has been written about Enlightenment. What is Enlightenment? Has anyone living now attained Enlightenment? Where can we see them? How can we talk to them?

Sages see with an equal eye the learned and cultured brahmin, the cow, the elephant, the dog and the outcaste.(B.G. 5-18) This balanced view of everything as One, everything as the Self, is a blissful experience, called *brahma-Ananda*. This was the continuous experience of a Ramana Maharishi, a *SadAShiva brahman*, a Ramakrishna and sages of that kind. It is naturally a state to be experienced internally, not by any external apparatus. It is a super-fortitude, an equal-mindedness so unfaltering that it results in feelings of deep happiness. At that ultimate level there is really neither good nor bad. The qualities of poise, perspective, peace of mind and patience all go with it. These are not just nice traits; they are the basic components of happiness. This after all is IT. This is the peace so sought by every one. This is the ultimate aim of it all.

God, the Reality Absolute, is not only transcendent – in the sense that He (or It) is beyond all finite conceptions – but He is also immanent in everything, animate and inanimate. This immanence aspect is a speciality of Hindu Vedanta. Whatever we see, hear, smell, taste or touch – everything is the Almighty. (M.N.U.)

The taste of water, the light of the Sun, the sound in space, the smell of the Earth, the glow of Fire, the lives of living beings – all these are nothing but that Absolute Itself. (B.G.7-8,9) "*rasoham apsu kaunteya prabhAsmi shashi-sUryayoH; praNavas-sarva-vedeshhu shabdaH khe paurushhaM nRshhu; JIvanaM sarva-bhUteshhu.*

It all looks like poetry, music. Yes, the music of the moving, the melody of poetry, the delicacy of dance – all this is the song of the Absolute! We are told by great saints that one obtains this kind of Realisation in the *samAdhi* state. Listen to one such description from the Tamil spiritual-scholar saint Kripananda Variyar (1906 – 1993):

The sages of antiquity who have been in that state revel in their equanimous vision and their Bliss of Equanimity and Compassion; they are conscious of nothing else but the fullness of that Consciousness. The vision knows no 'I' or 'Mine'. The little self is merged in the Supreme Self. Knowledge and Ignorance both get consumed in that oneness of the knower, the known and knowledge. There is no seer, no vision, nothing to be seen. For such a *brahma-jnAni*, neither time, nor action, neither merit nor demerit, neither pleasure nor pain, matters the least. In that state of Enlightenment, there is no distinction between one self and the other self. It is full of Grace and Light – no darkness, no confusion. It is the massive Light of Consciousness. No up, no down, no peak, no valley. It is a state that transcends speech and mind, a state that has no goings-on, no action, no reaction.

Who can describe such a state? Only a confirmed *brahma-jnAni* like Shankara can vocalise it into poetry thus. "No merit, no demerit, no happiness, no misery, no chants, no holy water, no scriptures, no rituals. I am neither the experiencer, nor the experienced, nor also the experience. I am Consciousness, I am Bliss, I am *Shiva*". This is the acme of Enlightenment.

> *"na puNyaM na pApaM, na soukhyaM na dukhaM*
> *na mantro na tIrtham na vedA na yajnAH/*
> *ahaM bhojanaM naiva bhojyaM na bhoktA*
> *cidAnanda-rUpaH shivoham shivoham//*

Jivanmuktas and *brahma-jnAnis* are difficult to identify by us ordinary people. A profane example may be given as one of us, visiting a lunatic asylum; we may think they are out of thie mind in the asylum, but that is what exactly they might be thinking of us; they may be thinking we are out of our mind! Only such *brahma-jnAnis* can show the world where the path lies for salvation. They are the ones who can talk authentically from their own experience. In our own times we had Ramana Maharishi, Ramakrishna Paramahamsa, Kanchi Mahaswamigal and a few others. All of them with one voice say the same thing. This universe is nothing but the Almighty Himself. Recall 'vishvam VishhNuH...' in the very beginning of *VishhNu sahasranAma*.

QUESTION C-37: Advaita Vedanta, I am told, establishes that Action (Karma) can never lead to *moksha*. Only Knowledge (JnAna) will lead to *moksha*. Is not acquiring knowledge also a kind of Action (Karma)? I feel there is a self-contradiction in the theory.

Very incisive question! There is no self-contradiction. When Vedanta says Knowledge (*jnAna*) it does not mean intellectual knowledge, which is got from books or reading or even listening to expositions (even vedantic expositions!). Intellectual Knowledge is what every one of us is familiar with. It is that mass of information, ideas and concepts that we absorb (and stuff in our minds) from Science, from books, worldly mixing and what not. The 'knowledge' that Vedanta speaks about should not be mistaken for this 'gathering, analysing and collation of information, opinions and concepts'. Knowledge in Vedanta means the emotionally satisfying conviction that 'I AM NOT THE BMI, I AM BRAHMAN'… Acquiring knowldege is only a *sAdhanA* which is certinly a *karma*. Emotional conviction is different from intellectual conviction. My father used to say when I was a boy of eight or ten, when I protested to get up at 4 AM in the morning to accompany him to go for a river bath and morning *sandhya-vandanam*, ' Then what do you mean by accepting that you are convinced that getting up at 4 AM is a good thing? It is not enough to be intellectually convinced. You must be emotionally convinced enough to act upon it'. This is exactly what happens in our learning from Vedanta that 'I am not the body'. We must have the necessary will-power to FEEL IT IN OUR BONES that when somebody pinches us, it is only the body (BMI) that has been pinched and that the real 'I', that we are, has not been pinched. Knowledge and Knowing are two different things. Knowledge begins with memory in the mind. Knowing in vedanta is the emotional conviction of that memory. It is existential; it is of the Being. Knowing is the very nature of this Existence; it is the core of human existence. It arises when you are in touch with your Being. So in the understanding of Vedanta let us be clear about the distinction between the 'intellectual knowledge' of 'I am *brahman*' and the 'JNANA' of BEING EMOTIONALLY CONVINCED AS BRAHMAIVAHAM-ASMI. Being *Brahman* (*brahma-nirvANam*) is therefore NOT an action! It is what we are!

QUESTION C-38: I have heard the 'story of the tenth man' from certain expositors of Advaita. What exactly is the lesson of this story?.

Well this story will be very apt for understanding the statement "One attains or obtains *Brahman*" which occurs quite often in the Upanishads and other scriptures. (B.G. 18-50 is one example where the word 'obtains' i.e. Apnoti is used). The word 'obtains' is only a way of saying. It does not mean that *brahman* is an object located in a far-off place and one goes there and reaches or obtains it. *Brahman* can never be the object of attainment, since it is itself the subject always. (He is the *kshetrajna* – cogniser, of all the *kshetras,* i.e., of everything which is an object). There is no question of 'knowing' *brahman* which is formless and attributeless. This is where Shankaracharya's analogy in the form of the story of the 'tenth man' is quite educative.

Ten fools who do not have any introduction to one another cross a flooded river and on reaching the other bank, find that one of them is missing. They count again and again and find only nine of them are present. Where is the tenth man? – is their cry. A passer-by notices their predicament and offers to help. He makes them count in his presence. Now one of them counts: one, two, three……nine, and he stops. The passer-by remarks 'you are the tenth'. Suddenly each of them realises that in each of their countings each has missed to count himself! This revelation, namely that the tenth man was never missing, he was always there, he was not "obtained" in any sense of the word, it was only the dispelling of the ignorance of not counting yourself that revealed to you that you are the tenth. **This analogy is a masterly epitome of the advaitic standpoint that the *brahman* which is our own Inner Self does not have to be sought after** – we have only to dispel our beginningless Ignorance. Shankaracharya in his *bhAshya* on this verse makes what seems to be a paradoxical plea that the effort should only be to discard the superimposition of Ignorance on the Self and therefore, 'no effort need be made to 'obtain' the enlightenment of *brahman*'. The tragedy here, says the Acharya, is that the differentiations are nothing but names and forms stipulated by Ignorance (= '*avidyA-kalpita*', an expression most often used by Shankara) and this misled our discretion and intellect – the consequence being

> What is most explicit (*prasiddhaM*) in us looks implicit (*aprasiddhaM*)

What is well-known (*suvijneyaM*) to us appears unknowable (*avijneyaM*),
What is nearest (*Asanna-taraM*) to us seems distant (*atidUraM*)
What is our own self (*Atma-bhUtaM*) turns out to be something other than ourselves (*anyad-iva*).

QUESTION C-39: What happens to the so-called soul when we go to sleep? If you say it gets merged into the Absolute which, like the ocean, has all the souls merged in it, how is it that the same soul comes out after the sleep.?

Every time we go into deep sleep the *JIva* (soul) becomes one with the absolute *Brahman* (Self) in us. This means there is nothing but *brahman* in our deep sleep. The Brahma sutra C-2-9 says that the same *JIva* wakes up after the deep sleep. In writing his Bhashya (Commentary) on this, Adi Shankaracharya gives three important reasons as a justification of this. Firstly this *JIva* continues to proceed with what he had left half done the previous day. Secondly he remembers what he had experienced in the past. And thirdly if we on the other hand suppose that each *JIva* becomes finally free from samsara on his becoming one with *brahman* during sleep and quite another (*JIva*) gets up, this would lead to the conclusion that any one becomes free as soon as one goes to sleep. And if this be the case, then would you tell me what is the need of undertaking a rite or a meditation that will yield its fruit in the future?. After giving these reasons, Shankara himself raises an objection from the opponent's side of the argument. Inasmuch as the *JIva* has become absolutely one with *brahman*, how can we discriminate any particular *JIva* from others? Is it not impossible to take the same drop of water after it had been thrown into a sheet of water since there is nothing to mark out its individuality? And he himself answers it: There is one's karma and Ignorance as the factors making the (individual) distinction; the two cases are thus different! — A digest from Adi Sankaracharya's Bhashya on the Brahma Sutra C-2-9.

QUESTION C-40: I saw myself in my dream last night. Was that my Self that I saw?

Not at all. It could not be so. The Self is not an object or something that you can see. The Self is beyond the senses. You may say that in the dream your senses were not active and so what you saw was beyond the senses and therefore it could be the Self. Please note that any language, English including, is so weak that it cannot find the proper words when talking about the Self. *'yato vAco nivartante'* says T.U., meaning, 'words retreat when trying to describe it'! 'See'ing the Self does not mean you see it as any object in your experience. The word 'understand' is also weak in respect of the perception of the Self. You understand Physics and Mathematics. You perceive the meaning of their most confounding statements. But all this is done by the intellect, i.e., buddhi. But even this buddhi was sleeping while you were dreaming. Only the 'mind' without the help of the intellect, was roaming rampant.

B.G. says Self is *buddheH param.* (3-43), i.e., beyond the intellect. V.S. also says: *'agrAhyaH'* (55th name) meaning it cannot be understood by any of the senses. That is why Krishna gives special 'divine sight' for Arjuna to enable him to see His *vishvarUpa*. But in Ch.6 – 21, it also says *'buddhigrAhyaM'*, the English meaning being 'grasped by intellect'. Again the language is failing and struggling. This 'grasping' is not 'understanding' in the usual sense of the word. The *'grAhya'* is an 'awareness by identity', i.e., awareness by becoming one with'. **All Knowledge of the Absolute is knowledge by identity.** Our ordinary knowledge of things, objects and concepts is either indirect or approximate. So 'seeing' or 'perceiving' the Self has to be by identity, – not any other way. This is the most abstruse concept of Vedanta, which trips us. Please don't be tripped by your dreams. But people do have experience of dreams where they have seen a *saguNa mUrti* of the Supreme, which is certainly, several steps below the Self.

QUESTION C-41: Modern Physics tells us that our consciousness is in some intricate way mixed up with the external world. Vedanta declares that there is no mixing up, in the sense there is only one consciousness everywhere; there is not even a subject and an object. But, when the subject and object disappear, are we not left with a complete blank, a void?

No. It is a mistake to think that when the series of presentations to consciousness comes to an end there is nothing left behind. Even the statement that there is nothing left behind is a piece of knowledge, presupposing consciousness. In the state of profound sleep without dream, we do not perceive anything. Next morning we exclainm that we slept well and do not know anything about what went on when we slept. This reminiscent experience of ignorance – and the usual statement about a happy sleep – would not have been possible if the state of deep sleep were a blank. While everything is presented to consciousness and is revealed by it, consciousness itself is not presented to anything else. It is never an object in relation to a subject. It is that which underlies both subject and object and can manifest itself without any aid. This is the Ultimate Reality which sages experience in the state of *nirvikalpa-samAdhi* – when they have left everything far behind. It transcends the three states of waking, dreaming and sleeping and it is known as the 'fourth' *turIya*. One can deny everything external to oneself but one cannot deny one's own self. The strength of advaita lies in the fact that it has identified the Nirguna *brahman* with the Atman or the innermost self of man. It is directly knowable. Anything that can be known as 'this' or 'that' is not supposed to be 'direcly knowable' (=*aparoksha*). Things that are known as 'this' or 'that' are all *paroksha* (=not directly knowable). This table, that sky, this tiger, this body, this book, this idea, this picture, that speech, this food, this pain – all these are only indirectly knowable; that is, they are all *paroksha*, because you have to see it, or feel it, hear it, taste it, touch it, or think of it, in order to know its existence. In other words you need one of the senses or the mind to make you know it. *Brahman* which is identical with the Self is the only one that is *aparoksha*, because you are yourself *Brahman*.

QUESTION C-42: Why is the concept of 'Equanimity' so importantly spoken of in spiritual teaching and practice?

Real knowledge begins only with the perception of Oneness in your bones; this is the effect of the *samAdhi* state in the Dhyana regimen of Yoga Shastra and also of B.G. Chapter 6. We are told by the great seers that once we experience the state of *samAdhi*, thereafter the perception of oneness will be more natural to us. Oneness – One matter, One life, One mind, One soul, playing in many forms. The declaration by the Vedas of this oneness is only an indirect knowledge (*paroksha-jnAna*) for us. The indirect knowledge becomes a direct (=*aparoksha*) knowledge only when there is direct experience. It is the experience of seeing the right thing, that is, *brahman*, behind the negated universe and the negated individuality of the Atman. This *brahma-bhAva*, being in *brahman*, automatically implies an equanimous view of every being in the world as the same self as the one that dwells in the seer. This balanced view of everything as One, everything as the Self, is a blissful experience, called *brahma-Ananda*. This was the continuous experience of a Ramana Maharshi, a SadaShiva brahmam, a Ramakrishna and sages of that kind. It is naturally a state to be experienced internally, not by any external apparatus. We know that in their cases, even after they came out of the *samAdhi*, they had an attitude of equanimity in their world perception. The following delightful explanation of this equanimity is found in a most unexpected context, namely in the description of the qualities of proper 'leadership' for Managers in the book, Reawakening the Spirit in Work, by Jack Hawley (p.175). Referring to it as one of the most important spiritual discipline, 'carrying a great cosmic secret' he says:

Self-possession is the root of it – knowing and being in control of self and senses, being composed and calm. It is a depth of composure that is foreign to most Western thought. The Sanskrit phrase *shama-dama-sukha* (roughly, same-minded, suffering, and happiness) helps define it. It alludes to an unaffectedness, a steadiness in the face of any circumstance whether 'good' or 'bad'. It is a super-fortitude, an equal mindedness so unfaltering that it results in feelings of deep happiness. The great secret in this is that at some ultimate level there is really neither good nor bad. It is a matter of how we react – and our reactions depend on our steadiness of mind. We create the opposite of a vicious circle: a victorious circle.

Why is equanimity so important for leaders? It is the qualities of **poise, perspective, peace of mind, and patience** that come with it. These are not just nice traits, they are the basic components of happiness. This after all, is It. This is the peace so sought by every one; this is the ultimate aim of it all. The four 'p's lead to the fifth 'p' i.e. permanent peace.

QUESTION C-43: In studying advaita, I am totally confused by the following questions that pop up in my mind. Unless *mAyA* is already present, neither concealment nor projection can take place. Is *mAyA* then coeval with *Brahman*? Do they exist side by side? Does this not contradict the non-dual status of *brahman*? Where does *mAyA* operate? What is its base of operation? Can advaita respond to these questions in a way an ordinary seeker like me can understand?

These questions raise profound issues, which take us to the very core of technical controversies with which the extensive vedantic literature of India is replete. We shall only very briefly touch upon Shankara's bold answers to these questions.

The base of activity of *mAyA* cannot be *brahman* because the latter is Absolute Luminosity and there can be no place in it for ignorance or darkness. Nor can the *JIva* be the base of operations of *mAyA*. For *JIva* itself cannot come into existence until *mAyA* has operated. Yes; there seems to be an unresolvable logical difficulty here. But the difficulty will vanish once we realise that we are making an implicit assumption which is not valid. We are actually assuming the prior reality of time and space before the appearance of *mAyA*. Otherwise we could not have asked the question: Where does *mAyA* operate? When does it come into existence? These questions are valid only if you have a frame of reference in time and space independent of *mAyA*. But time and space, points out Shankara, are themselves creations of *mAyA*! (cf: *mAyA-kalpita-desha-kAla-kalanA vaicitriya chitrIkRRitaM...* Shloka 2 of Dakshinamurti Ashtakam). Before the universe was made manifest, it was undifferentiated in its cause, *Brahman*, like the sprout in the seed. *mAyA* as grounded in *Ishvara* (=saguNa *brahman*), as an adjunct, posits (= takes as given) conditions such as space and time and produces the variegated world with beings bearing specific names and forms. The question whether *mAyA* as an adjunct of saguNa *brahman* contradicts the principle of non-duality does not arise, for *mAyA* as well as the created world, are *mithyA,* i.e. neither real nor unreal.. Only if it were a reality besides *Ishvara* there would be duality. The causality of the world which appears in *Ishvara* is structured by the beginningless indeterminable *mAyA* and so the causality is also *mithyA*. *MithyA* means neither real nor unreal; whatever comes and goes is *MithyA*

In fact this is also the answer to the physicist's question: When did time originate? Time did not originate in a timeless frame because we would then be begging the question. The very fact that we are conscious of the passage of time is a consequence of *mAyA*. So questions such as, Where does *mAyA* operate? And When did it start operating? are not properly posed. Time and space cannot claim prior existence. It is therefore wrong to ask whether *mAyA* is prior to *JIva* or later than *JIva*. Ultimate Reality is beyond space and time. In the words of Swami Vivekananda, time, space and causation are like the glass through which the Absolute is seen, but in the Absolute itself, there is neither time, nor space nor causation. As in the field of modern physics, so in the field of Vedanta, time and space are modes incidental to sense perception and should not be applied to what is trans-empirical. *mAyA* is different from both the real and the unreal. It is in this sense that we say that the world of perception, the common world of experience, cannot be rejected out of hand as totally false, like the hare's horn or the lotus in the sky; nor can it be taken to be totally real, because it suffers contradiction at a higher level of experience. It is real only in the empirical sense and unreal in the absolute sense.

QUESTION C-44: A dead body in a room would not know whether the room is lighted or not and would not even know that it does not know. Because the dead body is just an inert matter without the presence of consciousness in it. This much is understandable. But the dead body also should be Consciousness, because Consciousness as the omnipresent Absolute Reality is everywhere. Why then is it not knowledgeable about the lighting in the room?

Very intelligent and legitimate question! Although the Ultimate Self (Consciousnss) is present at all times and in all things, it cannot shine in everything. Just as a reflection appears only in polished surfaces, so also the reflected Self shines as Consciousness only in the intellect. Shankara's Atma-bodha, Verse 17 says:

sadA sarvagatopyAtmA na sarvatra avabhAsate.
buddhAveva avabhAseta svacchheshhu pratibimbavat.

This means, even though the Atman (The Supreme Self) is always and in everything, it does not shine everywhere. It shines only in the intellect, just as reflections show up only on polished surfaces!

The intellect (along with the mind) has already left the body in the case of a dead body! BhavabhUti in Uttara-rAma-carita says "though sunlight falls equally on a shining surfact and a clod of earth, only the former reflects and not the latter".

QUESTION C-45: How can a finite lamp of knowledge, such as ours illumine the infinite light of Pure Consciousness?

Certainly not. A torch, however big, however powerful, cannot illumine the sun. It is the sun that illumines everything including the torch. The answer to the question is explained by Swami Ranganathananda in his book 'Divine Grace' (1980). Far from the mind, through meditation and other spiritual exercises, however deep and profound they be, illumining or revealing the Atman, it is the Atman that overpowers the puny light of the mind and illumines it through and through. For, the Atman, is of the very nature of Pure Consciousness, infinite, non-dual and undecaying. There (in the Atman) 'the sun does not illumine, nor the moon, nor the stars, nor these lightnings, much less this terrestrial fire; when that (Atman) shines, everything else gets illumined from That; by that light, all this universe is lighted', says the Katha.U. (V.15: *tasya bhAsA sarvamidaM vibhA*ti)

If such is the nature of the Atman, it is preposterous for the human mind to hold that its realisation is effected through a series of spiritual practices. Therefore, Yama says in Katha U. (I-2-23) 'whom alone it chooses by him alone is It attained (*yamevaishhe vRRiNute tena labhyaH*)' to him this Atman reveals Its own (true) form'. It is true that initially, the seeker seeks the Atman; but finally it is the Atman that chooses the seeker, that chooses to reveal Itself to the seeker through an act of self-revelation. '*yamAtmAnaM eshha vRRiNute tena varaNena labhyaH*' says Shankara in his commentary. The sadhaka chooses only Self-knowledge, nothing else and this choice makes the true self reveal itself to the sadhaka. The seeker chooses the Atma alone, giving up everything else and it is attainable due to this choice.

QUESTION C-46: I was listening to an exposition of Mandukya Upanishad the other day. It is fascinating to know that the three verbal sounds 'a'. 'u' and 'm' reflect the three different positions of the tongue in the palate and they exhaust all possibilities of pronunciation of words and so it is quite natural that 'AUM' stands for all the Universe and therefore *brahman*. I wonder whether we can make a similar interpretation for the word 'GOD" in the English language. The letters 'G', 'O' and 'D' are the 7th, 15th and 4th letters in the English alphabet and since 7+15+4 is 26, which is the total

number of letters in the English alphabet and so 'GOD' represents the whole universe! What do you think of this argument?

Certainly the argument is ingenious! You sure have a proposal for something like a Mandukyopanishad for the English word 'GOD'! But I think you may be trapped by the fact that your logic also applies to the word 'DOG' and so 'DOG' also should represent the whole universe! This is where the Upanishadic seers score a point. In fact they talk eloquently about the silence that follows AUM. (That is another point of importance which you seem to have missed!) When they interpreted the three sounds 'a', 'u', and 'm' of AUM they did not fall into such a trap as yours! The only other word in the Sanskrit language with the same three sounds in a different order is 'UMA' (meaning the consort of Lord Shiva). And in this case UMA Herself is the Mother Goddess and the same esoteric interpretation that applies to AUM certainly also applies to UMA!

QUESTION C-47: I am told that Mind is the villain of the piece in our spiritual welfare. But whatever I do, I have to use my mind. Then how do I make my mind take the lead in changing my lower self into the higher self?

Very tricky question. Well, this is exactly for which Vedanta and Yoga are being taught as indispensable disciplines for proper sAdhana. By overcoming desire, vanity, violence and untruth by its own efforts, the normal mind, with discrimination as master, and an exercise of will-power, can train the lower self to rise above its barbarian nature and rise in spirituality. Purity of mind is just the state of being filled with divine consciousness. Vedanta helps us to approach the problems of life with clarity and firmness and thus loosen our spiritual ignorance and ultimately destroy it. B.G. also lays emphasis (6th ch.) on self-exertion for the sake of self-improvement. Divine sight does not mean seeing God in flesh and blood but seeing the one Divinity as both the material and the efficient cause of the world. A logical onsequence of this would be to be able to see in every other person a reflection of one's own self.

To quote from Ravi Ravindra's SCIENCE AND THE SACRED (2000), the mind is limited to modes of judging, comparing, discussion, association, dreaming, imagination and memory. Limited to these modes, it cannot know the objective truth about anything. The mind is not the true knower. It can calculate, make predictions in time, infer implications, quote authority, make hypothesis or speculate about the nature of reality, but it cannot see the objects directly, from the inside, as they really are in themselves. In order to allow direct seeing to take place, the mind has to be totally silent and inert so that the real subject, namely Purusha and the real object, namely Prakriti, are simultaneously presented to it. The seer and seen are then concurrently present in it and the seeing takes place without distortion. This is specificlly what takes place in a vedantic meditation or a yoga-sAdhanA.

(The following is a quote from a well-written book; but I am not able tolocate which): The four technical ways of fighting the weaknesses of the mind are: **Persuasion, Purification, Eradication and Subjugation.** Persuasion is the path of Reason as prescribed by JnAnayoga. Purification is through the path of Devotion. Eradication of the Ego is achieved by the path of selfless action, namely karma yoga. Subjugation of the will-power to make it srong is done by the path of DhyAna yoga of Ch.6 and Rajayoga of Ch.9 of B.G.

Habits of mind can be changed only by creating new habits. These new habits have to come from the above spiritual disciplines. The usual reaction to an imposition of spiritual discipline is to say: 'I am not in a mood to practise them; I will do them only on my own terms, not when told by somebody or forced by circumstances'. But the very moment you say this you have sacrificed your will to be dictated by moods and desires. The will must be strengthened by putting it to a self-discipline. Such strengthening takes place when we keep on pouring the clear water of the thought of God into the reservoir of the mind and thus diluting the impurities in it. Eventually the divine thoughts will completely fill up the mind, hopefully.

Swami Chin*mAyA*nanda in his book MEDITATION (1972) calls this disciplining of the mind as 'an inner guerilla war'. Says he: 'The enemy is never out in the open. We have to counter all his unexpected moves and surprise him in his own hideouts and catch him in his own acts. Alertness and vigilance alone can promise the final victory. A seeker must assume intelligently a get-tough stand with the mind. Deny the mind its full and uncurbed freedom and stand in yourself as a quiet 'witness' of the mind's demands. The tempo of the mind's revelry slowly will quieten. And in time it will come almost to a spent-out halt.'.

QUESTION C-48: WHAT does all the Vedanta mean to the layman of the modern world?

It is this. Every religion says that man should behave in a noble way with compassion, love and sympathy and should spread happiness everywhere. The Upanishads add a punch line to this and say: Man should behave in a divine way *because* his essential nature is divine. The animal instincts that he usually exhibits are the ones acquired by him through his thoughts and deeds in his several lives. But if he is himself, he can conquer these lower tendencies in him and bring out his natural divine instinct in him which will prompt him to love to be happy and to revel in that Inner Glory of the inherent Divinity in Him. Therefore, say the Upanishads: Don't seek happiness from outside. Be yourself, turn to the *Atman*, see the same *Atman* in every other self. And that way see the same positives and not the negatives of every other self. If only we set our mind to do this the Lord will help us; because, the Lord resides in us. He is not an absentee landlord; He is working with us all the time. This is the fundamental guideline of the Upanishads for practical living. It is necessary here to record the flexibility and frankness exhibited by the Upanishadic seers. The knowledge of *Brahman-Atman* elucidated in these ancient texts is of course a declaration of the great sages who 'saw it all'. But they never say it as a dogma. Nor are we supposed to receive them as dogmatic assertions. The beauty of their teaching is that they ask you to enquire within yourself and arrive at your own conclusions, step by step, checking with the Upanishadic revelations at each step.

To help us in this search after truth they give us their intermediate conclusions also. The final conclusion, according to them, is a realisable truth, which forms therefore an axiom – a single axiom from which the entire science of vedanta and metaphysics is built up by accepted forms of logic. This single axiom is enunciated in four different ways in the vedas. These are the four Grand Pronouncements (*mahA-vAkyas*).

Mahavakya	Location in Scripture	Literal Meaning
prajnAnaM brahma	Rigveda, A.U. 5.3	**Absolute Consciousness is** *Brahman*
ahaM brahma asmi	Yajurveda, Br.U. 1-4-10	**I am** *Brahman*
tat tvaM asi	Samaveda, Ch.U. 6-9-4	**That Thou art**
ayaM AtmA brahma	Atharva veda, M.U-2	**This Atman is** *Brahman*

Each of these pronouncements is subjected to an intensive analysis by the commentators belonging to each school of philosophy. However the differences in the interpretations by the different *AcAryas* should not matter in one's daily life. It is as if there exists a multidimensional Reality of which each individual perception has only an one-dimensional projection of the Reality before it, and, perhaps, each in a dimensional axis. You are free to choose that one which is appropriate to your taste, evolution, training and tradition.

QUESTION C-49: WHAT is meant by self-enquiry?

A reasonable reply (with which I agree) to this question is given by Dennis Waite in his book 'BACK TO THE TRUTH' (2007) (published by Winchester, UK). The following is a summary of the answer on pp 267-270 of the book:

Self-Enquiry (Atma Vichara) is the term usually given to the technique advocated by Ramana Maharishi in which the question 'Who am I' is repeatedly asked. We are not looking for an answer. Any answers that may arise will be from the mind and necessarily untrue. It might be a variant on the *'neti neti'* practice in the Br.U. but Ramana denied this, claiming that *'neti, neti'* is only an intellectual exercise and effectively saying that the ego could never eliminate itself.

Self-enquiry begins with the realisation that "I am not the body" and progresses thereon. To recognize what I am not is the beginning of the process of recognizing who I am. Self-effort channeled into self-enquiry brings Self-knowledge.. The Self does not do anything. All thinking or apparent action is through the mind. The very notion of 'I' itself is a mental *vritti* (modification), says Ramana Maharshi. He calls it *'aham-vritti'*. In the question 'Who am I', the 'I' is not the real Self; because the mind can never know the real Self. Mind can know only objects. The real Self is not an object. The purpose of the question-exercise is to try to discover the ego. The question is not to be used as a mantra but only as an inquiry. The mind may throw up an answer, but the answer is always wrong. So doubts arise. Cease to pay attention to them. Pay attention to the Self within. Instead if you try to remove the doubt or fear, another doubt or fear will arise. There will be no end to it. The best method to annihilate them is to ask 'To whom do they occur?'. Whenever an apparent answer is thrown up by the mind, it is turned around into another question. By separating the 'I' from the objects with which the identification is occurring, we are undermining the seeming reality of the ego. When all these *'ahamvrittis'* (thrown by the various answers) disappear, there is no longer any identification of any sort – no feeling that 'I am the doer, thinker, etc. or a person). All is seen as the Self.

QUESTION C-50: Is spiritual enlightenment same as Self-Knowledge?

No. For 'enlightenment' is an event in time. 'Enlightenment', 'Awakening', 'Realisation' – all these words imply something happening in Time. That is, there is a time when we are in bondage and then there is a time when we are liberated. This is not the truth.

We are always liberated!. Many believe that 'Enlightnment' happens suddenly, there is a flash of realisation and afterwards we live in a state of heightened awareness in which we are able to have the equanimous view of everything. This is not so. In fact our *samsAra* is an illusion (not unreality, but *mithya*, meaning, only an appearance which will vanish in due time) – not recognizing it is a mistake we have made for ourselves by sheer ignorance of the Truth. The mind must become the servant of the intellect, not the slave of the senses. It must discriminate and detach itself from the body. Like the ripe tamarind fruit, which becomes loose inside the shell, it must be unattached to this shell or casement which is the body. Strike a green tamarind fruit with a stone and you cause harm to the pulp inside. But do this to a ripe fruit and what happens? It is the dry rind that falls off, nothing affects the pulp or the seed. The ripe aspirant does not feel the blow of fate or fortune. It is the unripe man, who is wounded by every blow. So too, your ignorance must fall off through your own efforts. It will not come to you as a gift or miracle. Truth, Bliss and Peace that are won by your own struggle with untruth and injustice will be the lasting treasure for you.

It is worthwhile to quote Swami Vivekananda here. The spark of realisation and the onset of spiritual becoming have to come through faith and intuition, not through study of books. The Soul can receive impulses from another soul and from nothing else. We may study books all our lives, we may become very intellectual, but in the end we find that we have not developed at all spiritually. It is not true that a high order of intellectual development goes hand in hand with a proportionate development of the spiritual side of man. The Yoga VasishTa has a beautiful verse in this connection:

> *adhItya caturo vedAn dharmashAstrANyanekashaH/*
> *brahmatattvaM na jAnAti darvI pAkarasaM yathA//*

Meaning: Having studied all the four vedas as well as many dharma-shAstras, one may still not know what is brahman, just as the spoon does not recognize the taste of the soup.

In studying books we are sometimes deluded into thinking that thereby we are being spiritually developed, but if we analyse the effect of the study of books on ourselves, we shall find that, at the utmost, it is only our intellect that derives profit from such studies and not our inner spirit. This inadequacy of books to quicken spiritual growth is the reason why, although almost every one of us can speak wonderfully on spiritual matters, when it comes to action and the living of a truly spiritual life, we find ourselves so woefully deficient. To quicken the spirit, the impulse must come from another soul. The person from whom such impulse comes is naturally the 'guru'. (From Swami Vivekananda's Complete works. Advaita Ashrama Calcutta, 7th imprn. Vol.C.p.45)

As a result of Shravana, Manana and Nididhyasana – questioning everything until we have no further doubts about the Vedantic Truth, and then continually reflecting upon it, Self-Knowledge is established as a re-cognition. There are four stages of this re-cognition. We start with **Ignorance,** a sprouting in mud, the next is an **aspiration**, a yearning to the surface; the third is the **endeavour** to soar high and the fourth and last is **illumination**, which is the blossoming in the light. And we re-cognize we have always been and always will be Brahman. This is *JIvan* mukti, that is, Liberation even when the body is alive..

QUESTION C-51: I need to have explanations for the technical words 'anvaya', 'vyatireka'. 'adhyAropa' and 'apavAda' – which all seem to be very common in vedanta literature. In what way do they help the understanding/

Yes, these four words are really very significant for the understanding of Vedantic content. But I shall postpone two of them *'adhyAropa'* and *'apavAda'* for a separate question. We shall talk about *'anvaya'* and *'vyatireka'* now. On the very first day of Brahma's appearance it is the Absolute Himself who teaches these words to Brahma. Srimad Bhagavatam has this in the four shlokas (usually called *'chatus-shlokI bhAgavatam'* (II-9-32 to 35). The Lord Absolute taught the gist of the Bhagavatam in these four *shloka*s.

"It is I, who was existing in the beginning, when there was nothing but Myself. There was nothing else, neither Being nor non-Being nor anything which transcends them. That which you see now is also Me, and after annihilation what remains will also be Me. Whatever appears in the *Atman*, be it a reflection-like appearance where there is nothing of value, be it a darkness-like non-existence where there is existence, all this is to be considered as my *mAyA*. Know thou that just as the universal fundamental subtle elements appear to have entered into the cosmos but in reality there is no such 'entry', so also I appear to have pervaded into everything but in reality there is no 'pervasion'. By the two exercises of logic known as '*anvaya*' and '*vyatireka*' what is known to exist everywhere and every time is the only thing to be known by those who seek to know the truth of the *Atman*."

The logic terms '*anvaya*' and '*vyatireka*' are to be explained thus. Consider the Self as the string in which every non-Self is strung like beads. The fact that the Self is the continuity part of the string in all that is non-Self is called *anvaya*. The fact that the Self itself is separate from the non-self just as the string is separate from the beads, is called *vyatireka*. Said in another way, when the non-Self exists, the Self certainly exists; this is *anvaya* (continuity). When the non-Self does not exist, even then the Self exists; this is *vyatireka* (discontinuity). At the end of the four *shloka*s the Lord adds a rejoinder to BrahmA. Says He: Establish Yourself in this by the highest *mAyA*. Then throughout all your work of Creation in every *kalpa* you will never be deluded" (II–9–36). This can be taken as God's Commandment to all humanity in all their works. This is the highest teaching.

It is enlightening to note that the boy Prahlada when talking to his classmates, when their teacher was absent, gives them a sample of Vedanta (which he had already (as an infant in his mother's womb) learnt from Sage Narada. And Prahlada uses this very concept of *anvaya* and *vyatireka* then. He says: (Bhagavatam VII – 7: 23 to 25) "It is here in the body that the Self (*Purusha*) is to be sought for by discarding every non-Self as 'not this' 'not this', by men coolly reflecting on the creation, continued existence and dissolution of the universe with a mind purified through reasoning on the lines of '*anvaya*' (the all-pervasiveness of the Absolute) and '*vyatireka*' (the distinctness of the Absolute from everything else)."

We have a still down to earth presentation By Lord Krishna in B.G.(Ch.7 shloka 7). The Self is the string in which every non-self is strung like beads or gems. The self is the continuity part of the string in all that is non-self and this is called *anvaya*. The fact that Atman itself is still separate from the non-self just as the string is separate from the gems or beads is called *vyatireka*.

In Sum, Anvaya is the continuity part, AtmA, in all that is *anAtmA*; also the association of cause in all its effects. It may also be called the Immanence or *antaryAmitvaM* aspect of the Supreme. This is also the meaning of the very first word '*vishvaM*' (=universe – therefore indicating that He is immanent in everything) in V.S. When the non-Self exists, the Self certainly exists. When effect (non-self) exists, certainly cause (Self) exists. This is *anvaya* (continuity). When the non-Self does not exist, even then the Self exists. This is *vyatireka* (discontinuity). *Vyatireka* indicates that Atman itself is separate from the *anAtmA* (non-self). Cause is distinct from the effect. This is the *vyapakatvam* or transcendence aspect. This is the name '*VishhnuH*', (who transcends all transcendences) the second name in V.S..

The words '*anvaya*' and '*vyatireka*' are also translated into English as 'agreement/accordance' and 'contrariety/divergence'. Again, the existence of the Self in deep sleep while the BMI is dormant is *anvaya*; that the Self is Conscious independently of the BMI, as in deep sleep, is *vyatireka*.

QUESTION C-52: I found the following statement in Mandukya-karika 4-47. 'As a fire-brand when set in motion, appears as crooked, etc. so also Consciousness, when set in motion, appears as the perceiver, the perceived and the like'. WHAT is this about Consciousness being set in motion? Is Consciousness an object of Matter?

Your question is legitimate. Consciousness is not an object. But the analogy with firebrand being waved needs a detailed explanation. Let me lean on Acharya Shankara himself (and also on a book in English, entitled 'AUM – Awakening to Reality' by Dennis White, 2014) on this abstruse question. If a fire-brand be moved swiftly it makes a cirrcle or a straight line or a crooked line according to the movement. Shankara says, so does Consciousness appear as the perceiver, the perceived and the like. What is that which appears as the perceiver etc. here? It is Consciousness set in motion. Certainly there is no motion in Consciousness. Since there is only Consciousnes there is nowhere it could move to. It only appears to be moving.

The metaphor of the firebrand is deceptively simple. The firebrand, or torch, or stick, with a glowing tip stands for Consciousness. When the firebrand is moved, lines and patterns seem to be created. These patterns represent the world. When Consciousness 'vibrates' a subject perceiver and perceived objects seem to be created. This appearance, says Shankara, is due to avidyA or Ignorance. Consciousness is ever immovable; so no motion is possible in it. The ignorant only imagine illusory subjects and objects which are the basis of our sense-perception.

When the glowing tip stops moving, the patterns also stop; the firebrand complete with still glowing tip just sits there without any 'appearances' being created. Similarly when Consciousnessis is not 'vibrating' (that is, when the mind is still, in deep sleep) there are no appearances of forms of any kind. We simply rest in stillness and peace. Because there are no patterns when firebrand is still, we have to conclude that the firebrand itself is not the cause of the patterns. Similarly when Consciousness is still (in deep sleep) there is no world. Accordingly Consciousness itself cannot be the cause of either the waking or dream worlds. It has to be the movement, which is the 'cause' in each case and the patterns and forms are the 'effect' of the movement. Without the moving firebrand there are no patterns. Without the apparently-vibrating Consciousness, there is no world.

QUESTION C-53: If God's Grace is what ultimately decides what is going to happen to me, WHY does He not give me or grant me that bhakti which I seem to lack and need?

Yes, God grants you the right buddhi to develop that *bhakti*. But you have to receive it. Sage Ramakrishna gives a beautiful analogy. The rain may pour, but if a vessel is upside down no water will collect in it. Your mind is free; by your own free will you have to decide to receive what God is ready to give you. By your own volition you have to decide to trust in God and surrender to Him. If by supplanting your will, God has to give you what you need, then there need be no creation, no existence of the universe. This is the mystery of God's *lIla* (sport, play) of creation. Creation is a kind of play where God allows beings to have the feeling of separateness from Him and then waits and waits until the beings that have emerged from Him come back to Him. If they don't want to come back to Him, He allows them to go their own way and take their own time to discover that that is the Want which will finally rid them of all their wants. The 'agony of God' (see B.G. 7 – 26) in this great cycle of creation is that beings do not want to get out of this cycle. So sometimes He gives them all the petty things they want, so that in due time they would want what He wants to give them. All our temples, gods and goddesses and the innumerable ways by which we can propitiate the divine in these places of worship, as well as the uncountable methods by which we may offer our private prayers – all of them have that one objective, that we should ultimately want to go back to where we came from, that is, merge in Him and His Glory.'Even if he be a person of evil conduct' says Krishna in B.G 9-30, 'if he worships Me with devotion to nothing else, he too should be regarded as righteous, for he has rightly resolved'. In other words, the Lord seems to say 'You have taken the first step and I will take several steps to meet you on your own ground". (This is a quotation from Sathya Sai Baba.

Incidentally you might have noticed that throughout the scriptures, God is said to give you *jnAna, buddhi, buddhiyoga,* wealth and prosperity, and so many other things, but never it is said that he gave or granted Bhakti to somebody. Bhakti is a thing that we have to cultivate in ourselves by ourselves for ourselves. We can ask for guidance from Him for a proper intellect (buddhi) which thinks in the right direction. But bhakti as such, we have to develop through that right buddhi!

QUESTION C-54: As an advaitin, WHAT do you think of Shri Ramanujacharya and Shri Madhvacharya, the eminent propagators of the non-absolutist traditions?

Shri Ramanuja-AcArya (1017C.E.–1137C.E.) was the first propagator of *viSishTAdvaita* philosophy on a national scale. His followers are known as *Shri vaishNavas*. He was the third *AcArya* (= Master, Teacher, *Guru*, Guide) in the succession of *Shri vaishNava AcAryas* beginning from *nAtha-muni*. While the *AlvArs* represented the emotional side of Vaishnavism, the *AcAryas* who followed them represented the intellectual side. Ramanuja was not only a great thinker but an equally great organizer. Before he embraced *sannyasa* and took the headship of the Vaishnavas at Shrirangam he was a householder devotee but his wife's inability to tune herself to the spirit of his spiritual leanings made him renounce that life. He spent two years in studying the teachings of Yamunacharya from the specialists who had been trained by him. Once when he learnt the most sacred *ashTAksharI* (=the eight-lettered) *mantra* from a scholar at Tirukkoshtiyur, he disclosed it to a large mass of people, inspite of the *Guru*'s injunctions of secrecy and punishment of Hell for violation. Ramanuja's defence was that if the knowledge of that *mantra* would help all those people go to the abode of Lord *Vishnu* after death he would welcome going to hell for disclosing it to them. He carried on this war against intellectual, religious, snobbish arrogance unceasingly throughout his life.

Ramanuja toured the whole country to popularize his teachings. Wherever he went he won over the controversialists there and established his own monasteries. He divided the Vaishnava world into several subdivisions and appointed spiritual leaders for each one of them from among the householder devotees who flocked to him. He arranged for the central apostolic succession of the spiritual leadership at the temple of Shrirangam, which from now on became the headquarters of the

Vaishnava world. He displayed towards all, and in particular, towards the lower class, a unique compassion and sympathy and gave everybody a place in the Vaishnavite world by allowing them to wear the caste marks of Vaishnavism, to follow the Vaishnava customs and habits and to recite the Prabandhams.

That the Lord is both the goal and the path was convincingly established by him as the core of the teaching in the vedanta of both Sanskrit and Tamil. He revolutionized the thought processes of tradition-bound brahmins by preaching *mantras* and their meanings to seekers and devotees, irrespective of their caste. He was the foremost maker of modern Vaishnavism. His innovations in the rituals, practices, ideals and the norms of society were successful because, in the tradition of his two great predecessor-*AchAryas*, he combined the management of the Shrirangam temple with the duties of the apostolic head of Vaishnavism..

The lessons of the Visishtadvaita way of life and the message that Acharya Ramanuja left for posterity and the world went home not only in his home, the heartland of South India but in the entire country upto distant Kashmir. Many of the great medieval reformers of India drew inspiration from his teachings. He was the first to synthesize the teaching of the Vedas, Brahma Sutras and the Gita with those of the divine prabandhams of the Tamil land.

Individual souls are only expressions of the one and only unique *brahman*, according to Acharya Ramanuja's interpretation of the Upanishads. So his philosophy is called 'Qualified non-dualism' (*VishishTAdvaita* philosophy). When the Upanishads declare the nirguna nature of *brahman*, says Ramanuja, they only deny certain lower qualities, and do not deny its every quality. God, souls and matter form an inseparable unity which is one and has no second. In this sense ultimate reality is one. Matter and souls inhere in that Ultimate Reality as attributes to a substance. They exist before creation in the subtle phase and after creation in the manifest phase. While creation is only a phenomenon or appearance for Acharya Shankara, it is a real act of God for Ramanuja. To the former it is a movie-like projection and to the latter it is an actual play on the stage. Creation of life in Vishishtadvaita means the expansion of intelligence and the acquisition of a material body. Matter is fundamentally real and it undergoes a real evolution. All objects are bodies of Ishvara who is their Atman. Between matter and soul, the soul is a higher mode because it is conscious. It is also eternally real and eternally distinct from Him though dependent on Him. It is atomic in size whereas God is all-pervasive. Every visible expression of God is only an *amsa*, fragment of God. The souls use the senses to have their experience of pleasure and pain from material products. The Lord gives them the fruits of their actions according to their past karma.

Among his numerous unexplainable miraculous contributions to the greatness of Sanatana Dharma the most remarkable, in my opinion, may be his transformation overnight of Dhanurdasa, a wrestler by profession, of low birth. Spotted by the Acharya in a most lustful act of meanness, this Dhanurdasa became overnight into the noblest devotee of the Lord and in course of time one of the foremost disciples of the Acharya himself!

It is no wonder that today no Vaishnavite temple is considered complete without an image of his as the prince of devotees ever facing the Lord in His contemplation. Factions will forget their differences just at the mention of his name. His influence over all alike, brahmin or non-brahmin, southerner or northerner, poor or rich, the protagonist of Sanskrit or of Tamil, is remarkable. It does not matter whether they adhere to his school of philosophy or not. Throughout the Hindu world, the attitude of religious worship of a divinity or a Guru is in essence the one taught and followed by Ramanuja, namely the attitude of a servant to the Master, of one of insignificance to one of Infinite Compassion, Knowledge, Power and Grace.

MadhvAchArya (1238–1317) belongs to the triumvirate of spiritual giants along with Shankara and Ramanuja, through whose expositions of Upanishadic philosophy India's spiritual greatness became famous and continues to be so, throughout the world. His original name was Vasudeva, while in religious circles he is known as *PoorNa-prajna*, the fully enlightened. In his 37 treatises he signs himself as Ananda-tirtha. He is considered as an incarnation of the Wind-God, *vAyu*, also known as *mukhya-prANa*. He was born in a village near Udupi in Karnataka. Around the age of 25 he renounced worldly life. He was not only a scholar-Sannyasi but was also a giant in physical strength as well as in psychic powers. He studied the philosophy of *advaita* in the beginning but very soon was dissatisfied with the distance it keeps from reality. He started making his own interpretations of the scriptures. He used to declare that he remembered these ideas from his previous lives. His captivating powers of exposition, his originality and his untaught learning resulted in his being named as the head of the Monastery in which he was just a student. His philosophy is down-to-earth realism. He interprets the passage *tat-tvam-asi* as saying essentially that everything is under the direction and control of the Almighty, from whom we, the souls, are different. For this he invokes a vowel from the preceding word *AtmA* in the passage and reads it as *atat-tvam-asi*. He has written *bhAshyas* on the *brahma-sUtras*, the Upanishads and the *Gita*. It is said he mastered 21 rival traditions before he wrote all these. His *M.B.-tAtparya-nirnaya* (=the fixing of the purport of the *M.B.*) is a poem of 32 chapters. He also wrote a gloss on the *Shrimad-BhA..* He was probably the first one, chronologically, to use the *BhA.* systematically for philosophical expositions.

MadhvAchArya was an uncompromising theist. His devotion was coeval with knowledge and therefore more intellectual than emotional. His life was so full of miracles and miraculous devotion that we cannot separate his life from either his miracles or his devotion. The most unique of them all has a historical overtone. Once a ship while reaching the shore near Udupi faced a great storm and was in imminent danger. MadhvAchArya who was standing on the seashore, saw the scene, waved his cloth towards the ship and by the Grace of God the ship was saved. The first thing the captain did on landing was to prostrate himself before the AcArya and thank him for what he believed was the AcArya's miracle and request him to take something as gift. The AcArya by his inner vision saw a heavy lump of *gopi-candana* (a species of white clay) lying in the ship as ballast. He asked for that to be given him as gift. Surprised at this seemingly trivial request the captain obliged. The AcArya drove his hand inside the lump of clay and brought forth a *sAlagRama* stone idol of Balakrishna (Krishna in his childhood) from within. The idol was so heavy that the very fact that the AcArya could carry it all by himself was itself a miracle. But more miraculous was the information he gave on the idol. It appears it was originally made by the divine architect *viSva-karma* and was kept by no less a person than Rukmini hrself in Dwaraka in the *dvApara yuga*. When Dwaraka was submerged in the sea at the end of Krishna's time, the idol was lost. That was the idol which the AcArya had unearthed! It adorns the temple of Udupi even today.

The end of MadhvAchArya's life was equally miraculous as was his life. It is said that when he had completed his mission on Earth the heavenly beings showered flowers on him and under the cover of these flowers heaped on him, his body simply disappeared!

QUESTION C-55: If *Brahman* is nameless and formless, WHY are we expected to go to temples and worship the vigrahas or replicate such worship at home?

This is question number one of every atheist attempting to blast the faith of Hindu believers! Well, the atheist is so confirmed an atheist that he may not be moved by the argument that I present below. I don't hold a brief for this argument because this is a fundamental thesis of the subject of Vedanta. We can give a title to it, namely, *adhyAropa-apavAda* — about which an earlier question was there and I postponed answering it to a later question. This later question is now.

adhyAropa means super-imposition, wrong imputation, attribution of a false characteristic; assumption. When we are told to think of (and treat) the *vigraha* (either in the temple or at home) as God, we are doing an *adhyAropa*. Why are we asked to do this? Because, we are unable, in the beginning, to comprehend the Impersonal Attributeless Supreme. So we are given the *saguNa brahman* (*brahman* with attributes, form,, name, etc.). Then when we ripen in Vedantic wisdom, we are told to take it back (this is *apavAda*, negation, withdrawal, denial, rescission), because as an ultimate this is what is true. A shloka of Amalananda says this process has been initiated by the Shastras, mainly out of compassion for our poor understanding of Vedantic subtleties. The shloka is:

"nirvisheshham param brahma sAkshhAt-kartuM anIshvaraH/
ye manDas-te anukampyante savisheshha-nirUpaNaiH",

meaning, For the benefit of those who are unable to comprehend the Impersonal Supreme, the concept of *saguNa-brahman* is superimposed by the scriptures out of compassion.

The Tamil saint Tayumanavar has a picturesque way of presenting this:

kaDattai maNNenal uDainthapodo inthakkarumac-
caDalattaip-poy enal iRanthapodo collattarumam

Do we have to call the pot but clay only when it is broken? Do we have to call this body as false only when it is dead?. The body has to be called *jaDa* (inert) even before the so-called death occurs. The clay-pot is only clay even when it is not broken. By calling it the clay-pot we are still in the *adhyAropa* stage only. If we can remove the pot-idea, even when it is not broken, then we have done the *apavAda* of the *adhyAropa*. In the teaching of advaita also, they allow you to go on with the idea that the universe and all that we see, hear and feel are real along with the teaching and the teacher. This is the *adhyAropa* or superimposition on Reality. In fact even the Iswara concept and the Bhakti towards that Iswara are all part of this *adhyAropa*. At the end of it all they help you realise that what you have been through is nothing but part of the Mayic play of the Lord and so *apavAda*, the eradication of this mAyic goings-on even when it is going on, is what is needed to be *Brahman* itself!

QUESTION C-56: I have heard it said that if you are a real sincere seeker of spirituality, the Guru will come to you in due time! This is a little tricky; Can you explain?

Yes, it is enigmatic of course! In this connection I want to draw attention to the article on 'Self-Reliance and Discipleship' by Dr. Paul Brunton in his book ESSAYS ON THE QUEST (1984). My answer to your question borrows freely from that article.

The saying that the Master will come to you in due time is definitely not to be denied. But the Master referred to here may not be an embodied or an external one. He may be inside your own heart! Just as the seeker has to learn through disappointment and suffering to cast off the dependence on any human being for happiness, he has to learn though the same means to cast off sole reliance on any human being for guidance. Even Sage Ramakrishna has admitted: "He who can himself approach God with sincerity, earnest prayer and deep longing, needs no Guru" But he also adds: "But such deep yearning of the soul is rare; hence the necessity of a Guru". A teacher's instruction at best leads to mediate knowledge, whereas the realisation of the Truth must be immediate.

YogavAsishta contrasts two kinds of paths. If one follows without failure the path laid down by the Guru, delusion will wear away little by little and emancipation will result either in this birth as later. If on the other hand the mind being fortified with a stainless spontaneous knowledge, ceaselessly meditates upon it, there may alight a true enlightenment like a fruit falling from above.

Though the Buddha taught spiritual self-reliance, he did not intend his teachings on these things to be universally and eternally valid. A seeker should utilize the knowledge of those who in the past have gone before him on the road of life and of others, who, in the present, have gone ahead of him on the same road. However it is hard to find a teacher who unites in himself wisdom, compassion, experience, strength and the willingness to serve others without reward.

Your reason, rightly directed, says Swami Satprakashananda in his book 'Mind according to Vedanta', can lead you beyond its scope. Reason has a limited range, beyond that it is helpless. If you lose your way you ask a traffic policeman for directions. He will direct you, but will not take you there personally. Reason functions in the same way. A man of God tells you of the nature of God and the world and of the path to take to realize God, but exactly like the Vedas, he cannot take you all the way. You reason on his words and eventually reach the goal thus using reason to go beyond reason.

Any one can therefore reach the highest goal by his own power, continues Paul Brunton; but if he has a teacher to remove his doubts and correct his errors he will reach the goal probably more quickly. It is common sense to look for a teacher to whom one can appeal for help, encouragment, instruction, inspiration and direction. Without being too cautious on the one hand or too rash on the other one may adopt an ideal balance. And Paul Brunton closes with the following real story.

A very earnest western seeker once travelled to an Oriental country (not India) in quest of a guru. She selected the monastery of great repute and rented a cottage for herelf. She sought for tuition from the abbot but her request was not granted. After six months, as it seemed useless to stay longer, she began arranging for departure. Just then the comprehension stuck her, as in a sudden flash, that no one outside herself could do for her the work resulting in self-realisation. This seemed to clear the mind. She was ready to depart in peace. Lo and behold! The abbot came quite unexpectedly and told her she was now ready for his help!

QUESTION C-57: How is it that advaita which trumpets the attributeless (*nirguNa*) nature of the Absolute also strongly advocates

the daily worship (called *panchAyatana pUjA*) of five deities in the form of rock-formations of stones?

The panchayatana puja tradition may be taken as an intermediate stage between the worship of Godhead with form and the worship of the formless because the symbols of worship as rock formations have certainly a form but they are also formless in that they have no parts like face, eyes, body, hands or feet. It is as though the devotee trains himself to take the mind from the forms to the formless while at the same time allowing full scope for his devotional feelings.

Let me tell you the interesting information about where these rock formations are available as small stones for being used in personal puja are available. Each one of the five divinities has a specific place in India where it is available as such. They are regarded as already divine in their nature. No special invocation is required.

Surya, the Sun God (Aditya) is taken as inherent in certain crystals normally found in Vallam in Tamilnadu. Shakti, the Mother Ambika, is represented by the swarnamukhi stone found in the bed of the river of that name in the Andhra region. Vishnu is worshipped in the Salagrama stone that can be had in plenty in the bed of the Ghantaki river in the Himalayas. Ganesha is the red Shonabhadra stone found in the bed of the river Sone flowing into the Ganga. Finally Shiva is the Bana-linga which is found in the Omkarakunda of the river Narmada., near the island of Mandhata.

QUESTION C-58: We need to understand this concept of nirguNa. Can something exist without attributes? If *brahman* has a force of any kind, then that force is an attribute. If it does not have a force of any kind, then how can it achieve anything? If *Brahman* is a force, then force is an attribute of *Brahman*. If *Brahman* is everywhere then this is an attribute. The attribute is "being present everywhere". If *Brahman* is always present, then this describes an attribute of *Brahman*. The attribute is "presence always". Everywhere refers to

Space. Always refers to Time. *Brahman* is present in all the Space and in all the Time. Our present-day science does not know of anything that does not get transformed. It can then be concluded that science does not know the truth. There are multiple perceptions of Truth. In computer science, when a technical term has multiple definitions, we call it overloading. The word "Truth" is overloaded. Please put me wise on these statements.

Really a very complicated matter.. As a person soaked in the world of science you are talking of a force, which the nirguna *brahman* is 'expected' to have! Nothing of this kind. *Brahman* itself is the force. Yes, it is difficult to imagine or think of... Well, that is *brahman* – no attributes, no qualifications, no action! Science cannot deal with it

There is only *Brahman*. There is no matter. Existence of matter is a *mithya* that appears to us and vanishes in due time. There is no question of two facets of *brahman*. Sometimes when we 'think' of *brahman* we see Saguna *brahman* with name and form in our mind. There is no such at the transcendentl level. There is only *Brahman*.

The statement '*Brahman* is everywhere' is itself a mix-up between the transcendental and transactional levels. You cannot use the word '*brahman*' in any *vyAvahAric* (transactional) way. The term 'everywhere' involves concept of space and the word 'always' involves the concept of time. *Brahman* 'is'. That is all. Nothing else 'is'. That is all. 'Presence everywhere' or 'presence always' when used with *brahman* mixes up the two levels of conversation, namely ' transactional' and 'transcendental'.

Any object which has the *shaDvikArAs* (six kinds of transformations, birth, growth, decay, death etc.) is not Truly Existing. It is only a transactional or phenomenal (in the case of mirror image) existence. This is the fundamental principle of Advaita VedAnta. And, all objects of the ephemeral world have the transformations. Science deals only with matter that is subject to transformation, whether it is electron or black hole. Science does not (and cannot) deal with something which never goes through transformations.

There are no multiple perceptions of 'Truth'. When you say that science deals with multiple perceptions of truth, all of that is in *vyAvahArika* (trnsactional) level. At the transcendental level (which is not the concern of science) Truth is only one. There is no 'overloading' of Truth in the transcendental level. At that level there is only the Absolute Supreme (=*brahman*) and that is the Absolute Truth. Every other usage of the word 'truth' which science or ordinary conversation uses is only *mithyA* (which has no eternal existence).

QUESTION C-59: How can you renounce anything when you never own anything in the first place, says Ashtavakra Gita. I understand it only vaguely. Can you explain?

Yes, the fifth chapter of AshtAvakra-Gita starts with the shloka:

> *na te sango.asti kenApi kiM shuddhas-tyaktum-icchhati/*
> *sanghAta-vilayaM kurvan evameva layaM vraja//*

I am sure you are referring to this shloka which means: "You are not bound by anything; What does a pure person like you need to renounce? Putting the complex organism to rest you better go to your rest"

I have seen a funny explanation for this shloka, but with pregnant vedantic meaning, given by Acharya Sadananda in his book SELF AND THE SUPREME (2020). Let me share it with you verbatim:

"It is like the story of Mr. Jones and the rat. For some reason Mr. Jones thought he was a rat. Since he understood that he was a rat, he was hiding in the closet whenever he saw a ferocious-looking cat. Somehow his wife came to know his problem and took him to a psychologist who showed him that he could not be a rat since he appears more like a human being while rat looks different. After many sittings Mr. Jones understood that he is a man and not a rat. With understanding he went home. To his horror he saw the terrible looking cat was sitting as usual on the porch, as though waiting for him. Mr. Jones ran back to the doctor and said, I understand that I am a man and not a rat, but I am not sure if the cat understands that I am a man and not a rat. Mr. Jones has to renounce that he was never a rat and claim himself to be a man. That knowledge does not depend on anybody else other than himself. In addition whatever he did while thinking he was a rat has no bearing on him since he was never a rat, at any time. Mr. Jones has to recognise that 'I am a man all along' and that understanding has to be abiding in a sense he will never be afraid of facing any cat at any time, anywhere."

In Vedanta also a more realistic story runs around. The King of a Kingdom died without any issue. The Minister and other courtiers had now the major responsibility to name the successor. And the Minister remembered that twelve years earlier a son was born to the King but the child was kidnapped and till now nothing has been heard of him. So now the Minister made some elaborate efforts to chase the tribesmen who kidnapped the child, finally found them and also found the twelve year old boy living with them as one of their tribe. The Minister recognized the boy by his resemblance to his father, called him separately and slowly divulged the truth to him. "You are actually the Prince of this kingdom; because you have grown with these tribes you think you are one of them. Change your mind and come with me and I will make you the King". The boy could not easily get over his thinking that he was one of the tribesman, but after the Minister pounded the truth on him repeatedly he agreed" Vedanta uses this to tell you that you are *brahman* and you are wrongly thinking that you are a separate human being in this body.

In the same way says Ashtavakra, you don't own anything in this material world, no possessions, not even this mind-body-intellect. You are wrongly wedded to this BMI and this universe. So what are you renouncing?

QUESTION C-60: The universal message of the Upanishads is that *Brahman* is nirguNa without attributes and the individual self shines because of the presence of *brahman* as a sAkshi (Witness) in us. In the presence of these statements which are the highest truths of Vedanta, it is difficult to understand the following:

angushTamAtraH purushah antarAtmA
(Katha.U. II – C – 17; also II-i-12)

padmakoshapratIkAsham   *hridayaMcApyadhomukham;*
adhonishTyAvitasyAnte nAbhyAmupari tishTati (M.N.U.) and **B.G.
13-23:** *upadrashTAnumantA ca bhartA bhoktA maheshvaraH.* **The
first one seems to say that** *brahman* **has a form; the second one
says it is an inverted lotus sitting in the cave of the heart and the
third one seems to testify that it has an action of** *'anumantA'.* **How
is this?**

A very sensible question. I shall try to carefully (and hopefully) navigate
you through the answers. First let me start with an example which may
light up our understanding. Suppose some seeker asks the question:
What should I do in order to understand the Ultimate Truth? And
suppose a Vedantin answers as follows: " There is no seeker and nothing
to be sought; there is no 'you' who can do anything". What do you
gather from this seeker's question and the Vedantin's answer? The
seeker is wihin the *vyAvahAric* (transactional) level of thinking and the
Vedantin's answer is in the *pAramArtik* (transcendental) level. Thus they
don't match. This is exactly what happens in many cases of expression
and clearance of doubts.

Now come to our question. All the three quotations mentioned are
in the *pAramArthik* level. There is no lotus in the heart; but there is a
lotus-like blank space, the space that may fit an inverted thumb and
the Upanishad says *brahman* is to be imagined as occupying this space
like a flaming torch of fire. You cannot search for all this by medical
surgery on an operation table. The metaphor is extended to the analogy
of *'angushtamAtrah'.* All this is in the language of the *pAramArthika*
(transcendental) level. They should not be brought to the transactional
level of understanding. This mix-up between the transcendent and the
transactional is the origin of all the three parts of the question.

Let us come to some specifics. B.G. Ch.13 – shloka 13 says: His hands
and feet are everywhere. His eyes, ears and mouth grasp everything. His

face is in all directions. He is the transcendent spirit enveloping all that exists in the world.

All this is said at the transcendental level; if you want to check it out at the *vyAvahArik* level, you will not get anything. His is the energy which gives the power to all our hands and all our feet for all of us. This is the kind of meaning we have to give when he says 'I am the *upadrashtA* and *anumantaA*. He is sitting in the cave of the heart means His is the shakti which gives the heart and all the body the power or energy that it needs.

To understand the difference between the two levels – transcendental and transactional – here is the standard doubt of novices to Vedanta: If the Absolute Supreme is without form and name, how come you are all worshipping deities with name and form?

QUESTION C-61: You have been writing about Advaita all along. But you have not told us anything about the life of Shankara, who was the greatest propagator of Advaita. Can we have a short account of the life of Shankaracharya?

One of the earliest mystic Masters of India is Shankara more properly known as *Adi ShankarAcArya*, the prefix *Adi* meaning the prime, the original, the first. Shankara's interpretations of Vedanta have so dominated the intellectual life and thought of the country and has become so well-known in the rest of the world that his work has almost become synonymous with Vedanta inspite of the fact that other interpretations exist and are followed widely. One measure of Shankara's influence is that it is very difficult for any one either Hindu or non-Hindu to read Indian religious texts without unconsciously seeing them through the general interpretation given by Shankara. The great temples and holy places of India where he lived, preached and prayed, have made his name legendary and have left an indelible image in the Hindu mind. His greatness is not only in the context of Hinduism and Indian philosophy. His exposition of *advaita* has a relevance to the cultural history of the entire world philosophy. This is because *advaita* does not need for its validity the symbolism or the prop of the religion and mythology of Hinduism. The one fact that comes to the mind of a non-Indian the moment the country of India is mentioned is its contribution to the spiritual evolution of the human species over the centuries, particularly through its Vedic and Upanishadic thought processes But if any single individual Master is to be associated with this contribution one of the earliest such is Shankara. It goes back to as early as the second century BCE. Even this date of Shankara is controversial. In fact anything that is connected with Shankara is mystifying, if not controversial.

Shankara was not only a great philosopher who professed a sophisticated philosophy with precision and clarity but he was a great reformer also. In his short span of 32 years he achieved what no one ever before or after him achieved. At the age of three he had mastered the language of Sanskrit. At the age of six he had already learnt whatever formal learning there was to learn. At the age of eight he was ready to renounce the mundane world along with its glamour and he did. Before the age of twelve he had found his formal *Guru* at whose feet he reached the shores of all existing knowledge at that time. By the age of sixteen he had already written his famous commentaries (*bhashyas*) on the Upanishads, B.G., the *Brahma-sUtras,* V.S. and *SanatsujAtIyaM.* These commentaries have stood the test of time for more than a millenium and will so stand for several more millenia to come. Before the end of his life he had toured by foot the entire subcontinent three times and more, established several religious organizations called *mutts,* of whom five are the most famous and are still carrying the torch, carried on verbal debates with almost 76 other schools of religious thought and brought them all under his banner of *advaita,* left behind him scores of devotional poems, at least one for each deity or temple then known in India, wrote five unique expository works: *viveka cUDAmaNi, aparoksha anubhUti, Atma-bodha, upadeSa sAhasri* and *prashnottara-ratna-mAlikA,* each one of which constitutes, in its own way, a concise, encyclopaedia of *advaita* vedanta and, finally, reorganized and streamlined the daily worship of the individual Hindu in such a way that it has survived him for centuries till now. His immediate disciples whom he later nominated to lead the mutts he established were: *sureshvarAchArya, HastAmalakAchArya, Padma-pAdAchArya* and *ToTakAchArya.* Incidentally, there is a raging controversy (yet unresolved) regarding the number of mutts established by Bhagavadpada. Some say it is only four, representing the four mahavakyas of the Upanishads. Others say Kanchi mutt was not only established by Bhagavadpada but he was there, pointing out to the statue in the Kamakshi Amman temple.

Shankara was also an acclaimed poet. His compositions both in prose and poetry excel even some of the greatest literary poets India has known. He was not only one of the deepest thinkers of the world but he also had the unique distinction of being very lucid in his expositions (both written and oral) of his thoughts. He was a profound and well-read scholar but was in addition a blessed saint who had the grace of God in all its fullness. He exhibited, even in his childhood, marvellous powers of spirituality and scholarship. He was already known for his genial disposition and kind heart. On one of these days when he was studying in his *Gurukula*, (the abode of the teacher where the disciples become resident students), he went to a poor brahmin's house, as was usual with all celibate students, to receive his *bhikshA*, the daily food offered as a service. The poverty stricken housewife was unable to give him anything substantial. She brought and gave him an *Amalaka* (a fruit of the *embylic myrobalan*) as a humble token of her contribution to the *bhikshA*. Shankara's heart was moved at the sight of her poverty on one side and her readiness, on the other side, to give away even the very little she had. He prayed to Lakshmi, the Goddess of Wealth by composing his famous *kanaka-dhArA stotra*. Lo and behold, her house was immediately filled with a heavenly downpour of gold in the form of golden *Amalaka* fruits. Thus was born one of the most popular hymns of ancient India, which, even today is repeated very often by young and old for the obvious purpose of pleasing Goddess Lakshmi for Her grace to descend and bestow wealth and prosperity. This poem containing 27 verses not only offers this prayer but it also describes the three deities *Sarasvati, Lakshmi* and *DurgA* as manifestations of the one Mother Goddess.

Shankara was further a great mystic and Yogi who had a direct perception of the Infinite Consciousness and at the same time he was also a practical, socio-cum-religious reformer. His knowledge and felicity in law, logic, rules of grammar and etymology were as supreme as his devotion. Thus Shankara synthesized in his one personality the superlatives of a philosopher, writer, thinker, poet, scholar, blessed devotee, mystic, reformer, humanist, lawyer and logician, and the beloved of the Lord. This unique combination of so many excellent achievements of his in his short life has not perhaps been paralleled by any one in the history of the world either before or after his time.

QUESTION C-62: Regarding the topic, whether Karma or jnAna is important, as per some lectures we hear, karma is important for *chitta suddhi* (purifiction of mind) but cannot give you *moksha* or show *Brahman*…it is only jnAna that can help. What is your view?

My view is not my view. It is what I understand from the Gita. So it is Krishna's view that I am writing about. The first time he seriously compares the different types of seekers is in shlokas 46 and 47 of chapter 6. No.46 says yogi (of the 6th chapter) is the greatest. Then in the very next shloka he emphasizes the bhakti aspect and so He says: 'Among all the yogis, the one who has got faith and trust (*shraddhAvAn*) and worships Me (*yah mAM bhajate*) with his inner Self immersed in Me (*madgatena antarAtmanA*) is the one who is the best of all those integrated in Me (*yuktatamo mataH*).. So Bhakti is at the top.

Now come to the 12th chapter. Levels of Bhakti are detailed methodically. Shlokas nos.3,4,5 are at the topmost level of bhakti. Shlokas 6,7 and 8 are the next lower level of bhakti. Then shloka 9 and then shloka 10. Shloka 11 is at the rockbottom.

But Krishna, the mischief-lover as He is, reverses this order in shloka 12 and says *karma-phala-tyAga* (i.e. *karma yoga*) is the best. Commentators have agreed that this is a compromise shloka, given just to encourage the lowest level of bhaktas, so that they may do at least this much and come up.

Also the two shlokas at the end of the 14th chapter has a symbiosis of the four yogas of the Gita. Bhakti yoga by #26, karma yoga by the words '*shAshvatasya dharmasya*' in #27, Raja yoga by the words '*sukhasyaikAntikasya ca*' of # 27 and jnAna yoga by the first half of #27. None of the four paths is to be discarded.

Now come to the 18th chapter. As His own summary of the whole Gita He extols jnana path in shlokas 49 to 53; shloka 54 says the *brahma-jnAni* gets the suprememost Bhakti and in 55 He says it is bhakti that leads to the knowledge of *brahman*. And again in shloka 56 He raises *karma yoga* to the same level.

So what is the conclusion? It is this. at the highest level of spiritual understanding, all three – Karma, Bhakti, JnAna – coalesce. There is no distinction. I hope you understand. It is Krishna speaking, not me

QUESTION C-63: In the Gita Krishna takes the stand that He is the sovereign Lord of the Universe, namely Ishvara. In what way is this Ishvara different from *Brahman* the Absolute Reality? According to advaita, are we ultimately *Brahman* or Ishvara?

This actually is not one question; it encompasses several lessons on advaita. However, briefly we can summarize the interrelationships of *brahman, Ishvara* and *JIva* as follows:

> *Brahman* is *nirguNa*, attributeless; is not the predicate of anything, cannot be pointed at, is neither this nor that – and thus it goes on.

So there is no way of 'worshipping' it. No, we cannot even talk about that except by giving it a name, though not a form. Therefore Upanishads give it a name '*tat*', just for purposes of referring to it and to say that '*tat*' has no attributes.

But our intellect wants to do something with the Almighty Supreme. A worship, a prayer, a meditation, an offering or whatever. All these involve a duality of the worshipper and the worshipped. The moment we think of *Brahman* as an object of worship or prayer or meditation, immediately, the concept of *brahman* is automatically jeopardized. Thus the intellect has created *brahman* with attributes – a saguna *brahman*.

The very fact that our intellect has come in the picture implies that *mAyA* has done its job. It is *mAyA*'s effect that there is an intellect and we begin to think of objects through our intellect. Thus *Brahman*, with the *upAdhi* (impact, coating, influence, superposition, covering, conditioning,… – choose your word) of *mAyA*, is called *saguNa brahman*. You can go on debating now whether we (through our intellect) created the *saguna brahman* or whether it is somewhere there, if not an object, as a subject. That question is neither relevant, nor will it take us anywhere.

That *saguNa brahman* is the *Ishvara*. Now *Ishvara* has all the superlative qualities that any religion associates with Almighty God. But *mAyA* did not create *Ishvara*. It is *Ishvara* who has *MAyA* in His control. It is like a snake having poison but is never affected by its own poison. *Ishvara* is not affected by His *mAyA*.

On the other hand, the spark of *brahman* which is the core essence of beings, ('*JIva-bhUtAM*') is the creation of *mAyA*. So all *JIvas* are under the influence of *mAyA*. To get out of this *mAyA* we need the Grace of that *Ishvara*, who, by His magic wand, can take us out of the grip of *mAyA*.

Thus *Brahman* and *Ishvara* are the same, except for the way we look at them. If we don't look for *brahman*, but knowing we are *brahman*, if we 'are' *brahman*, then there is nothing more to say or do. '*aham brahma asmi*'. Period.

On the other hand, if we want to look 'at' *brahman* in some way or other, already we have made *brahman* an object and thus it is already only the *saguna-brahman* that we are talking about. So we can 'look at' it, meditate on it, aspire to 'reach' it and all that sort of thing.

JIva on the other hand, so long as it is in the grip of *mAyA*, is separate from *brahman* and also separate from other *JIva*s. Once it transcends *mAyA*, it is *brahman*. This is the *JIva-brahma aikyam* that advaita keeps trumpeting to us. When *JIva* identifies itself with *brahman* there is no need to bring in an *Ishvara* now; because the very identification of *JIva* with *brahman* already includes the identification of *brahman* and *Ishvara* – because the identification itself is something that transcends *mAyA*. So the *upAdhi* of *mAyA* is gone from both *JIva* and *Ishvara*.

A FOLLOW-UP QUESTION & ANSWER: 'When *JIva* identifies itself with *Brahman*, there is no need for Ishwara'. The BIG question is 'How do we get to that state?' Is it only through religion or is there a path outside of religion (all religions) to do this by supreme consciousness?

Answer: That is exactly what Self-Realisation means. You have to follow everything said in the Gita, namely, Karma (Actionlessness), Bhakti (Devotion and Meditation) and JnAna (Acquiring of Knowledge and trying to live it). The attitude of actionlessness eradicates the ego. The meditation disciplines your mind. Devotion purifies your mind. And then persuade your mind to disassociate yourself from your BMI. (SIMPLE. IS'NT IT?!!!)

QUESTION C-64: Vedanta says it is the science of the Inner Self. Though its axioms are different, its methodology is the same – experiment, observation, conjecture, further experiment, etc. All this however goes on in the realms of the inner world. As this experimentation goes on, the inner self unfolds itself, as it were. But the question arises: How can I believe it when I have no such experience?

The answer to such doubts is this. You are like my village astrologer, who does not believe that Saturn has rings. I tell him: 'Come to my

University, we have a telescope there. Come on an evening when Saturn is visible in the night sky. Then I will show you Saturn's rings'. But he says: 'No, they can't be the real thing; they are your hallucinations. Probably they are created by your own equipment. Unless you can show me Saturn's rings for my own plain eyes to see I will not believe in them'! Your disbelief of the mystic's word is exactly like this. What right do you have, to tell mystics like Aurobindo that what he says is a figment of his imagination? Do I doubt you a physicist when you say that you have 'observed' the bizarre wave-particle duality of light by the famous two-hole experiment though I have not myself done the experiment? If you are a good scientist, the most that you can do is to quit by saying: 'Well, I don't understand your Aurobindo's experiment'.

What is a miracle? Miracle is an event which goes against one or more of the known scientific laws. Until the scientist sees the miracle with his own eyes and has tested it under several circumstances he would not believe that it happened. Fair enough. But let him not be unscientific enough to say that miracles can never happen. In order that such a statement might be true we have to accept a universal law to the effect that 'Everything in the world has to happen only according to scientific laws'. But there is no such law! It can only be a dogma of the uninformed scientist. Miracles, for all we know, may be the visiting cards of God's presence. You may ask: 'Whose assertion is it?' Well, certainly not that of Science. Firstly the wisdom that one learns from life's experiences is sometimes beyond Science. Secondly 'miracles' rarely repeat themselves or at least do not seem to be repeatable on call. Just because there are frauds in the religious world (the proportion does not seem to be larger than in the secular world) let not the scientist be arrogant enough to assume that he should be able to explain everything. A scientific 'Theory of Everything' is still in the future. Even if it is properly formulated and accepted as law, scientific research will still continue to improve it and polish it for being applied for the benefit of mankind (or for the destruction of 'the enemy'!). This itself means there would be something still unexplained. Yes, it is an infinite regress. When the scientist sees a miracle 'happen' right before his eyes, the most scientific statement that he can truly make is: 'It is difficult to believe it; I do not understand it'. That would be the right scientific temper.

For sceptics to believe that there is truth in spiritual experimentation and revelations, I am giving you, the following long list of 126 names (and many many more whom I have not quoted) over the past 3000 years; Google their names and find out for yourself!

The twelve Alvars and sixty three Nayanmars, Tiruvalluvar, Tirumoolar, Nathamuni, Shankara, Ramanuja, Madhva, Jayadeva, JnAneshvar, Vedanta Desika, Pillai Lokacharya, Namadev, Swami Ramananda, Vidyaranya, Chandidasa, Kabirdas, Ravidas, Guru Nanak, Vallabhacharya, Surdas, Krishna Chaitanya, Narsi Mehta, Purandaradas, Tulsidas, Appayya Dikshidar, Narayana Bhattadri, Tukaram, Swami Bodendra Saraswati, Samarth Ramadas, Sri Raghavendra, Sadashiva *Brahman*, Bhakta Ramdas, Bhaskararaya, Tayumanavar, Ramaprasad, Tyagaraja, Shyama Shastri, Swami Narayan, Swami Dayanand Saraswati, Jothi Ramalinga Swamigal, Ramakrishna Paramahamsa, Swami Vivekananda, Aurobindo, The Mother, Dr. Annie Besant, Swami Shivananda, Mahatma Gandhi, Ramana Maharshi, Kanchi Mahaswamigal, Ma Anandamayi, J. Krishnamurti, Paramahamsa Yogananda, A.C. Bhakti Vedanta Swami, Swami Chin*mAyA*nanda, The Sai Baba Phenomenon.

QUESTION C-65: Vedanta revels in reiterating the quote: 'Neti, Neti' (from Br.U.) to impress upon us that *Brahman* is neither this nor that to say that *Brahman* is attributeless and therefore no name, no form, no attribute, in other words 'nirguna'. I certainly get it. But what puzzles me is: Why everybody (including the Shastras) use or say the 'neti' twice; Is not one 'neti' enough? Is it just for emphasis?

You yourself tripped in your question. Why did you use the words: 'neither this nor that'? You could simply have said 'not anything'.

Well, this is just to make a funny rebuttal to your question. Br.U. as well as other Upanishads and Shastras and expositors, do mean 'neti neti' as a double denial necessary for both 'the gross' and 'the subtle'. *Brahman* is neither anything gross, nor anything subtle. In our own experience, we have two kinds of things to deny supremeness or eternality or infiniteness to them. One is our external associations like our possessions, friendships and relationships; and the other is our own BMI with all its contents as well as its koshas. The former is the denial of the gross and the latter is the denial of the subtle. In fact you can note Acharya Shankara's meticulousness in most of (maybe all) his vedanta stotras, in his use of neither 'this' nor 'that' always one denial for the gross and another for the subtle. For instance, in his *nirvAnashaTkaM*, the very first shloka is

Mano buddhyahaMkAra-cittAni nAhaM na karNaM
na jihvA na ca ghrANa netre/
Na ca vyoma-bhUmir na tejo na vAyuH cidAnandarUpaH
shivo.ahaM shivo.aham//

I am not the mind, nor the intellect, nor the ego, nor the reflections of the inner self in the mind, I am not the ears (which hear), nor the tongue (which tastes), nor the nose which smells, nor the eyes which see. I am not the space, nor the earth, nor the fire, nor the wind I am indeed, That eternal knowing and bliss, Shiva, love and pure consciousness.

The first line is the denial of ceverything connected with our BMI. And the second line is the denial of the universe around us. As human beings overloaded with our beginningless Ignorance, we are swallowed by two kinds of superimposition (thinking wrongly of something), namely 'inbuilt superimposition' (*tAdAtmya-adhyAsa*) and 'associated superimposition' (*samsarga adhyAsa*). Both are caused by our ego. The first one is our attachment to the false Self in us, namely the BMI. The second one is the attachment to anything which has or had a connection or association with us in the outside world (which includes all relationships and whatever we call mine). Both the *adhyasas* have to be negatived if we are to recognise ourselves as *brahman*. This is what is reflected by the two 'neti's'.

Again, within the first line of the shloka, the first quarter is the denial of the subtle within ourselves and the second quarter is the denial of the gross in our personality.

And in the second line, which is the denial of the universe, *vyoma and vAyu* represent the subtle while *bhUmi and tejas* stand for the gross.

Again, in the shloka (first of his advaita-pancharatnam):

> *nAhaM deho nendriyANyantarango nAhaMkAraH*
> *prANavargo na buddhiH/*
> *dArApatyaH kshetra-vittAdi dUrah sAkshI nityaH*
> *pratyagAtmA shivo.aham//*

the first half (except the word '*dehah*') is the denial of the subtle (within ourselves); *nAham dehaH* is the denial of the gross thing visible and perceivable by us, namely, the body; and the first quarter of the second half is the denial of our (gross) external associations. Thus he carefully separates the two denials and reverberates with 'neti, neti'.

QUESTION C-66: Once a bevy of housewives who were listening to my lectures on the B.G., unanimously raised the following question: Sir, what you are saying on detachment as a sine qua non for karma yoga may be alright from the point of view of the text of the GItA. But look at us. We are all housewives. Each one of us has a husband, family, children and parents to be taken care of. We love them all. We all have tremendous affection and attachment for our children and their welfare. How are we supposed to be detached? If we are not attached to our family what will happen to them? Is it not our duty to serve and take care of our family? It is almost impossible for us to detach ourselves from our family and carry on our lives. All of you GItA-expositors say the same thing about detachment. But we cannot go and ask great Swamijis this question of ours. Please tell

us whether you really mean that we should practise non-attachment even in the midst of our family duties, or wait for us to reach age 50 or 60 and then start your ideas of detachment. Is there something called 'detached attachment'?

The answer to this legitmate question has been given by Kanchi Mahaswamigal in one of the Tamil books of 'Deivathin Kural' and also in his lectures. Yes, says the Mahaswamigal. 'What you ladies say is legitimate. But who asked you not to pour your affection on those to whom you are attached? Pour all your affection, as much as you can, and more if you so wish, on all your children, kith and kin and whomsoever you are attached to. Simply flood them with your affection. No problem. But remember this. **Do not ever expect anything as a result or reward in return**. Do not pour your affection on your children expecting them to do something for you in return. Do not keep any such expectation as a motive for your pouring affection on them. So long as you totally avoid all expectations of 'fruits' or 'rewards' either immediately or in the future, you are within the norms of the GItA. In fact by doing like this, your minds will in due course of time develop the maturity for a healthy detachment!' This healthy detachment towards your kith and kin may therefore be called 'detached attachment'!

Incidentally, Swami ChinmAyAnanda has a remarkable way of telling us what is the peculiar flavour of the word 'attachment' (rAga or sanga) in the Gita. He gives the following arithmetic: Ego + Ego-centric desires = Attachment. Now you can see the meaning and value of 'detached attachment' which the Mahaswamigal recommends. Duty with affection to children and kith and kin, without the Ego or ego-centric desires playing their part, is what 'detached attachment' means! In fact this summarises for us what is 'Vedantic Living'.

QUESTION C-67: Why is GayatrI the 'Queen of all Mantras'?

'The Queen of all mantras' is only a modern way of saying it in English. The Vedas themselves call the Gayatri as 'The Mother of all Vedas' *(chhandasAM mAtA)*. The simple meaning of the word 'GayatrI' is: that which protects the one who chants it.

The Sun is the most practical example of God's immanence in everything. The Sun-God is the Ultimate Godhead itself. There are three formal scriptures for the worship of the Sun. The Gayatri Mantra, Aditya hridayam in V.R. and the Aruna Prashna of K.Y.V. Of these the Gayatri Mantra is universally acclaimed as the most fundamental. Gayatri-upAsanA is actually the upAsanA of *brahman*, that is taken as imbedded in the region of Savitri, the Sun.

The very word Gayatri means that it protects those who chant it. Protecting here is for the sake of the Ultimate. Recall the use of the word '*naH*' (ours, to us) in the mantra. So the protection and grace of God is not only for the one who chants it, but it is for all those included in 'us'. It may therefore mean the whole universe if you have the right attitude of universal oneness when you chant. In spite of the fact that the responsibility of japa and dhyana of the Gayatri has been allotted to only a tiny fraction of the total population, the power of the Mantra is so much that it has been protecting the entire civilisation for mankind. But many of those who had this privilege have defaulted, in recent times, to discharge their responsibilities and so they have gone in evolution, far below those that did not have the privilege but only did the chanting of the names of God.

The essence of Hinduism, namely, that Divinity is everywhere, it is that Divinity which provokes us into thought and action and it is only with the help of that ever-present Divinity that we may ever hope to have a discerning intellect with which we may feel the effervescence of the Godhead that is inherent in all the universe, including ourselves – all this is built into that Mantra of three quarters, the Gayatri. Creator Brahma declares: There is nothing greater than the Gayatri, whether it is for japa or for tapas or for dhyana or for sacrificial offering into the Fire. By massive repetition of the Gayatri one obtains the power to turn his mind inward toward the Light within. It harmonises the constituents of the inner body, quietens the mind and and stimulates the latent spiritual qualities.

The three-fold presentation of Reality, as *sat, cit* and *Ananda* is also reflected in the *GAyatrI*. The three lines of the *GAyatrI* mean, literally:

That – of the Originator – Most excellent;
Light – of God – Let us meditate;
Intellects – He who – Our – May prompt.

tat-savitur-vareNyaM; bhargo-devasya dhImahi;
dhiyo-yo naH pracodayAt

The word *savituH* in **the first line**, which indicates 'Origin' or 'Birth', suggests Creation and makes it characteristic of the '*sat*' or the '*satya*' facet of the Absolute Reality. This line is a *glorification of the Absolute*. A glorification of a deity simply praises the Lord as Lord, does not ask for anything and does not do anything in the wake of that praise. It is like a subordinate visiting his superior (or a party worker visiting his leader) purely for courtesy and simply offering words of praise without expecting anything to be done by the superior. The first line of the *GAyatrI* does simply this. **The second line** asks us to meditate as if it is the be-all and end-all of life. Yes, because the meditation itself gives the bliss, immanent in the Absolute Reality. Meditation on the Absolute is communion with or worship of, the Divine. It is therefore the *worship aspect* of the *mantra*. It corresponds to the *Ananda* (or the *ananta*, infinite) aspect of the Absolute; because the very meditation of the Absolute is Bliss. Bliss is not something that you attain after you have achieved something as a reward from the Lord. To think of Him is Bliss! It is a communion with Bliss! The use of the words *dhiyah* and *pracodayAt* in **the third line** show that this line is indicative of the *cit* facet of Reality and is also the *Prayer aspect* of the *mantra* imbedded in the *GAyatrI*. It is the *cit* (Knowledge, *jnAnaM*) facet of the *sat-cid-Ananda* form or the *satyam-jnAnaM-anantam* definition of *Brahman*. It is significant that in this line it is the intellect that asks for the prompting of the Absolute and that is why this line is the *cit* facet. A deeper enquiry into the meaning of the *mantra* will take us into the analysis of the state of sleep and our memory of it. In fact the *sat-cid-Ananda* form is our true nature, though we don't know it. But every day when we go to sleep and come back with the memory of a happy sleep, it is because we have gone and touched that true nature of us without our own volition. Thus the three lines together, of the *GAyatrI* incorporate, in a sense, the three-fold universal practice of all Religion, namely, **Glorification of the super-natural, Worship of the Supra-mental and Prayer to The All-mighty**. The three lines represent the three different types of propitiation of the Absolute. All the different connotations of the *GAyatrI* may now be summarised in a Table as below:

'tat savituH…'	Glorification (or Creation)	I	*ahaM*	Experience	*sat*
'bhargo…'	Communion (or Merging)	happily	*sukhaM*	Happiness	*Ananda*
'dhiyo…'	Prayer (or Realisation)	slept	*asvApsaM*	Awareness	*cit*

In Srimad Bhagavatam there is what is called Dhruva-stuti (a hymn of 12 shlokas, by boy Dhruva on his memorable darshan of the Lord).

tvaM nitya-mukta-pariSuddha-vibuddha AtmA
kUtastha Adi-purusho bhagavAn-stryadhISaH/
yad-buddhy-avasthitim-akhaNDitayA svadRshTyA
drashTA sthitA-vadhimakho vyatirikta Asse//

satyam jnAnaM anantaM is the definition of the Transcendental Absolute. *satyam* (Truth) is the same as *sat* (Absolute Existence). *jnAnaM* (Knowledge) and *cit* (Consciousness) are the same. *anantaM* (Infinite) and *Ananda* (Bliss) are the same. These three facets are presented in *EACH* of the lines (lines 1, 2 and 4) of this 10th verse of *Dhruva-stuti*. Since the *GAyatrI* itself is a presentation of these three facets of the Absolute in its three lines, this 10th verse is taken to represent the *GAyatrI*. **For the same reason, it is said that those who**

do not have had the privilege of being inducted into the *GayatrI* (like women, for instance) can take this verse and recite it and use it for meditation purposes; and they will have the same benefit as they would if they had done the *GAyatrI*. This is the *mantra* power of this verse. This interpretation beautifully dovetails with the description by commentators of *Dhruva-stuti* as representing the 12 *Adityas*, namely the twelve manifestations of the Sun-God. These twelve are, in order, *mitra, ravi, sUrya, bhAnu, khaga, pUsha, hiraNya-garbha, marIci, Aditya, SavitA, arka,* and *bhAskara*. The relevant one here is *SavitA*. It is the tenth facet. Each verse of *Dhruva-stuti* represents one of these. The manifestation *savitA* is represented by the tenth verse, namely the present one. *SavitA* is the manifestation that is deified in the *GAyatrI* (right in the first line itself) as representative of the Absolute. Thus this tenth verse is representative of *SavitA*, therefore of GAyatrI. Each epithet introduced here by Dhruva deserves elaborate comments. We shall attempt to give only a few.

kUTastha: The Immutable or The Immovable; that which remains like the unchanging iron-piece (anvil) on which the blacksmith does all his hammering. In Vedanta literature *kUTastha* is used to denote the *akshara purusha,* the imperishable Self, (B.G. 15-16) who is the changeless non-participating witness of the doings of the outer self. The outer Self, which is called the *kshara purusha,* 'the perishable Self', is involved in the actions of Nature, reflects the varied workings of the *Gunas* of the individual's *prakRti*. This outer Self identifies himself with the play of personality and assumes the doer-ship of all actions. He is under the constant spell of *mAyA;* whereas the *akshara purusha,* the *kuTastha,* is the inactive non-doer and is only the witnessing Self. It is the Lord that appears as both the *purushas.*

drashTA: The seer. Actually this word has to go along with the entire third quarter, meaning: He who watches, uninterruptedly, by His own Cosmic Vision, the state of intelligence. But He never undergoes any *vikAra* (transformation) because of what He sees. cf. *Br.U.* (4-3-23):

'Indeed there cannot be any impact of the seen or the seeing on the Seer, because the latter is immutable'.

He is actually the *kUTastha* or the *akshara purusha* witnessing everything. It is because of this existence of a continuous witness, that the outer Self when it goes to sleep along with its BMI, has however a memory of the sleeping act ('I slept soundly and happily') when it wakes up after sleep. This is a daily phenomenon that happens without our noticing it carefully. In *K.Y.V., taittirIya-AraNyaka*, 10-1-67 there is a *mantra*: '*aham-eva-aham-mAM-juhomi svAhA*', meaning, 'I make myself (the finite self) an oblation into the fire of the infinite *Brahman* which I am always'. This *mantra*, truly enunciates the refunding of the individual self into its source, the Supreme Self, or the realisation of the identity between the *JIva* and the *Ishvara* when the adjuncts created by ignorance are removed (by the oblation of the lower self into the Fire of the Higher Self). The outer Self goes and 'merges' as it were with the Inner Self during sleep and that is what makes it conscious of the sleep *after the event*. It is this daily event that is the proof of the theory that the *kshara purusha* and the *akshara purusha* are *essentially* the same.

tryadhISaH: The simple meaning is 'Lord of the Three'. Here the 'three' could be any one of several possibilities. In fact every such possibility is so apt for the Lord that all of them apply and that is what makes the epithet one of the richest epithets for the description of the Lord. He is Lord of the three worlds. He is Lord of the three *Gunas*, meaning, He transcends them. So He is *guNAtIta*. He is Lord of the Trinity – meaning, He is the absolute of whom each of the Trinity is only a manifestation. He is the Lord of the past, the present and the future – *bhUta-bhavya-bhavat-prabhuH*. He is Lord of the three states of Consciousness – waking, dreaming and sleeping; in other words, He is the fourth level of Consciousness, that transcends the three and is the substratum for all three. In the same manner He is represented by the silence that follows the three syllables '*a*' '*u*' and '*m*' in the chanting of '*aum*'. He is the One who is sung by the three vedas. He is the One who is attained by the three yogic paths – *karma, bhakti* and *jnAna*. He is the One who is 'born' in all the three *yugas*. He is the One who has three eyes. He is the One who made three strides to span the three worlds

vyatirikta Asse: The Inner Self which is the *akshara purusha* also known as *kUTastha* is totally unaffected by any of the concepts that are generally known to create differences between individual and individual, namely, *jAti* (species, like bird or reptile animal or human, man or woman), *kriyA* (nature of work or profession), *guNa* (quality, like white or black, lean or stout, short or tall, etc.) and *sambandha* (relationship, like rich or poor, possessor of property or not). So He stands aloof from everything that individualises the outer self! He is the substratum or the base. Everything else is a superposition. The *adhishTAna* (base) has always the extra status (*adhika-sthAna*), both in terms of time and in terms of existence. For a pot made of clay, clay is the base; the pot lives for lesser time than the clay of which it is made. The Seen is superimposed on the Seer, *drashTA*. No doubt the latter stands aloof.

We shall end this long account with the traditionally ripe shloka:

> *gangA-gItA ca gAyatrI govindeti catushhTayaM/*
> *catur-gakAra-samyukte punarjanma na vidyate//*

meaning, There are four things which begin with the alphabet 'ga'. The combination of these will ensure the end of transmigration – namely, the GangA, the GayatrI, the Gita and the name Govinda.

This is the age-old advice of our Guru – which word also begins with a 'ga'!

A BASIC SURVEY OF THE MESSAGE OF ONENESS

The scriptures are innumerable; the things to be known are many; the time at our disposal is short; the obstacles are too many. It is therefore important to grasp the essence and essence only'

ananta-shAstraM bahu veditavyaM alpashca kAlo bahavashca vighnAH/
yat-sAra-bhUtam tad-upAsitavyaM hamso yathA kshIram-ivAmbhu-
rAshau//

It is in this sense that we should approach the message of one-ness taught by the Advaita school led by Shankara. The philosophy that Shankara propagated was not his own. It was already in the Upanishads. What he did was to focus his searchlight on it and prove to us that it was the central and only teaching of the Upanishads as well as their collective last word. But the ordinary layman who remembers Shankara now does not know enough about him or his philosophy to understand him well. The only thing he can say is that Shankara taught about *mAyA* or illusion. 'Illusion' is a wrong translation of *mAyA*. By translating *mAyA* as illusion we have done the greatest disservice to Shankara. It is not being said that the world does not exist. It is only being said that the world is an appearance, not totally real. Shankara distinguishes three orders of reality.

▲ The Absolute Reality, that is *Brahman* and *Brahman* alone.

▲ The complete unreality, like the horns of a hare, or like squaring the circle if one wants to use the modern scientific language.

▲ In between these two extremes there is a phenomenal (or subjective) reality which is the apparent reality of the dream world, and an empirical (or operational) reality which is the 'reality' of the world of experience by the senses. Both these realities are classified as MithyA in advaita vedanta, because the reality is not absolute. MithyA is a technical word in advaita, not to be understood as 'illusion'. It is that which is neither unreal (because it appears) nor real (since later it disappears). Therefore it is anirvacanIyA, 'indescribable'.

A dream is neither real nor unreal. It is real to the person who dreams. It is unreal to the same person after he wakes up from the dream. This is the most important point. A dream is not a dream or illusion to the dreamer. So long as we dream, so long as we are seeing only the plurality of this mundane world, it is as real to us as the dream is to the dreamer. The world is unreal only to the seer who has waken up to the reality of the Absolute – like a Ramana MahaRshi or a SadaShiva Brahmendra. For them the only real thing is the Absolute *Brahman*. What they see before them is also *Brahman*. They see *Brahman* everywhere. So the world has not vanished absolutely. The world has vanished from their point of view. So if they keep on telling you that the world is an illusion or mithyA, it is like someone appearing in your dream and telling you, you better wake up from the dream and wake up to the reality. We are so much engrossed in our dream (namely, world-experience) that we are not prepared to listen to the advice of the guru or the Upanishads or to Shankara. Thus between the Ultimate Reality of the formless and nameless Absolute and the total unreality of non-existence, there is the intermediary apparent reality of this phenomenal world – which appears to be real but is not absolutely real. This appearance of the world as a reality has been given several analogies by philosophers. The most telling example of this is that of a rope appearing in twilight as a snake. The snake was never there. Even when the snake was being seen there was only the rope. The rope appeared as the snake. So also *Brahman* appears to us as the world. Even when the world is being seen it is *Brahman* that is being seen as the world (just as the rope is being seen as a snake). This the seers do know and so what they see is not the world but *Brahman*. One may object to this analogy as follows. I realise that there was no snake. So the snake no more appears to me. In the same manner I realise that there is only *Brahman* and there is no reality of the world. But still the world is appearing to me. For this Ramana MahaRshi asks you to go to the example of the mirage. The water in the mirage is only an illusion. I see the water in the mirage. I go near it and realise that there is no water. But once I come back I see there is again the appearance of the water. This analogy is to tell you that how even after realisation, the illusion may still appear as real.

Let us accept that any analogy has its own limitation. The analogies have to be taken only to that extent where we do not overdo it. Once the point of the analogy is made, there is no use in continuing the analogy. Thus here the objection is raised as follows. The water of the mirage does not quench my thirst, but in this supposedly unreal world, I have my thirst, hunger etc. and all these are quenched by the happenings in this world. For this Ramana asks you to look at the analogy of the dream. Within the dream you may have thirst, and it may be quenched by the water in the dream; so also hunger. Dream analogy is a great blessing. What else is a dream for? In God's creation, the value of a dream seems to be only this: To tell you how unreal is the world. Without the dream analogy it is impossible even to mentally conceive of the possible unreality of the phenomenal world from a different point of view, namely the absolute point of view. A dreamer wakes up usually only when something unpleasant happens within his dream. No dreamer ends up his dream while still in the happy state, except when an external force acts. This is because man's natural state is happiness. Realisation of one's natural state of happiness is *moksha*, according to Shankara. A complete absorption of the BMI in this eternal state of knowledge and happiness is realisation of one's self. In order to do this one has not to chase it or do anything else, says Shankara. The removal of Ignorance is the only thing to be done. Automatically our natural state will be realised.

So what are we supposed to do at all? Shankara says: Do an introspection and investigate about your self starting the probing from a ruthless analysis of your own mind and its vagaries. Try to get away from its external occupations and make it preoccupied with questions like; What is making the mind think? What is really behind it? Who is the thinker? Why are you not able to control the mind? What is more permanent than the mind? Wherefrom does the mind derive its strength? Besides the physical brain where the external hardware processes the thoughts of the mind, what is the software that forms the source for all the vibrations of the mind? Whence does it spring forth? Who is operating this software? If the answer comes up saying that it is you who are operating the software, then is that 'you' different from the 'you' which stands behind, watching the mind? Can you watch the mind unperturbed by any of its goings-on? In that sense can you still the mind? Now who is this 'you'? Shankara and all the other exponents of advaita vedAnta plead with us to keep on asking these questions and try to get convincing answers within oneself from oneself. Certainly they also ask us to go to a teacher and go through the shravaNa discipline.. But a teacher can only point the way. The final analysis has to be done by oneself on (and for) oneself by *manana* and *nididhyAsana* (introspective contemplation). Seers have declared emphatically that the quality and intensity of the internal struggle to get at these answers differ from person to person and it depends upon one's stage of spiritual evolution and the struggle he has already put in through all his various lives.

The person who is already spiritually ripe because of his earlier *vAsanA*, will probably get the enlightenment just by one listening to the teaching from the guru. But for the rest of us who are still far below this stage, Shankara says:

'Occupy your mind with God rather than with such secular pursuits as learning the gymnastics of rules of grammar'.

(bhaja GovindaM bhaja GovindaM GovindaM bhaja mUDhamate;
saMprApte sannihite kAle na hi na hi rakshati dukRngkaraNe).

'Seek the company of the good. Through the company of the good (sat-sangam) there arises non-attachment; through non-attachment, there arises freedom from delusion; through delusionlessness, there arises steadfastness; through steadfastness, there arises liberation in life.'

(satsangatve nissangatvaM nissangatve nirmohatvaM;
nirmohatve nishcalatatvaM nishcalitatve JIvanmuktiH)

In this context, it is important to note that, throughout the length and breadth of India, and through all the centuries, the concept of sat-sangh has been emphasized in every scripture and almost every literary work, that one cannot miss to note it as the sine-qua-non for spiritual uplift. Listen to the noblest of the noble souls, Tulsi from his Ram-charita-mAnas: 'Of the various creatures, both animate and inanimate, living in this world, whether in water or on land or in the air, whoever has ever attained wisdom, glory, salvation, material prosperity or welfare anywhere and by any means whatsoever, know it to be the result of association with holy men; there is no other means either in this world or in the Vedas'.

Do not be proud of wealth, kith and kin, and youth; Time takes away all these in a jiffy. Leaving aside this entire world which is transitory, and knowing the state of *Brahman*, enter into it –

(mA kuru dhana-jana-yauvana-garvaM harati nimeshAt-kAlas-sarvaM;
mAyA-mAyAm-idam-akhilaM hitvA Brahma-padaM tvam praviSa
viditvA)

continues Shankara in his Bhaja-Govindam. Sing the song of the Gita. Recite and revel in the one thousand names of Vishnu. Meditate on the form of the Goddess. Take the mind into the company of the good.

Distribute wealth among the needy. Be devoted completely to the lotus-feet of the Master. Then, through the discipline of the mind and the control of the senses you can behold the Absolute who resides in your heart. Make no difference between the God Absolute and the Master to whom you have surrendered. Even matters that have not been explicitly declared in the scriptures will become manifest to such a seeker. It is interesting to note that this meaning comes out from a famous verse in Sv.U.6-23: Whoever has superlative bhakti in God and as to God so to the Guru, to that great soul will the meanings spoken of here will sprout

Yasya deve parA bhaktiH yathA deve tathA gurau/
tasyaite kathitAhyarthAH prakASante mahAtmanaH)

But great exponents split the words '*tasyaite kathitAhyarthAH*' as '*tasyaite + akathitAhyarthAH*' (the grammar allows this!) and now it means:… even unspelt meanings sprout in him!

So it all comes down to Devotion to the Absolute, or devotion to the guru who is nothing but the Absolute. In such a devotion, there is to be no distinction between God and God. The usual talk among the masses about the worship of Shiva or Vishnu (the two major Gods of the Hindu trinity) being two contrary disciplines does not make sense to Shankara. There is not only no difference; they are one and the same. The Absolute in two garbs, that is all. Shankara is so convinced about the importance of this non-difference that he prays to God in his Gangashtakam, verse #8,, as if he were afraid that he himself might get lost and lose his conviction in this maze of confusion prevalent in this world! The first step in understanding the non-dual philosophy of Shankara is this non-difference of Shiva and Vishnu. The next step is to realise that this one God is not only transcendent but also immanent in every one of the living beings. This makes Shankara define bhakti as nothing but the contemplation of one's real self. (Viveka-chUDAmaNi #32:

svasvarUpAnusandhAnaM bhaktir-ity-abhidhIyate).

As oil dwells in the oil-seed, as curd in milk, as water in a ground-water source or as fire in firewood so does He dwell in the Universe – says Sv.U.. 1-15

(tileshu tailam dadhinIshhu sarpiH Apas shrotashvaraNishhu cAgniH).

This Absolute is everywhere, in front of us, behind us, above us, below us, to the right of us, to the left of us – the scriptures do not tire of repeating this kind of refrain. And all this is in oneself, i.e. one's Self. This Self is everywhere. That is why the I.U. says: It is already there before even the fastest mind goes there. In the entire philosophical thought process of the world this thought that the whole universe is immanent in oneself is a giant leap for mankind. When the universe dissolves in the Ultimate, it is a stepwise dissolution. From earth to water, from water to fire, from fire to air, from air to space – these are the stages of dissolution. Finally what remains is Space. Even that space finally will dissolve in the Atman, says the scripture. Can we imagine this situation when there is nothing, not even space? It is to help us attempt the mental gymnastics of comprehending this that all the scriptures cry hoarse on this topic.

Great devotees and exponents of the Advaitic school (of Shankara) have extolled the qualities and pleasures of bhakti so eloquently that for the ordinary man there should be no doubt about the fundamental role of bhakti in advaita. But critics of advaita as well as laymen who have not cared to take the effort to understand what advaita is, do sometimes declare that bhakti is not concordant with the concept of advaita and to be a devotee is not the forte of an Advaitin. Their question is: how can bhakti coexist with advaita? According to them, the teaching (of advaita) that the Self of each individual is the same as the Supreme Self is contradictory to the duality implied in the concept of bhakti. In the process of devotion there is always a duality involved – namely, the worshipper and the worshipped. If God or the Supreme Reality does not have a separate status other than our Selves, then who is to worship whom? advaita means non-duality. There is no second object in existence other than the Supreme Godhead. So where is the leeway for any worship or devotion? Recall his S.L. Verse No.81. It is the same Shankara who declares through all his commentaries and prakarana-granthas that Knowledge alone – neither an integration of Knowledge and Works nor an integration of Knowledge and Devotion – that leads to *moksha*. But to get to that state of Knowledge where one perceives nothing else, because there is only the Perceiver, he strongly recommends the doing of Works in a desireless unattached way and with a one-pointed devotion to the Ultimate. In order to impress upon us laymen that this is the only way to ascend to spiritual heights, he tours the whole country more than once, visits almost every important temple and place of pilgrimage and sings his compositions in praise of the revered deities of that place in the most eloquent poetry. He it is who has established the tradition of ritually worshipping together all the five divinities – sUrya, the Sun-God; Shakti, the Mother; Vishnu, gaNeSa and Shiva – of the Hindu tradition through the pancAyatanapUjA way. It is because of this worship of the formless as if it has a form, that invocation mantras in the advaitic tradition contain effectively the following idea as the core of the mantra. 'Oh God! I know you are omnipresent. But, for the purpose of my concentration and worship please condescend to make your presence felt here in this idol (image, picture or stone or whatever) for the period of the pUjA; maybe I am insulting your omnipresence by requesting you to confine yourself to this form and space, but please pardon me; I know no other way'.

The ascent from our physical, vital, emotional and intellectual being into the supermind of spiritual being is spiritual evolution. The technology of this ascent is Spiritual Love. There are at least three stages through which one has to rise. The first is *bAhya bhakti* or external bhakti. This is adoration of something outside ourselves. It is based on the unenlightened tAmasik feeling that God is external to us and that He dwells in a particular locality – a temple, a shrine or a holy place or bathing ghAT. Popular religion does not usually rise above this level. The second stage of bhakti is *ananya bhakti*, the exclusive and passionate (rAjasik) worship of one's favourite deity.

It is in fact an intense monotheism. The entire Ram-carita-manas of Tulsidas is a monumental example of the purity and majesty of *ananya-bhakti*. The third stage of bhakti is *ekAnta bhakti*, the purest (sAtvik) form. Here the worshipper loves God for His own sake and not for His gifts, not even for *moksha*. It is free from the feeling for any other object. It is the service of the Lord – an adoring service that implies centering of the mind on Him, expecting no gain either here or hereafter. It is a constant flow of mind, brimming with love towards the Lord and His creation, without any selfish desire. All his activities are sublimated into worship of the Divine. Whatever he does, whatever he eats, whatever he offers, is all a dedication to the Divine, not just as a formality, as ordinary virtuous people profess to be doing, but in total reality. Such a devotee appears to be doing external activities but since his ego is in total sublimation to the Divine he is not doing anything for himself. Even the distinction between sacred and secular activity disappears in such a soul. Every work is sacred to him inasmuch as it is an expression of his love of God. This supreme love of God was expressed by the cowherdesses of Brindavan. Their love can be understood by us only if, in the words of Swami VivekAnanda 'we can forget our love of gold, name and fame and this little material world of ours'. Their love, even though it originated in a kind of physical desire, rose up to the highest plane of self-effacing love of God, because of the holy association of the Divine, and thus in its final stages became the pinnacle of perfection of bhakti. The artistic manifestation of this bhakti can take place in one or more of nine ways – says Prahlad, the Devotee par excellence. This statement of his occurs as a spirited reply of a boy of five years old to the arrogant father's seemingly innocent query about the former's progress in his study-in-residence with the guru. It is one of the grandest pronouncements of the Hindu religion, that has since been quoted across the world millions of times.

It is not the name of the deity, Vishnu or Narayana, that is important here. The name is not there to distinguish it from the other names of

God. This is the purport of advaita. Whether it is Shiva or Vishnu, all the references are only to the One Supreme God – this is the intent of the Vedas. 'They are the same; just as the same actor appears in different roles, one is the Paramatma (Transcendental Supreme) dressed as Vishnu and the other is Paramatma dressed as Shiva, says the Mahaswami of Kanchi. Throughout the vedic literature one will find various divinities Varuna, Indra, Soma, Agni and Surya each glorified at one point to the exclusion of everything else. Any attempt to dissect the meanings and find a logical hierarchical explanation in the worldly literary sense of characters in literary fiction, would fail miserably. The entire mythological set-up embedded in the multitude of our PurANas, if taken at their story-value without any feeling for the under-current of the oneness of the Almighty, will create nothing but chaos in our intellectual understanding. The different hymns eulogising the different gods and goddesses are couched either in simple language with complex meanings or in complex language which perhaps hide simple ideas. It is very easy to misunderstand their significance and meanings. Western interpreters who have not got into the spirit of the religion have erred in a colossal manner. If you carefully look at the superlatives being used in the Vedic literature in the same manner and language for each Vedic deity and if you look at the exact imitations of these eulogies made by the PurANas for the various other manifestations of the Ultimate Divinity, one cannot but conclude that the last words of the Vedas are those passages where each such deity is considered as only one expression of the same many-faceted supreme Almighty. One such passage from the A.U. (III-1-1) raises the question: Who is this Self, whom we desire to worship? Is he the self by which we see, hear, etc.? Is he the heart and mind by which we perceive? No, says the Upanishad (III-1-3). These are but adjuncts of the Self. The Self itself is Pure Consciousness. He is *Brahman*. He is God, He is BrahmA, He is Indra, He is all Gods; the five elements – earth air space, water fire; all beings, great or small, born of eggs, born from the womb, born from heat, born from soil; horses, cows, men, elephants, birds; everything that breathes, the beings that walk and the beings that walk not, the beings that fly and those that fly not. The reality behind all these is *Brahman*, who is pure Consciousness. Consciousness is *Brahman. prajnAnaM Brahma.*

The natural state of each individual is the state of being *Brahman*, say the scriptures. Shankara therefore defines bhakti in specific terms as contemplative living in one's natural state, that is, the divine state. This *brahma-bhAva,* being in *Brahman,* automatically implies an equanimous view of every being in the world as the same self as the one dwells in the seer. This balanced view of everything as One, everything as the Self, is a blissful experience, called *brahma-Ananda.* It does not come out of studies or scholarship. It is a state to be enjoyed internally, not by the external apparatus. When that experience crystallises, there is no more knowledge, no more ignorance, no perceiver, nothing perceived, no perception. All that is seen by these enlightened souls is the godliness of Infinite Love and the loveliness of the Omnipresent God.

Shankara talks unceasingly about such a state of supreme bhakti, which we call advaita bhakti, in glowing terms. This poetic but precise description of Shankara is very often quoted as the thesis on bhakti. It is verse no.61 of S.L. It gives five analogies for bhakti or Devotion to Divinity. The first one cites what is called an ankola tree which has the characteristic that when its seeds fall from the tree on the ground and mature, they travel to the base of the tree and join the roots by their own nature. Just as these seeds reach the tree with a one-pointed purpose, so also the devotee should be devoted to his God of devotion – is the theme. The second analogy is that of iron filings that are drawn to a magnet. In these two analogies the duality of the components of the system involved is all but obvious. The next two analogies are that of a chaste wife being devoted and drawn towards her husband and that of a creeper which winds around a parent tree. In these two cases the quality of the relationship is certainly different from that of the first two analogies but still some duality remains. The fifth analogy is that of a river which is irrevocably bound to a path towards the ocean, its ultimate destination. It appears it is this analogy that is closest to the heart of Adi Shankara as far as his definition of bhakti is concerned.

Think of a golden ring. Does gold have the form of a ring? Goldness has nothing to do with the shape of a ring or roundness. The roundness of the ring is extraneous to gold. Do not see the ring, see only the gold, they say. This is why even words fail when the Vedas want to describe the Ultimate. 'What is not uttered by speech but that by which speech is revealed is *Brahman*, not the thing that is before you', says Kena U. I-5.

(yad vAcA anabhyuditam yena vAg-abhyudyate;
tadeva brahma tvaM viddhi nedaM yadidaM upAsate)

It is something which the words cannot describe, eyes cannot see, the ears cannot hear. Even the senses cannot sense it. How can the Seer see himself? How can the Knower know himself? So somehow out of all the multiplicity that is visible to us we have to see and sense the unity which is our own Self.

In short, we can quote frm Srimad Bhagavatam (through the voice of T P Ramachandran in Voice of Shankara, 2005) the lesson from the message of Oneness as follows: The concept of bondage (bandha) and release (*moksha*) are discussd in Srimad Bhagavatam in many places as its final teaching. These concepts are relevant only to the *JIva* and not either to the world or to *Brahman*. The essence of bondage is that the *JIva* out of beginningless Ignorance identifies itself with limiting factors like the physical and subtle bodies. As a result, it considers itself as a finite individual separate from the physical world and other *JIvas* similarly situated. In this state it engages itself in good and bad actions, undergoes a series of births acording to its karma and experiences pleasure and pain appropriate to those births. Therefore release consists in overcoming avidyA and realizing non-difference from *Brahman* and thus experiencing eternal and perfect bliss. Since avidyA is the root cause of bondage, the direct means to release is jnAna, which is nothing but direct experience of one's non-difference from *Brahman*. The preparation for jnAna lies through other disciplines like nishkAma-karma, upAsanA on saguNa-*Brahman*, and disinterested bhakti towards that Ishvara. This is the point of advaita and the Bhagavatam fully subscribes to it, though there are also theistic ways of presentations in BhagavataM.

AUM TAT SAT